Steps Along The Hunter's Path

Volume 1

A rich mixture of hunting wisdom
from a "who's who" of today's
top deer and turkey hunters;
plus trophy contest results;
wild game recipes
and more
from five Deer & Turkey Expos
produced by Target Communications

TARGET COMMUNICATIONS CORPORATION

Copyright ©1998 by Target Communications

Published by
TARGET COMMUNICATIONS CORPORATION
7626 W. Donges Bay Rd.
Mequon WI 53097

All rights reserved, including the right to reproduce this book or portions thereof – except for brief quotations in book reviews — in any form or by any means, electronic or mechanical, including photocopying, recording, or by any information storage and retrieval system, without permission in writing from the publisher. All inquiries should be addressed to Target Communications, 7626 W. Donges Bay Rd., Mequon WI 53097.

Printed in the United States of America

Volume 1   Published 1998

ISBN   0-913305-14-6

Cover photos by Troy Huffman

Library of Congress Cataloging-in Publication Data

Steps along the hunter's path.
    p.   cm.
    Contents: v. 1. A rich mixture of hunting wiscom from a "who's who" of today's top deer and turkey hunters -- Trophy and contest results -- Wild game recipes and more from five Deer & Turkey Expos.
    ISBN 0-913305-14-6 (pbk. : v.1)

    1. White-tailed deer hunting. 2. Turkey hunting.
  I. Target Communications
SK301.S754   1998
799.2'7652'0973--dc21   97-52714
                                          CIP

Introduction

Nothing in the natural world is more graceful, more magical, more heart stopping than the whitetail deer ... nothing that will cause befuddlement more quickly than the leaf rattling, thunderous gobble of a mature wild gobbler. And nothing, year after year, is more challenging to the hunter than these two.

Even better, they're the two most widespread, most adaptable, big game species in North America, and the hunting challenge most of us take up.

That's why "Steps Along the Hunter's Path" was created. It offers the kind of scouting, preparation and hunting advice you can "take to the woods", advice that can make the difference on any hunt.

The heart of "Steps Along the Hunter's Path" consists of greatly expanded versions of seminars given by nearly 20 top deer and turkey hunting experts at the five 1998 Deer & Turkey Hunting Expos (Illinois, Michigan, Ohio, Tennessee and Wisconsin) produced by Target Communications. The speakers are a "who's who" of deer and turkey hunters. From them, there is page after page of timely, productive hunting information that could not -- simply because of time constraints -- be included in the seminars.

And there's more —
- A complete list of all trophy contest winners from all five of our 1997 Deer & Turkey Expos. Looking to admire huge antlers? These five states are some of the best rack producers.
- County-by-county maps of each of the five states, showing where the record book bucks were taken.
- Directions to get your trophy measured, scored and entered into state and national record books.
- A mouth-watering, nicely-seasoned chapter of venison and turkey recipes.
- Photos of hunting scenes . . . of hunting tips . . . and of Outdoor Photo Contest winners.

Every page is another step along your Hunter's Path to greater enjoyment of the outdoors, in all the things it has to offer. We hope you enjoy the book and the hunt.

About The Publisher....

TARGET COMMUNICATIONS

TARGET COMMUNICATIONS produces Deer & Turkey Expos in Illinois, Michigan, Ohio, Tennessee and Wisconsin. The company also publishes, in its "On Target" series, books on deer hunting, archery, muzzleloading and wild game cooking.

This book —"Steps Along the Hunter's Path"— is our first effort at producing an "added value" book to complement the things you learn at the shows which help your hunting and add to your enjoyment of the outdoors. We intend to do this annually; additional projects are planned.

GLENN HELGELAND

Target Communications' President Glenn Helgeland was editor of *Archery World* magazine (now *Bowhunting World*) 11 years — 1970-1980. He is the founding editor of *Archery Retailer* magazine (now *Archery Business*). He has been a columnist for *Bowhunting World, American Hunter, North American Hunter* and *Archery Business* magazines. His hunting and natural history articles have been published in the above publications, plus *North American Whitetail, Field & Stream, Outdoor Life, Sports Afield, Bowhunter, Bow & Arrow Hunting*, plus state publications.

He was the Editor of the Pope and Young Records Book, 2nd Edition; co-author, with John Williams, men's 1972 Olympic archery gold medalist, of the book "ARCHERY FOR BEGINNERS", and author of the "COMPLETE BOWHUNTING" book for the North American Hunting Club.

Helgeland was Associate Editor of *NATIONAL WILDLIFE* magazine 1968-1970.

He has won awards for his writing and publishing from the National Shooting Sports Foundation and the National Archery Association.

Helgeland is an individual member and past director of the Outdoor Writers Association of America (OWAA). His company is a supporting member of this same organization.

Target Communications is a member of the National Association of Consumer Shows (NACS) and the International Association for Exposition Management (IAEM). Helgeland is chairman of the Wisconsin Chapter of the IAEM.

CONTENTS

SECTION 1: THE SMARTER YOU HUNT, THE LUCKIER YOU GET   **1**

Topo Maps / Compasses / GPS: Hunting Terrain Navigation Made Simple & Safe	Phil Johnston	3
Prepare For Success	Kathy Butt	11
Camouflage Vs. Concealment	Ralph Cianciarulo	19
Where to Hunt Suburban Fringes & How To Get Permission	Gen Ebert	27
Pre-Season Blunders — They're A Growing Problem	Greg Miller	31
Handguns for Big Game	Phil Johnston	37
Biggest Buck of Your Life With Black Powder	Richard P. Smith	45
Inside the Tracks	Tony Kemnitz	51

SECTION II: IMPROVE YOUR HUNTING CONDITIONS   **61**

A Clear Guide to Personal Deer Management Practices	John L. Sloan	63
Formula For Herd Calculation	John L. Sloan	69
PDM Means Button Buck ID	Stan Potts	73

SECTION III: WHITETAILS, WHITETAILS, WHITETAILS   **79**

Are You Hunting A November Stand in October?	Tony LaPratt	81
Buck Core Areas— Fact & Fiction	Greg Miller	89
Take The Water Trail To Deer Hunting Success	Les Davenport	95
Harvesting the Exceptional Buck	Les Davenport	101
Finding Big Country Bucks	Richard P. Smith	109
To Rattle Up Bucks, Easy Does It	M. R. James	119
Give It Your Best Shot	M. R. James	125
Hunting Pressured Bucks	Tony LaPratt	129

SECTION IV: THE GREAT FEATHERED BIRD   **137**

Building Blocks for Success	Greg Abbas	139
To Hunt Turkeys Successfully	Bob Clark	145
Locating Techniques for Spring Gobblers	Gary Sefton	151
Pterodactyl Pturkey Ptalk Pfriction Calling Pfacts & Pfundamentals	Gary Sefton	157
Tactics For Silent Gobblers	Bob Clark	163
Outsmart Gobblers With Your Instincts	Greg Abbas	169
Hunting Midwest Gobblers	Steve Puppe	175

SECTION V: OF BEAR & ELK — **181**
Elk Tips For Flatlanders   *Jay Verzuh*   183
Black Bears ... Baiting & All   *Vicki Cianciarulo*   189

SECTION VI: THE ROAD AHEAD — **197**
Affordable Adventure   *Ralph Cianciarulo*   199
How Michigan Almost Lost   *Richard P. Smith*   209
   Its Bear Hunting
Watchable Wildlife - Family Fun   *Chip Gross*   215

TROPHY CONTESTS / OTHER AWARDS / DEER DATA — **219**
Illinois Deer & Turkey Classic   221
   1996 County-by-County Big Buck Tally
   1997 Trophy Contest Winners
   1997 Best of Show Awards
   1997 Outdoor Photo Contest Winners
Michigan Deer & Turkey Spectacular   226
   1996 County-by-County Big Buck Tally
   1997 Trophy Contest Winners
   1997 Best of Show Awards
   CBM Best of 1996 Awards
   1997 Outdoor Photo Contest Winners
   1997 Beards & Spurs Winners
Ohio Deer & Turkey Expo   232
   1996 County-by-County Big Buck Tally
   1997 Trophy Contest Winners
   1997 Best of Show Awards
   1997 Outdoor Photo Contest Winners
Tennessee Deer & Turkey Expo   239
   1996 County-by-County Big Buck Tally
   1997 Trophy Contest Winners
   1997 Best of Show Awards
   1997 Outdoor Photo Contest Winners
Wisconsin Deer & Turkey Expo   244
   1996 County-by-County Big Buck Tally
   1997 Trophy Contest Winners
   1997 Best of Show Awards
   1997 Outdoor Photo Contest Winners
   1997 Turkey Calling Contest Winners
How To Enter Your Trophy   *Richard P. Smith*   251
   In The Record Book

FROSTING ON THE CAKE — **257**
Deer & Turkey Recipes   259

SECTION I:

THE SMARTER YOU HUNT, THE LUCKIER YOU GET

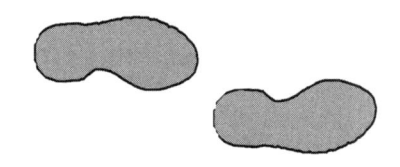

• A GPS (Global Positioning System) unit combined with a good compass and topographical map – and knowing how to use them – add up to great navigational skills, which can give you the confidence to range as far as practical in your search for good hunting terrain ... and then safely find your way back out.

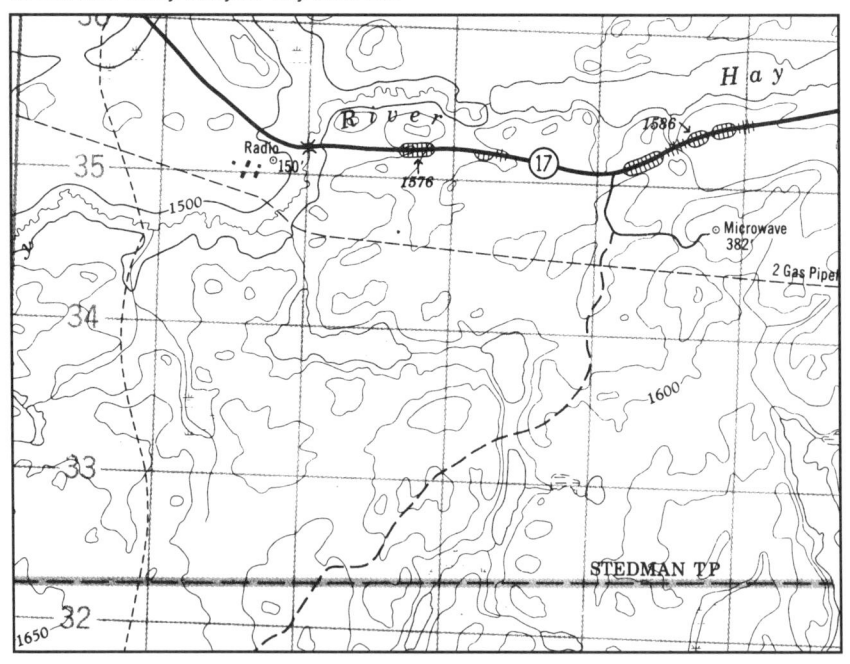

Steps Along the Hunter's Path

> Knowing how and where to get around in the woods can make you a "luckier" hunter.

by Phil W. Johnston

Topo maps...Compasses ...GPS: *Hunting Terrain Navigation Made Simple*

Two scenarios come quickly to mind here:
1) It's not a huge area, but it doesn't have roads and there still are swamps to get around, ridges and saddles and bottlenecks to pinpoint and check, and a creek bottom to explore. You study the topographical maps, and in doing so prove for the umpteenth time that the place you want to hunt never is in the middle of one map but, instead, at the corner of four maps. You also mark a couple of splendid-looking terrain changes that might be prime spots to hunt.

That weekend, marked topo maps in hand, you park your pickup, take a compass reading and head out. One hour of efficient high-ground travel later – scouting as you go – you're checking out those spots. They look good. On the way back out, you leave a few judiciously placed trail markers that will be easy for you to find but won't be immediately obvious to anyone else.

At daylight on opening day, you're at a dry-ground bottleneck between two swamps. Bingo! At 8:27 a.m. you tag a fine 10-pointer which was headed back into its swampy lair for the day but now will be redirected to your freezer.

2) The local paper carried the tragic story. Another young hunter had left his camp in familiar territory in northern Michigan for a quick deer hunt that, instead, due to a sudden storm, carelessness and lack of preparation turned into a tragedy. A quickly organized search party failed to find the young man in time.

Stories like these, or variations of them, happen every year. They are the good and the bad of finding your way in the woods. **Navigation is such a simple thing that everyone who goes outdoors ought to know it and be comfortable with it. This skill can make you a much better and more confident hunter. This skill can take** you where many hunters will not go. This knowledge can save your life. It's hard to beat a filled tag and staying found.

Many hunters sacrifice good hunting opportunities because they aren't able to get around in the woods like they should, which means they're scared of getting too far from a road. So they stay where the people are and grouse that there aren't any big bucks or great hunting conditions to be found.

The flip side of this sees hunters, hikers and other outdoor people heading off into the wild expecting to be gone for a few hours, instead ending up terrified, confused and sometimes in danger of losing their life. Daniel Boone supposedly said he'd never been lost, but he had been confused a couple of times in his wandering. As funny as that sounds today, there is only one reason Daniel's confusion didn't become a tragedy – he was prepared, and he was woods wise. All we have to do today to put ourselves in Daniel's shoes is to prepare. The way to get started is to learn how to navigate. We can learn that in our back yard, but we can use it anywhere on earth.

Navigation on our shrinking earth is not rocket science, although some of our most affordable and sophisticated navigation today is possible because of rocket science. Today we have maps and compasses, but we also have GPS.

As easy as it is to find our way today, it is easy to forget how difficult it was to navigate on our planet just a few years ago. While early navigational efforts went unrecorded for a variety of reasons, we do know that men began traveling beyond sight of their homes as astronomers were beginning to take note of the movements of the sun and stars. Although they didn't realize that the movements they were charting were due to the earth's rotation, it mattered little for their purposes anyhow.

Astronomers have gazed into our sky for thousands of years but the first attempt to record our sky took place in AD 150. An astronomer named Ptolemy established the Tropic of Cancer (23 degrees, 26 minutes N), the Equator (000 degrees) and the Tropic of Capricorn (23 degrees, 26 minutes S). These latitudes correspond to the northern-most and southern-most latitudes of the sun's movement over our earth, from the summer solstice to the winter solstice. With the establishment of latitudes, early navigators could begin traveling east and west on a straight line. Columbus was said to be navigating "on a parallel" when he bumped into North America. Ptolemy also was interested in establishing lines of longitude, fully aware that one would never know where he or she was on a line of latitude until longitude could be measured. For the next 1,500 years or so, man struggled to establish the Prime Meridian and subsequent lines of longitude.

The Prime Meridian would be moved all over the world by political winds until finally taking up residence in Greenwich, England, under the hand of Nevil Maskelyne, England's fifth astronomer royal, in 1765. The Prime Meridian would permanently originate at each pole and run through Greenwich. The problem of determining additional longitudinal points running east and west from Greenwich still hadn't been solved, however.

The Longitude Act of England was passed July 8, 1714, under the reign of Queen Anne. Passage of the Longitude Act was due, in no small part, to the loss of four of five warships of the British fleet October 22, 1702. More than 2,000 British sailors lost their lives because they didn't know their longitude. They literally didn't know where they were, so they didn't know what to expect nor when to expect it nor where to expect it from. They were hammered. In a nutshell, the Longitude Act proclaimed large cash awards which would go to the individual or individuals who found an accurate way to determine longitude.

Our earth rotates once every 24 hours, covering a rotation of 360 degrees. That works out to 15 degrees per hour. After passage of the Longitude Act, it didn't take long for early navigators to realize that if they had an accurate clock, they could begin navigating with precision. The first clock that was accurate enough, portable and fit for sea duty was built by John Harrison. The clock aptly was named Harrison's #1. Navigation was never the same, fortunately.

Although we likely won't be using a sextant to navigate in the field, it is nice to know how and from whence came lines of latitude (running east and west on the earth) and lines of longitude (running from pole to pole, north and south). Since star fixes or the angle to the sun can't always be measured, man needed another tool to navigate, one we now routinely use in the field – the compass.

Early compasses consisted of a magnetized needle which was inserted into a shaft of straw. The combination was then placed on a bed of water. The crude needle would swing to the north, and our early navigators were off and running ... or sailing.

We've improved a bit on the original design, but the principle remains the same. Originally, it was a mystery that a compass pointed north. Today we realize that the compass needle aligns itself with the magnetic field of the earth. In reality, the needle of the compass points to magnetic north – a point south and east of the North Pole, northwest of Hudson Bay. The difference between magnetic north

True north is the map direction toward the geographical North Pole, magnetic north is the compass direction toward the Magnetic North Pole.

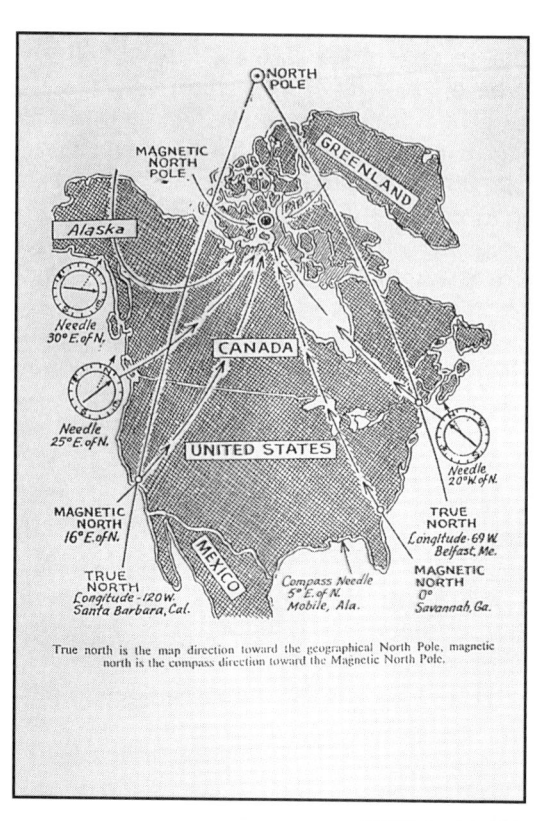

- *The magnetic compass aligns itself with the magnetic field of the earth. Magnetic north is in alignment with true north (the North Pole) only along the line which runs from the western edge of Hudson Bay to eastern Florida. The difference between magnetic north and true north is called declination or variation.*

- *The compass indicates a "bearing" of 270 degrees (due west). Note the "north" arrow aligned over the shadow.*

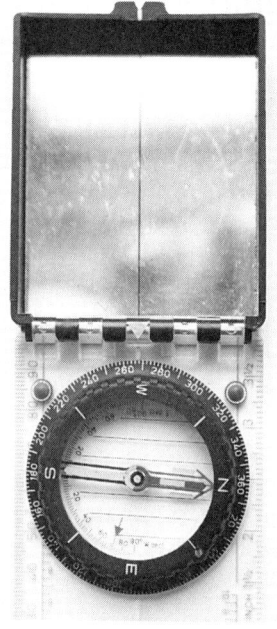

6 Steps Along the Hunter's Path

and true north (the North Pole) is called declination or variation. Where I live in eastern North Dakota, true north lies 8.5 degrees west of magnetic north. Declination or variation for where I live is thus said to be 8.5 degrees east (the compass points east of true north). To convert magnetic north to true north here in eastern North Dakota, one simply subtracts 8.5 degrees from the indicated compass reading. True north for my residence is, thus, 351.5 degrees.

An easy way to remember this simple rule is "east is least – subtract declination from the compass reading to show true north; and west is best – add declination to the compass reading to show true north". The imaginary line of zero declination – the line on our earth where magnetic north and true north are one and the same – passes through the United States near the Georgia/Alabama state line. West of this line, declination or variation is east, so subtract the declination. East of this line, the declination is west, so add the reading to the compass indication to arrive at true north.

Learning to use a compass is easy. Practice with it before you venture into the field, for just a few minutes, and you'll understand how it works. Believe me, reading any written instruction takes much longer than doing the compass reading. So don't be put off if these written directions seem intimidating.

Our compass today is an affordable, accurate and indispensable tool. Compasses come in all shapes and sizes and range in cost from a couple of bucks to hundreds of dollars. Some compasses can be adjusted to compensate automatically for the declination of the area being navigated. It's a good idea to clip or otherwise attach the inexpensive, back-up compasses all over – jacket zipper, pack, etc. Carry a main, precision tool around your neck or wherever it's always handy and safe.

Today's compass typically has two moving parts – the magnetized needle or pointer, and a rotating azimuth ring, set into or onto a fixed baseplate. In use, you hold the compass reasonably level to allow the needle to stabilize on a northerly bearing, keeping it well away from any metal object which could adversely affect the tool. With the needle indicating magnetic north, it's a simple matter to rotate your entire body (holding the compass in front of you) to "point" to magnetic north. So far, so good.

The azimuth ring rotates on the compass body or baseplate. This allows you to "take a bearing" to an object or navigate on a heading. To walk a line, or heading, of 300 degrees, for instance, you simply rotate the compass azimuth ring until 300 degrees lines up under the direction-of-travel line in the middle of the baseplate.

Then rotate your entire body until the magnetic pointer in the compass lines up over the red "shadow". With body and compass so arranged, you're now pointing 300 degrees, as long as the magnetic pointer is over the designated "shadow", which typically also is indicated with red markings. Anything lying ahead of you – trees, mountains, etc. – also will "bear" 300 degrees, if you're still lined up as above.

To take a bearing on another object, point yourself and the compass baseplate toward the object in question, then rotate the azimuth ring until the red pointer again lines up over the red shadow. The bearing can then be read under the direction-of-travel line. Taking a couple of accurate bearings on points also shown on a map allows you quickly to plot your position on a map after laying the map out pointing to the same north you're using on the compass. With the map so arranged, you can use the edge of the compass to draw a line back from the points you took bearings to until at least two lines cross. Where the lines meet, that's your location. Remember to draw the lines without moving the map or the azimuth ring for each point.

The second portion of the mix is a good, accurate topographical map of the area you intend to navigate. Maps of all types are available from the USGS Map Sales Office, Box 25286, Federal Center Building #810, Denver CO 80225. To order any map for the United States, one needs to obtain a "Catalog of Published Maps" and an "Index to Map Coverage" for the state or states in question. These two booklets are available free from the USGS.

Although it's possible to get 1x2 degree maps, 30x60 minute maps or county maps from the USGS, the 7.5 minute topographical map best offers the detail we need in the field. The 7.5 minute maps currently sell at the bargain price of $2.50 each.

One other map note is worth mentioning: when you're planning an outing, start early. It'll take a month or more just to get your maps.

Today, precise navigation is a snap because of the rocket science I mentioned at the start. The Department of Defense currently maintains a fleet of 24 satellites orbiting our earth twice a day, 10,000 miles above our heads. Twenty-one of these satellites are maintained on an active status at any time. They transmit two types of electronic data to our military troops and anyone else who "listens". This data, in a nutshell, allows receivers to plot their exact position from geometrical calculations based on the time difference of pulsed signals. Not unlike the old land-based Loran A and C systems, the current Global Positioning System (GPS) is state of the art – and getting better each day. When the satellite transmissions are combined with land-based transmissions, the GPS becomes so exact that GPS-based instrument landings soon will be commonplace in the airline industry.

While the GPS allows pinpoint navigation and targeting for our military, it at the same time allows us to navigate in the back country with uncanny precision. Today, for less than $200 in some instances, we can purchase a portable GPS receiver that fits in a pocket, which will locate itself precisely come rain, snow or fog, as long as it has a clear view of the sky! These units likewise will routinely store up to 500 waypoints or locations (such as your tree stand locations) as well. These little GPS receivers will plot distance and direction to another stored location, and they'll tell you your speed getting there as well as the estimated time of arrival. This space-age technology makes it impossible ... IMPOSSIBLE ... to get lost or be confused, as long as the batteries are up, of course. If you love the GPS as much as I do, you'll always leave on a trip with fresh batteries in the unit – plus a second set of fresh batteries in your pack.

However, having a GPS receiver in your pack or pocket does not eliminate the need for and knowledge of a good compass and map. If you rely on batteries for all your navigation, leaving the GPS unit on all the time, the batteries will fail long before the outing ends. I caution everyone to use a GPS unit for an occasional location "fix" or heading only, relying on a compass and map for the remainder.

With a good USGS map in your pack, a good compass around your neck, and a GPS unit handy, you'll navigate like an expert, regardless of the terrain. You'll know the easiest and safest way to get from Point A to Point B, and you'll know the way back to camp or home. Daniel Boone would be impressed, I'm sure. Your friends will be, too.

If you would like to read and learn more about navigation, these are excellent information sources:

• *A Comprehensive Guide to Land Navigation With GPS*, by Noel Hotchkiss. Published by Alexis USA, 1037 Sterling Rd., Suite 203, Herndon VA 22070

• *Longitude*, by Dava Sobel. Published by Walker & Company, 435 Hudson Street, New York NY 10014

Check with your local bookstore. If the store doesn't have in stock the title you want, the store will order it for you.

• *Map Reading and Land Navigation*, a Department of the Army Field Manual dated September 1987. Reference Number: FM 21-26. Publication Number: 1988 0 n-222-165:QL 3. The 178-page book costs $38. You can order it from National Technical Information Services at 1-800-553-6847. Credit cards accepted. Use the reference number first when ordering; the people we talked with found the book faster by using the reference number than by using the publication number.

PHIL JOHNSTON

When you want to talk about handguns and big game hunting, you talk to Phil Johnston. He took up the challenge of the limited range of the shortguns many years ago. He has written hundreds of pro-gun, pro-hunting articles in all the major outdoor magazines, written a book titled "Successful Handgun Hunting" and co-edited "The Encyclopedia of Firearms". With a handgun, he has taken black bear, brown bear, Dall's sheep, caribou, mountain goat, elk, mule deer, whitetail deer, coyote and red fox.

He also has roamed the continent -- staying found & finding trophy game -- w/GPS, maps & compass.

Here's a solid list of tips to help you have a good time and avoid physical, hunting equipment, hunting conditions and trophy care disasters.

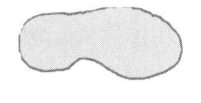

by Kathy Butt

Preparing For Success

We spend a great deal of time, effort and hard-earned salaries to bag big game. That's all the more reason we hunters, especially traveling hunters, should do our homework months in advance of that scheduled trip. With proper advance planning, something as simple as packing a few special items or visiting our taxidermist will insure that our hunt results in a memorable adventure, instead of The Hunt From Hell.

However, success doesn't just happen. You've heard the statement "The harder I work, the luckier I get." It's the same with all hunt preparation, not just the scouting part. Doing our homework includes being prepared physically, making equipment checklists, knowing the area we'll be hunting, being prepared for weather conditions and higher altitudes, or even something as simple as knowing how to repair our own equipment.

Whether you're hunting whitetail deer close to home or traveling great distances for even bigger game, you can do a number of things to insure success. For instance, the traveling hunter must pay special attention to packing the proper gear, being absolutely sure all essentials are included (without overloading), and then sorting out and taking the useful items, setting aside the gimmicks. Take advantage of those which work; they'll save you time and effort.

There's no doubt that experience is the best teacher, but why should hunters suffer "negative adventures" when it isn't necessary? We're not trying to reinvent the wheel here. The following suggestions and tips have resulted from years of experience which my husband and I have gained firsthand as professional taxidermists and as big game outfitters.

1) PHYSICAL CONDITIONING

Elk hunting? Mountains? High altitudes? Or just plenty of walking on a home hunt? Packing or dragging out a game animal? Day-after-day stick-to-it effort, while maintaining a positive attitude? Sore muscles and exhaustion take the fun out of a hunt and keep you from hunting effectively or hunting long.

Being prepared physically is something which cannot be accomplished overnight. Hunting in high altitudes can be dangerous if you're not prepared, and it even can do strange things to those who are prepared. Preparing your muscles for climbing steep terrain, as well as for miles and miles of walking, will prevent days of agonizingly sore muscles. As for preparing your lungs for the higher elevation, up there where the oxygen is thin, the best advice is to arrive a day or two early, if possible, and give your lungs time to acclimate. Go slowly and drink lots of water.

Take care of your feet. They'll be your best friend or your worst enemy when hunting in mountainous terrain ... actually, any terrain, anywhere. So break in new boots before making the trip. Pack moleskin and carry it in your backpack. At the first sign of a sore spot or blister, completely cover that area. Painful blisters on your feet can end your hunt faster than it started.

2) TROPHY CARE

This is especially critical in warm and hot weather. Archery seasons kick off in late August or early September when weather can be really hot. That makes **quick** game retrieval and field-dressing imperative. Whether you're hunting early season archery hunts for elk, mule deer in the Rockies, bear in the wilderness areas of Canada or whitetail deer at home, when 80 and 90 degree temperatures prevail, hides and meat can ruin in a very, very short time.

Meat Care: It is essential to field-dress your big game animal as soon as it is recovered and cool the carcass as quickly as possible. Cool and dry are the key words. Getting big game out of the woods is never easy, and quite often you may hunt in areas which don't allow ATVs or motorized vehicles for game retrieval. This is where using a two-wheel game carrier comes in handy. It really takes a load off your back.

Completely cape out the carcass and lay the hide, flesh side up, flat on the ground in full shade. Get that hide off the carcass; I can't stress that enough. It is the fastest way to cool the meat. Lay meat quarters on the fleshy side of the hide while quartering the animal, but hang meat quarters for cooling as quickly as possible. It's important to keep meat clean, but should you happen to get a little dirt or debris on meat, simply wipe it as best you can. Water encourages meat spoilage, and it's best just to brush or trim the debris away.

If evening temperatures drop low enough to completely chill meat quarters, it's a good idea to hang the skinned meat quarters and backstraps for even better cooling. Meat can be protected from insects either by covering it with special game bags or by rubbing meat completely with a product called "Liquid Game Bag", a peppered oil which seals meat and discourages flies and bees.

A word of caution – check hanging meat often to insure the meat is cool to the touch. If it isn't, find a processor quickly. The prepared hunter, especially the traveling hunter, will have checked out options for meat processing prior to opening day. Locate a professional game processor in the area you'll be hunting and discuss cost, processing options (cuts, specialty processing such as deboning, summer sausages, jerky, etc.) and shipping options.

If you take pride in butchering your own game, be sure to take the following items: A good selection of sharp knives, sharpening steel, plastic-coated freezer paper, freezer tape and permanent felt tip pens. Always start with clean hands and utensil when butchering meat. Deboning removes bulk and extra weight, making transport much easier. Just to give you an idea of how much processed meat you'll glean from, let's say, an average-sized bull elk (600 pounds), you'll end up with approximately 250 pounds of meat. That's a lot of weight to carry out.

Each year we advise our hunters to pack their clothing in two extra-large coolers, along with an empty duffel bag in each. These coolers can be used for meat transportation and the duffels for clothing on the return trip. When flying home, the meat coolers can be checked as baggage and duffel bags shipped UPS (if you don't want to pay the expensive extra baggage fee). Most airlines allow a 70-pound weight limit per each bag and charge anywhere from $45 and up for each bag exceeding the three-bag limit. These restrictions vary with each airline, so be sure to check ahead and know what to expect.

Hunting at home also requires careful attention to game taken, especially during the early portion of archery season. There once was a time when Ol' Joe tied his big buck on the hood of his truck and drove to town to show off his trophy. Not only did it give the wrong impression to those who don't hunt, it sure didn't do much for cooling the carcass. Thank heaven we've gotten smarter. Put that tailgate up when hauling your trophy in the back of your truck and cover the carcass with a light tarp. This will do two things – it will keep the carcass out of direct sunlight and prevent wind damage to the hair, and it won't draw attention from those who are turned off by the sight of a dead animal.

Trophy Care: There's additional special work if you want to preserve your big game trophy for a beautiful mount. Visit your taxidermist and learn first-hand how to properly cape out your trophy and

- Above. Hunting in higher elevations and in cold weather conditions present special challenges. Nasty weather can take its toll on you and your hunting equipment. This is the author with an Idaho mountain lion.
- Upper right. Hang carcass, skinned if possible, to chill meat and protect it with some sort of pepper and game bag if insects are a concern.
- Right. Proper hide care means fleshing, then salt, salt and more salt.

- On fly-ins, if you need it, be sure you've packed it.

Steps Along the Hunter's Path

care for the hide. Even if you plan to hunt with a professional outfitter, it doesn't hurt to know how caping should be done, and I suggest you watch as they cape your trophy out. After all, it's your trophy and you have every right to see that the job is done correctly.

If you plan to hunt mule deer during the early portion of September, be prepared to preserve the velvet-covered antlers. Again, your local taxidermist should be more than glad to prepare for you a special kit of formaldehyde and syringes, as well as demonstrate how to inject this solution into the velvet covering. Or you could find a professional in the area you'll be hunting and pay him to take care of this for you.

Hides must be thoroughly salted immediately after excess meat and fat are trimmed from the fleshy side of the hide. The big word, the important word is ... SALT! Lots of salt! Take it with you or buy it when you get there; it really doesn't matter as long as you have it in camp. You cannot use too much salt. So don't worry about overdoing it. Fifteen to 20 pounds of salt is adequate for a big game animal such as an elk. Any kind of de-ionized salt will work.

Rub it in thoroughly on all areas. After you've completed the salting process, lay or hang the hide (salty side up) in the shade and allow to dry. To transport the salted hide home, fold the salted sides together and place the hide in a bag in a cooler. Keep the hide as dry as possible during transport to prevent the formation of bacteria which cause hair slippage. Remember to remove the hide from the bag as soon as you return home; hides deteriorate in air-tight bags.

Transporting antlers as airline baggage requires careful homework. Be prepared to cover the tips of your big game antlers with cardboard, pieces of garden hose, or even spent shotgun shells, all of which can and should be wrapped with duct tape. These will protect the tips from being chipped during transport. To reduce excess baggage costs, large antlers, such as elk and moose, can be cut in half down the middle of the skull plate and tied together, but only if your trophy is NOT a record book animal. If there is any chance you plan to register your trophy in the record book, you must keep the skull plate intact, i.e., in one solid piece).

3) EQUIPMENT REPAIR

Do you know how to make simple adjustments and repairs to your hunting equipment? Whether you're hunting with archery tackle, blackpowder or centerfire arms, you should be familiar with your equipment and pack the necessary items for quick field repairs.

For instance, do you use a compound bow which requires a bow press to change the string? If so, purchase that press and learn how to use it. Having an extra string set up exactly as the one on your bow, complete with peep-sight, kisser button, silencers, etc., will save you time and frustration in hunting camp. Pack a tackle box with all the necessary tools for making quick repairs, items such as a nocking pliers, extra nocks, string wax, etc. — anything you normally use to make simple equipment repairs or adjustments.

Quite often we fail miserably in preparing for the unexpected, especially in the repair department. Make equipment checks upon arriving in camp; be able to make necessary adjustments and carry the tools required to make those adjustments. And above all, take the time before making the trip to learn how to care for your hunting arm. In addition, take a back-up firearm or bow, if possible.

4) THE FLYING HUNTER

Traveling by airplane requires preparing hunting arms for rough handling. If you've ever watched baggage handlers transfer (throw) baggage onto conveyor belts, you know. I cringe every time I watch the baggage guys toss my archery or gun cases from one cart to another.

When packing your archery case, remove the sight bracket from your bow and carefully wrap it in bubble wrap or a piece of clothing. Never place arrows tipped with broadheads in your case during travel. Always enclose sharp broadheads in a hard plastic case before packing in bow case, or tuck them safely away in another piece of checked baggage. As for packing guns and ammo, ammo must be packed in a hard case and carried separately from the gun case. I pack my ammo in a hard case and tuck it in with my checked baggage.

Hunting with blackpowder? Arrange for a canister of blackpowder or Pyrodex to be shipped ahead, as airlines are particularly fussy about passengers flying with explosive materials. Check your airline regulations ahead of time and be aware of their restrictions.

Lock your cases, and for extra security wrap duct tape around the case and over the locks. (Duct tape wrapped around meat coolers helps hold the lids tight, too.)

If you can make or buy cases which do not look like firearms or archery cases, so much the better.

5) PHOTOGRAPHING YOUR HUNT

To bring home great photographs that show the entire hunt instead of just the usual grip-and-grin photo of hunters and tagged animal, consider the following:

• Take two cameras, if you can, and use both. Don't own two cameras? Purchase one of the new disposable cameras. They take great pictures and are fairly inexpensive, while offering many features to choose from. Since you can't always use flash, consider getting film in 100 and 200 speeds and use both to cover sunny and gray weather. (Film speeds of 100 and 400 will give better opportunity to cover all light conditions; the higher the number, the faster the film reacts to light, meaning you can get better images from 400 film than 200 film in low-light conditions.)

• The professionals compose photos on the Rule of 3. Imagine a tic-tac-toe game's crossed lines. Center of interest should be at any one of the four points where those lines cross. The center of interest should never be smack in the center of the photo frame; such a photo looks static, lifeless.

• Put some color into the background, such as colorful fall leaves, blue sky, unusual dead tree, anything which adds to the picture's composition.

• Get close to the subject, while being sure you have everything of importance in the photo.

• Clean all blood, dirt, tongues hanging out, etc. from the trophy – anything which distracts from a beautiful photograph and a dignified animal.

• Look through the viewfinder before taking any photos and compose the picture. If the pose doesn't look right, rearrange your set-up until it does.

• Keep the sun off your shoulder or to left or right side, so the sun won't be in the subject's eyes. If possible, don't have the sun directly at your back; people looking into the camera will squint, and that doesn't look good.

• Use fill-flash when there are shadows across the subject's face. One of the most infamous facial appearances is the upper half of the face in deep shadow of the bill of a cap and the bottom half of the face in bright sunlight, producing a two-tone face with no details in the top half. Kind of makes the subject look like a raccoon, but with less eye definition. The eyes must be visible and show clearly; our mind won't like a photo of people or animals whose eyes are not shown clearly.

Planning ahead for a successful hunting season gives you peace of mind, helps avoid unnecessary problems and provides memorable and enjoyable hunting experiences. Something as simple as a checklist can and will save you time and money, as well as keep you safe and comfortable. No matter whether you're a traveling hunter or hunting close to home, be prepared so you can enjoy your success to the max.

Kathy Butt

Kathy Butt and her husband, Foster, have been in the professional taxidermy business for more than 20 years. She became enthusiastically involved in big game hunting 15 years ago and has hunted elk, whitetail deer, black bear, mountain lion, turkey and wild hogs with archery, black powder, rifle and shotgun. Kathy has written for nearly all the bowhunting and black powder publications. Many of her articles are geared toward encouraging women and children to become more active in the hunting world. She also assists in archery instruction classes at the Becoming an Outdoors Woman workshops in Tennessee.

• Use fill-flash to illuminate the subject's face under a hat or cap brim and fill the frame with the subject to create more interest and show detail. Action photos of other activities add interest to the photographic record of a hunting trip. This is a way to show what you got without making it look like another "hero" shot of a filled game bag or fishing stringer.

Don't think camouflage is total concealment. It's only one little part. Read on....

by Ralph Cianciarulo

Camouflage...Good Concealment...Better

Now you see me ... now you don't. Now you know I'm there ... now you don't. Boy, if it were that simple, all of us would be making ourselves invisible. However, it takes more than just a cool-looking pattern to help you blend in, although, in today's market, many hunters feel that if they have all the right camo and everything matches, they can't lose. This is the world of concealment, not camouflage fashions and looking right as you strap on your daypack. Many think because they bought the hottest camo out there they don't have to think about anything else regarding camouflage, and they mistake camouflage for concealment.

Wrong!

The art of **concealment – this term should apply whenever you enter the woods, because it applies to more than you and your camo.** A lot more...such as setting up a tree stand, a ground blind or even stillhunting or stalking, i.e., being aware of and preparing for how you move, when you move, and how and when you don't move. The depth of this factor – concealment – is something most hunters forget. There's much more than camo when it comes to concealment. Camouflage clothing is only one element, a small element, of concealment.

What are the elements of concealment? Here's a list:

• Your silhouette, partial-body and full-body, when you're still and when you move.
   • Where you stand or sit in a blind.
   • Stand or blind positioning.
   • Camouflage clothing, of course; body, head and hands.
   • Your scent, or lack of same.
   • Wind direction.

SILHOUETTE / POSITIONING / MOTION

Let's start with a man's silhouette. Take this upright standing man and have him walk through the woods. Have him stop and look around. Does anything in the woods look like this silhouette? No!

Another question: Does anything sound like this man walking through the woods, make walking noises like this man walking through the woods?

Take this small test the next time you go into the woods –

Dress up in your favorite hunting clothes, grab your bow or whatever hunting tool you're using, and have your hunting partner follow you with a camcorder. Have him/her film you walking around, getting up into your tree stand or ground blind. When you are settled in, be sure the camera person walks completely around you, filming you close-up and far away, from all sorts of angles. Draw your bow and come to full anchor a few times.

Then go home and plug this camera into your TV set. Now turn the color off your set and sit back and watch what you look like and sound like. Now we're talking concealment. Why turn the color off? Because, to the best of any scientist's knowledge, animals see in four-color poorly.

The part of our body that moves the most is our head, and there is no shape in the woods which resembles this. One of the best ways to help conceal the human head may look a bit crazy, but it really does work. Make your head become a small pile of brush.

A few years back, we found a great natural funnel loaded with sign. The problem was the prevailing winds stopped us from setting up in a tree. Due to the narrow funnel, we had to stay on the ground. Knowing we couldn't change the terrain, we did the next best thing and modified the vegetation a bit. We constructed a small deadfall blind.

As Brian sat in the blind, I walked around filming him. When we watched that tape we immediately noticed that even though Brian was in full camouflage, we could still see the silhouette of his head. Changing hats helped, but attaching small branches with leaves worked much better. Another solution is to buy stick-on leaves and dress up a favorite hunting hat. After seeing the problem on film, and then seeing how well the modifications worked, I am convinced that this technique breaks up the headline. Hats do help, but when you add these leaves there is no better way.

So never make fun of a ghilly suit. They look odd, but put one on and you'll disappear. You'll look like you're a complete piece of shrubbery, especially in a slight breeze.

Pay attention to what's behind you, because that's where the best concealment exists. Sometimes you can be best concealed simply by sitting in front of a bush or some brush and grass, or sitting in amongst it, instead of having vegetation in front of you. When the vegetation is in front of you, you MUST have a shooting lane through it. If you don't, you'll have to lean to the side or rise up to shoot. That's a giveaway, and that's why it's most important to be sure you're covered at your back.

Does your bow limb stick up above your concealment? If so, then you're not fully concealed.

When you're stillhunting, do you stop next to something which breaks your outline? You should. Do you stop in the shadows? You should. Do you stop your feet instantly, in shooting position? You should. Too many people shuffle their feet when they stop, or take an extra half-step, or stop with their feet positioned incorrectly for shooting. All of these factors cause extra, man-sounding motion and thus reduce the concealment factor.

Our faces are one of the shiniest parts you will see in the woods, as shiny or shinier than undersides of light green leaves turned up on a windy day. Due to the oils in our skin, plus perspiration, we positively glisten. We can be noticed a long way off. Exposed hair often shines, too. And if we notice it, what do you think the animals will do?

A friend of mine, several years ago on a Colorado pronghorn hunt, thought wearing a visor instead of a cap or hat would be a great way to keep cool because heat would escape off his scalp better. That it did, but his hunting partner in a blind 70 yards away at the opposite end of a dam on the water hole said his head looked like a shiny rock. Since there weren't any pronghorns around, they traded a couple of shouted, friendly insults, and then my friend removed his visor and put on a camo hat.

"The shadows in my blind weren't as deep as I would have liked," he told me. "So every time I turned my head to look for goats, my hair twinkled. That wasn't good for concealment, and it gave my buddy too many chances to get lippy. I guess I'd suspected the hair would be too shiny; if I hadn't, I wouldn't have had the camo hat in my pack."

Face masks work great, with one exception. Many archers do not like to shoot with a mask on. They say they can't shoot with a mask on, but what they're really saying is that they won't shoot with a mask on.

I always have liked using camo make-up instead of wearing a camo mask. A mask holds some heat; it bothers my vision, and I don't like the feel of the mask when I'm at full anchor. Yeah, I know you're thinking "He should be concentrating enough at full draw that he won't even notice the mask." You're right, but I do.

Many times while hunting , the make-up wears off or smears. Either way, the camouflage effect is gone. This is why I always carry a camo make-up kit.

Years ago, camo make-up was hard to get off. You would have to scrub for a long time and your face looked and felt like Rocky's after his big fights. That's not the case today, for there are good camo make-up kits available, with camo which stays on when it is supposed to and comes off painlessly when it is supposed to. Robinson Labs has a nice kit of this type; there are others, too.

I carry a small container of baby wipes in my pack. This takes the make-up off with no problem and also moisturizes my skin. Camo make-up removes the natural skin oils.

One time years ago, I shot a good buck and was so excited that I forgot I had the make-up on when I pulled up to the drive-up window at a fast-food joint to order a soda. The girl's eyes just about came out of her head. She thought I was going to rob her. I realized what I had done and quickly told her not to worry.

I make a concession to cold weather. As the temperature starts to drop, I pull out my spando-flage headnet. This keeps my face warm during cold days afield, and it fits snugly enough – without being too tight – that I don't have an anchoring problem. If you go this route, I highly recommend you practice shooting with this headnet on. For that matter, practice with any headnet you may wear.

I have found several neat things on the market designed for bowhunting in cold weather, but most of these items either take too long to get out for the shot or they just don't allow a proper anchoring point to be established.

SCENT

Scent has been discussed and cussed for years. There are attractant (to game animals) scents and cover-up (our odor) scents. The stories we've all heard make you wonder what is effective and what isn't, when is it effective and when isn't it, is there any particular pattern? Let me make this strong statement before we go any further – the only way to eliminate the human odor completely is to jump into an airtight body bag and zip it up. I don't think I have to tell you how long you will be able to hunt in such a set-up, but the game will not smell you, not even when you're lying there gasping for oxygen..

Let's take a domestic dog and train this dog to smell out drugs. Now take this dog and walk him through a warehouse of goods. Among all the conflicting odors, this domesticated dog can smell out a bag of drugs wrapped in plastic and taped up. And we think we can eliminate our odor completely from a wild animal that has to make life-saving decisions based on its sense of smell? Nope.

There are, however, things on the market which do help. Carbon-loaded garments work when used right. However, if you do not use the headnet you might as well not use the suit. Remember that most of the heat loss from our bodies escapes from our head and neck, and not using the headnet will allow scent to escape. That's all the more reason to wash your hair frequently and wash the hat or cap you wear. They're tremendous human scent collectors. They also collect cooking odors, smoking odors, etc., quickly.

Washing hunting clothes with scent blockers or with unscented detergent helps. So do the scent-blocking sprays. I have seen deer, elk, bear and many other game animals come onto me from downwind.

Have I been winded? You betcha, but I truly believe that trying to be as scent free as possible does help. But don't temp fate. Position yourself downwind. The scent concealment aids are just that – aids.

Taking a shower just before hunting is good. Washing with unscented soap and a rough wash cloth to remove dead skin cells….that's good concealment.

Wearing boots that have no foreign odor….that's concealment. Rubber boots help a lot. Just be sure to tuck your pants legs in, to hold scent in. If you're uncomfortable wearing high rubber boots all day, buy chest waders and walk in in them, then take them off at your tree stand. Rubber boots will leave some scent. Everything does.

Wearing latex gloves so you don't leave your scent on branches and leaves and tree steps – everything you touch – that's concealment.

How alarming are all the human and other scents? That's a good question. It varies with the individual animal's experiences with humans. Scent loses its strength over time, and the fresher it is when animals smell it, the more it will be detrimental to your hunting plans. How far is far enough and how far is too far? That's a good question. Let the game animal tell you; it's the ultimate judge. If it makes you, and you don't get a shot, then you didn't go far enough.

Concealment

TREE STAND / GROUND BLIND CONCEALMENT

Here is a good one I'll bet you never thought of. How many of you have ever used those little plastic cable ties. I carry them with me all the time. When I set up my stands, I use these to attach branches to my stand. I have switched from sitting in a small stand and being uncomfortable to using larger stands and sitting comfortably and quietly. (Sitting quietly is just an additional element of concealment. Fidgeting gives us away.) By adding branches to the stand you literally make great tree blinds that truly help to make you blend in.

Using foliage in your favor will help you every time, such as when you approach an area to glass out, or you want to see what is over the other hill. The best way to do this is with the wind in your favor and using the existing terrain to your favor. Any time you could silhouette or sky-line yourself, use whatever cover is available and look through it, not around it. You might even have to crawl or squat on your approach, but doing so will allow you to go undetected.

Assume you know the direction from which game will approach the majority of the time at any particular stand. Consider positioning your stand on the off-side of the tree, so you're facing the same direction the game will be facing as it approaches. Resist the urge to turn and look. The tree trunk blocks most or all of you from the animal's view. That's one benefit. You're not looking at the animal, and that will help you remain a little calmer. So simply wait for the animal to walk past you, offering you a quartering-away shot. This doesn't always work according to the script, but it works often enough to make this a useful concealment tool. I don't know whether you believe in brain waves, but when you're staring at an approach animal, really giving it your undivided attention but not moving a muscle, too often that animal makes you. Why? That's debatable, but.....

Concealment is avoiding being sky-lined. I saw a couple of tree stands one time which told a complete story without any help from the hunters using them. The guys said deer were making them at long range. No wonder! They had hung the tree stands on trees right over the deer trails they were watching, and they hung the stands on the side of the tree so they were completely silhouetted. The deer were unintentionally looking right at these hunters as they approached on their trails.

Remember, camouflage works as long as you pay attention to all the other factors which help you stay CONCEALED. The very best tool we have is our ability to think and remember. Remember this – we are a predator and must remember to think and act like one.

• Above. Look through or just over vegetation to keep yourself hidden. The thicker the cover behind you, the less visible you'll be to the game you're watching. Right photo. Keep low and crawl when needed. Keep your rear-end down and hitch forward on elbows and toes, with your head down. Look up only when you need to. This gives you maximum concealment when there's little cover.

RALPH CIANCIARULO
Ralph Cianciarulo promotes archery and bowhunting for a living as a video producer, seminar speaker, television personality and international bowhunter. He also is a guide/outfitter and has served as guide and shooting instructor to such athletes and celebrities as Bo Jackson, Walter Payton and Kurt Russell. Ralph was the first bowhunter to harvest a Eurasian brown bear, which he took in 1991 in Russia. He has made several hunting safaris to Africa. He is a member of the Hoyt "USA Hunting All-Star Team" and is on the field staffs of Hoyt USA, Beman USA, New Archery Products, Bowhunters Discount Warehouse, Fine-Line Inc., Loc-On Treestands, Trebark, Scent Shield and Spence's Targets.

Concealment

• Upper left. Full camo – face, hands and gear. Leather on quiver hood helps quiet it and absorbs light, eliminating reflection.
• Upper right. Be aware of light and dark areas and the high contrast. Most places have more light tones than we realize. A camo bag keeps bright fletches covered.
• Above left. Match the light/dark tones and the pattern to the situation. If you have snow, you'll need light areas.
• Above right. Eliminating or masking human scent is an effective tool for best concealment.

26   Steps Along the Hunter's Path

Great hunting opportunities come with great responsibilities in this situation.

by Gen Ebert

How To Get – and Keep – Permission to Hunt
Those Productive Suburban Fringe Hotspots

*H*unting on the edge of the urban sprawl can be exciting. You will see more deer, bigger deer with larger racks and much larger does. But to get and keep hunting opportunities in such a potentially wonderful site, there are five points to follow: 1) Ethics; 2) asking permission; 3) learning to read maps; 4) reading a compass and 5) the ability to scout the hunting land.

ETHICS

Great hunting opportunities in such areas come with great responsibilities, because problems can be magnified under the microscope of nearby, dense human population, some of it highly critical of us and of hunting before we even set foot in the woods.

What you do as a hunter will reflect on you and on all hunters, so what you do affects the future of all hunting. This means our children and all of our families which are coming up ... many fine years of hunting. This can be a big problem. People tend to have their own set of ethics, and times have changed. With this change you are going to have to adapt, to drop any bad habits you may have.

PERMISSION

The first bad habit that many hunters have is the reluctance to ask for permission to hunt. Unless you hunt on public land, you will always need to ask for permission to hunt. Private land is owned by someone; do your very best to find out.

Go to the local municipality first. Get the necessary plat book(s). Then call the owner(s) and start from there. Usually, they are helpful and polite. You'd be surprised how helpful the local farmers are. Absentee owners, or non-farming landowners, may not be as helpful and/or friendly. They don't have the same feel for the land and the stewardship of the land and everything which lives upon it.

Farmers, however, have crop damage from deer. They want to keep their deer herd down. Some of them have turkey problems, so they will be willing to let you in.

Along with access permission comes an obligation to the owner of that land. You will want to offer him some venison or you may want to help him do some fence work, or work around his place. Whatever it takes. Maybe he would like you to cut some logs for him if he has a fireplace, or he may be in need of tree planting, or digging a pond or whatever. Offer your skills; don't be shy about it. That will get you into the little woodlot on the edge of the urban sprawl. That will get you into some of the open fields. There's often fine pheasant hunting around such areas, too. If you just ask permission … just along the hedge rows … you might get permission to go in there and do some hunting. Some landowners will give you permission to hunt small game and upland birds and turkeys long before they will give you permission to hunt deer on their property. Deer is and most likely always will be the Number One game, and many landowners have family members returning each Fall to hunt deer on their property. In such instances, there simply may not be space for you.

Women and families may receive permission to hunt before men asking for themselves. Dress well; dress cleanly. Be polite and respectful. This is not a quiz nor an interrogation. Let the landowner know you're responsible. Many people aren't aware that closed gates are to remain closed gates, and that grassy fields are a valuable crop instead of a vehicular turn-around place.

MAPS

Several kinds of maps can be purchased, or you might be able to go to the town hall and copy them at no charge. There are topographic county maps and sometimes recreation-area maps. There may also be survey maps. There also may be companies in your area which sell maps; look in your local Yellow Pages. There might also be an exhibitor or two at these Deer & Turkey Expos who are selling the maps you need. Check it out.

COMPASS READING SKILLS

Why do you need a compass in suburban areas? Because you need to know exactly where you are at all times. People in such areas often feel like they've been violated if anyone steps foot onto their property. In addition, in such tight quarters, you can run afoul of no-hunting laws and trespass rules if you step out of the property you have permission to hunt.

I know so many people who do not know how to read a compass, nor do they know the direction once the sun goes down. Since it is easy to get lost if you are in an unknown area, a good compass and the skill to use it are essential.

I prefer one that can be suspended on a cord around the neck. The one pinned to your jacket can come off in rough brush, and then you're in a real predicament even if the trail is clear. The situation is worse if it snows and you can't backtrack or find a trail.

I'm noticing, too, some fellows are using orange surveyor's tape to mark a trail. That is a no-no. The surveyor uses orange; if you want to use another color, fine. But as you are walking out, take it with you. Don't leave it strung up in the trees; that really irritates a landowner (and gives away your trail to everyone else hunting there.) If you want to leave a little marker on the side of the road for the next morning when it is dark so that you can find your spot, that's fine. There's also a little reflective button you can buy for sticking onto tree bark. Don't forget that when you're walking into the woods you're going to see them, but when you turn around and go back out you're not going to see them. So double-side the trees. This will make it easy to get back out.

Bowhunting is, of course, almost exclusively the hunting tool of choice in most suburban areas because of safety and fear of firearms among the general population. You must be a better hunter, you must be an excellent judge of distance; most of all a clean, swift kill is necessary. You must practice, practice, practice, and be extremely careful of the shots you take.

The deer should not be seen dying in the neighbor's yard or in the green area of the local industrial park. You must, or should, maintain a low profile and be neat about the entrails when you field dress a deer. Don't leave them alongside the road or a path others may be using. Leave them back in the woods.

Take your tree stand down each night, if possible. Some places won't let you leave them up overnight. Then, the next morning you hunt there, there is this problem of courtesy to other hunters. Some hunters are in there really, really early. If you go clanging and banging with all your ladders and equipment in the early morning darkness, you've blown the hunt for yourself and the others around you. You'll have to figure out what to do. There are many ways to use a tree stand without it being cumbersome, plus steps and ropes and ladders. Do some research to determine what will work best where you hunt. That is part of hunting on the edge of the urban sprawl.

If local people come to see your deer, be polite and answer their questions. There will be a lot of questions, I'm sure. I've found there will be many more questions of curiosity than of accusation or anger. People will want to see what you have; they will ask what you will do with that deer.

You eat the meat, use the hide for garments or gloves or something, and the entrails are a gift to nature. Explain that entrails are fine food for some birds and animals ... the weasels, hawks, eagles, foxes, coyotes and many other species that eat meat.

Nothing goes to waste, not even the hair from a deer that is found in the spring. Little birds weave that into their nests. I saw the most incredible thing ... a spider carrying a long piece of deer hair. He wove it into his web. It was there most of the summer; we checked that little spider about once a week. It was beautiful.

SCOUTING

Putting a compass to good use while scouting is an excellent way to learn the woods...and learn quite a bit about yourself. It's best, anyway, to scout year round, or at least in the summer. Scouting just a couple of weeks before the season is inadequate and pressures the game.

We scout all year round. The game trails change. Some become old, some aren't used and new ones are taken. Those are the ones you want to keep an eye on.

RESPECT

Treat all game ... all wildlife ... all the natural world ... with greatest respect.

If you are taking pictures, clean off whatever blood shows, put its tongue back in its mouth, hold its head up in a respectful way and then take the pictures. It's a gift to you from nature; all effort must be made to show respect.

GEN EBERT

Gen Ebert is president of AWARE (A Wisconsin Alliance for Resources and the Environment) and advisor to Becoming An Outdoors-Woman. She sits on the board of directors of the Waukesha (WI) County Conservation Alliance. Outspoken and active, she has received the Educator of the Year Award from the Wisconsin Conservation Congress, plus several other awards from the WDNR and other conservation organizations. She is an avid hunter and all-around outdoor person.

Video cameras are the best thing and the worst thing to hit deer hunting in quite some time.

by Greg Miller

Pre-Season Blunders ... A Growing Problem

My deer hunting career eclipsed the 30-year mark a couple seasons back. As you might imagine, the sport has undergone many and important changes during those years. One of the most noticeable of these changes has to do with hunter attitudes. Deer hunters truly have become discriminating and selective, to the point of pickiness. This is especially true for those individuals who limit their pursuits solely to mature bucks. When it comes to trophy whitetails, the majority of serious hunters have learned that there's no such thing as working too hard.

I've also noticed a disturbing trend regarding the exhausting work some people apply to their bowhunting efforts. Simply put, **their gung-ho attitudes are getting them into serious trouble, trophy deer-wise. What's even more disturbing is the fact that, more and more these days, this trouble is starting before the archery season ever opens.**

I'd like to state for the record here and now that I am a vocal proponent of pre-season scouting. However, there is a right way and a wrong way to go about things at this time of year. If my recent observations and conversations with hunters are any indication, there's a growing number of hunters who routinely go about things the wrong way. In short, they're continually breaking a couple of the basic rules for successful trophy hunting.

Too Many Footprints

One aspect of pre-season scouting that seems to be growing in popularity is the "walk every square inch of your hunting area" approach. Don't get me wrong, you should be intimately familiar with your hunting area. However, the pre-season period is the worst of all times to be stomping around in the woods attempting to familiarize yourself with the lay of the land. It's also a terrible time to try to learn more about the animals you'll be pursuing during the upcoming season.

Maybe people like me are partly to blame. Writers often mention in their articles and seminars that hunters should strive to become intimately familiar with their hunting areas. The only way you can hope to accomplish this task is with topographical maps, fly-overs and by walking literally every square inch of the area concerned. I've stressed the fact that **the best time to so this walking is during the off-season. In my defense, I was referring to the post-season and spring periods, not the pre-season.**

In any event, I believe many hunters are under the impression that big bucks don't pay much attention to their surroundings during the pre-season. Therefore, under that same reasoning, it stands to reason that this is a great time to do some extensive scouting. Right? Wrong! **Mature deer miss very little of what's going on around them at this time of year. In fact, they are probably more in tune with their environment during the pre-season period than at any other time. This is especially true for that time frame I often refer to as the late velvet stage.**

Look at it this way. The bucks aren't doing any rubbing yet. They aren't doing much in the way of scraping either. And they certainly aren't being sidetracked by the sweet smell of estrous does. What this means is that the bucks are able to tune 100 percent of their survival instincts to the woods and fields around them. I seriously doubt they'll fail to notice when a human invades their turf. This is especially true when you consider some of the other variables that come into play at this time of year.

First of all, it most likely will be quite warm. So it's not likely you'll be able to walk through the woods without working up a sweat. Any time you sweat, you're leaving behind a trail of odor that a deer with a bad head cold could follow days later.

Oh, and then there's the problem of mosquitoes and other biting insects. No problem, you say. You'll spray a little bit of repellent on your hands and face – just enough to keep the bugs away, but not enough so the deer will smell it. Hmmm ... and exactly how much repellent would that be?

I've always found it interesting that anyone would even consider walking around in their hunting areas during the pre-season period. Now, I'm not talking here about slipping into the woods, putting up a tree stand for opening day, then slipping out again. I'm talking about all day, all-encompassing walks. Walks that are specifically designed to cover as much of a targeted area as humanly possible.

What's wrong with this approach? Well, as I already mentioned, you'll be doing a lot more to educate the deer than to educate yourself. Also, the underbrush and foliage is going to be summertime thick, which means your visibility is going to be extremely limited. Of course, this means you really will have to walk every square inch of your hunting territory. Once more, the more you walk, the more you sweat. I really fail to see where the benefits that might come from these pre-season walks could possibly outweigh all the risks involved.

There's something else to keep in mind about scouting during the pre-season. It's entirely possible that, because of the thick foliage, the bucks in your hunting areas could be bedding much closer than normal to their food sources. What this means is that even a short walk-around in the woods could put you face to face with an antlered animal.

Provided it only happens one time, jumping a bedded buck or having a big buck follow your trail through the woods really isn't all that big of a deal. Unfortunately, the gung-ho attitudes that I spoke of earlier seem to prompt a lot of hunters to make repeated walks through their favorite hunting areas during the pre-season. **A fair number of these people are turning this already costly mistake into something even worse. They're taking a buddy with them each time they visit their hunting areas.**

It should almost go without saying at this point, but here goes anyway. Two people means your hunting area will be contaminated with twice as much human odor. Two people means there's twice as much chance of having a face to face encounter with a big buck. Two people means you'll be causing twice as much disturbance in a particular area. In short, two people means there's one too many.

So how can you expect to be successful during the early part of the archery season if you're not supposed to scout during the pre-season? Hey, I didn't say you couldn't scout. I'm merely implying that you should put thought into your scouting efforts. For example, don't take regular and extensive walks through the heart of your favorite hunting areas. Even though the temptation to do otherwise sometimes is great, don't take a buddy along when you do decide to do a bit of pre-season scouting.

Remember, mature whitetail bucks possess the ability to quickly and efficiently pattern the activities of any of their natural predators.

- Video cameras are one of the worst things to hit hunting in recent years. Videoing a big buck from several hundred yards away in pre-season is one thing. Filming that same deer from a stand site you plan to use during the open season is quite another, yet many hunters do just that, destroying any chance they might have had of harvesting that deer.

- It's true, big bucks often display carefree and even careless behavior during the late summer. But be forewarned; their behavior at this time of year is not an indication that they're totally ignorant of what's going on around them.

Steps Along the Hunter's Path

This includes the human predator. Believe me, the way you treat your hunting areas during the pre-season can have a tremendous bearing on your chances for success well into the open season.

The Problem With Videos

Things like thick foliage, extremely warm temperatures and hordes of biting insects can make it impractical to do much in-woods stuff during the pre-season. In cases like this, hunters usually revert to another form of scouting. They drive around in late afternoon and spot-check known food attractants. Since big bucks usually become quite visible during the late summer period, this can be a great way to get a handle on both the quantity and quality of the antlered animals residing within your hunting areas.

However, it's this very thing, the sighting of one or maybe even several big bucks, that prompts many modern day hunters into making what often turns out to be a costly mistake. These guys aren't content with watching those bucks from a distance. They just have to get a closer look. In recent years, especially, a growing number of hunters are doing whatever it takes to get some up close and personal video footage of "their" bucks. Big mistake!

Video cameras are both the best thing and the worst thing to happen to the sport of bowhunting in some time. On the positive side, thanks to video cameras, there are some top-quality instructional hunting videos on the market today. There's no doubt in my mind that these tapes have helped quite a few people become better hunters.

On the negative side, however, the popularity of video cameras (and hunting videos) seems to have given a bunch of hunters the impression that it's okay to routinely invade a big buck's turf – especially during the late summer and early fall. These individuals further justify their actions by telling themselves that the big bucks they see at this time of year aren't displaying their normal survivalist mentalities, that they actually are behaving more like antlerless deer than big bucks. With archery season still a couple of weeks away, what harm could come from shooting some up close footage of the bucks now? Why not film right from the stand site you plan to use opening day? What a story it would be if you then managed to arrow one of those bucks?

I personally know of dozens of cases where bowhutners have sat on one of their stand sites during the pre-season and filmed big bucks. How many of these guys have then managed to arrow one of those bucks they had filmed? The answer is a resounding NONE!

It really isn't all that difficult to figure out why most amateur whitetail deer videographers have failed to score on big bucks they filmed during the pre-season. Hey folks, those bucks caught on that they were being watched. Now, I realize that it's the pre-season and opening day is still weeks away. I also realize that big bucks don't seem to be displaying much in the way of standard survival behavior, but as I pointed out earlier, mature deer are aware of everything that's going on around them at this time of year. It takes a big buck very little time to detect the presence of a human visitor. Mature whitetails are not crazy about being watched by one of their most feared predators – not even during the off-season and not even if it's only "in fun".

Capturing a big buck on film from a couple hundred yards is one thing. Filming that same deer from a few dozen yards is quite another. **In case you don't already know, mature bucks are seldom tolerant of such invasions of their privacy.** They have a couple choices to help them avoid future confrontations with a human intruder. They can wait until dark before making their way to the feeding area where the human has been spying on them. Or they can start utilizing an alternate food source located in a totally different area. In either case, the hunters who have been filming those bucks will suddenly find themselves out of the game.

I know there are a select few hunters who have managed to arrow a big buck while sitting on the same stand where they filmed the deer from during the pre-season. For every one hunter who has managed to accomplish this task, there are thousands more who have failed. Maybe you can justify taking a chance with odds like that, but I can't.

It's tough enough trying to get a big buck to walk by within bow range when that deer has no idea he's being hunted. That task becomes nearly impossible once the buck becomes aware of your presence. Believe me, the deer you're hunting will always be aware of your presence if you continue to make pre-season blunders.

For a close-range hunting challenge demanding finely honed hunting and shooting skills, try this.

by Phil W. Johnston

Handguns for Big Game

Long ago a bull elk was the reason I switched from a rifle to a handgun for all my hunting. Fresh out of the US submarine fleet, I longed for a great western adventure. An elk hunt on Granite Creek between Yellowstone and Grand Teton National Parks seemed just the ticket.

Money was tight and booking an elk hunt with a recognized outfitter like Bud Nelson took all the spare cash we had and a bit more besides. To make a long story short, I paid for and booked a 10 day adventure and ended the hunt in two days after knocking down a great 6x6 bull at long range with a .300 Winchester Magnum. The shots were some of the best of my life, to be sure, but slinging lead at long range left something to be desired. I hung up the rifles and have been carrying a variety of handguns ever since.

Handgun hunting is nothing new. Typical of the way history works, early handgun hunts went unrecorded for the most part. The Tower of London exhibits several early flintlock handguns which feature ornate hunting scenes engraved into the metalwork, suggesting that they might have been intended for the field.

Handgun hunting really got off the ground in the 1800s. When doing the research for my book "Successful Handgun Hunting", I came across some great old handgun hunts. Washington Irving was one of our first true handgun hunters. Irving wrote "I urged my horse sufficiently near, when, taking aim, to my chagrin, both pistols missed fire". Murphy's Law worked in those days, too. Irving was later to write "...pistols are very effective in buffalo hunting, as a hunter can ride up close to the animal, and fire at it while at full speed."

Back in those days handguns lacked the power and accuracy we've come to expect today. If a handgun was effective then, as

Irving wrote, I submit that today's handgun is perfect for hunting big and small game.

Today we're blessed with a variety of handguns, ranging from single and double action revolvers that generate half a ton of muzzle energy to single shot tack drivers that shoot better than some custom rifles.

All this technology and progress does not make handgun hunting easy, however. **The challenge of hunting with a handgun is surpassed only by bow hunting.** Like the archer, today's successful handgun hunter will shoot all year long, with hunting ammunition, and he or she will work far harder in the field, too. Like the archer, the handgunner has to get close, very close. To be successful in the field, the handgunner has to learn a complete basics package. Today's successful handgun hunter must add range estimation and target animal anatomy to the mix, plus a few items that protect our eyes and hearing.

Let's **look at the basics**, one by one.

Precision with a handgun comes after long hours of practice and just a bit of frustration along the way. To shoot "10s", a competitive handgunner knows that the basics on the range consist of sight alignment, trigger control, breathing and position.

Sight alignment typically refers to the alignment of the front sight in the square notch of the rear sight. When shooting open or metallic sights, we struggle to align the front sight so the top of the front sight is even with the top of the rear sight while showing an equal amount of light or "space" on either side of the front sight. The point of concentration is the front sight or just a portion of the front sight. One of our most successful international shooters tells himself "front sight, front sight, front sight, front sight" before each string of rapid-fire competition. This emphasizes the struggle required to perform this task in split seconds.

Open sights are fun to use in the field. An open-sighted revolver is the most compact, portable package that can be carried. I've taken bear, elk, antelope and many deer with open-sighted revolvers. Open sights are a short-range proposition, however, and should be restricted to 40-50 yards in the field. Because the shooter's concentration must always be on the front sight, it's easy to forget about all the other variables that we hunters face every day in the field. In addition, unfortunately that darned front sight gets harder to see clearly every day as we age.

When one decides to discard open sights in favor of optical or even electronic sights, there's a whole new world out there. When we slip a scope or electronic sight on one of our rigs, we instantaneously eliminate sight alignment problems while adding little weight or sacrificing little portability in the process. Revolvers look and handle great with a low power scope in place, and there are some good holsters out there for such rigs. Since our straight wall cartridge revolvers are limited range tools, we don't need lots of magnification. I still like a 2X scope on a revolver for much of today's hunting. In addition, I've been messing with one of the latest electronic sights these days, and my .454 Casull shoots great so equipped. Sub-two-inch groups are common with this futuristic red dot centered in the 50-yard target. The rig still fits my old shoulder holster, too. I'm so impressed that I'm going to try the sight on an elk hunt this fall.

If you're interested in shooting small groups or small things at long range, don't think that handgunners are excepted, either. There are several good bolt action and break action handguns around that are fully capable of half-inch groups at 100 yards and even better in the hands of a benchrest shooter. Prairie dogs and called predators aren't safe in these parts, believe me. All bets on sight equipment are off in this area. I've seen and used extended eye relief scopes up to 10X on occasion, and I've even resorted to a 24X rifle scope from time to time. Putting a high magnification scope on a handgun sets up a whole new array of problems, however, with critical eye relief and limited field of view for starters.

Trigger control refers simply to the act of squeezing the trigger without disturbing the "aim". This, too, is much more difficult to practice than preach. The best advice is to practice, practice, practice. Grab a gun you can safely dry fire (drop the hammer on an empty chamber) and then dry fire until you can squeeze the trigger without shifting your aim. Practice often. At the range, occasionally have someone else load your gun, secretly leaving an empty chamber or two in the process, before handing you the loaded arm. It's not uncommon to see the gun recoil nearly as much on an empty chamber in this drill. Squeeze the trigger; take seconds to apply an even pressure and remember that if you're doing it correctly the discharge will almost catch you by surprise.

Breathing refers to the act of taking a full breath and then letting about half of it out before you deliver the shot. You don't want to be straining to hold a breath.

Position on the range is dictated by the rules of the "games" we play. **Position in the field** refers to taking a rest, always taking a rest. Mother Nature supplies all kinds of rests out there, and any capable marksman knows that we must use them. In addition, take the time to find a stable position. Go prone if there's time. Take a rest.

Range estimation is critical to the handgunner, too, just as it is to the archer. While I don't feel that range finders have a place in the field during hunting season, I do think they're great for the rest of the year. Today's laser range finders are accurate and affordable and it's duck soup to guesstimate a range and then measure it. You'll get good, fast. As with many things, it's a matter of practice.

Anatomy refers to the way our quarry is built. We've got to hit 'em where they live, so to speak, and that typically consists of a 4" to 18" box (depending upon the size of the critter, of course) that is arranged immediately behind the shoulder. The heart is toward the bottom of the box and the lungs are on the high end. Simply said, if you run a .44 caliber or larger slug completely through both lungs, you've got a quickly dead critter. That's what we want to do.

Remember to look at position of the animal before you shoot, and visualize that box behind the shoulder. If you're shooting an ample gun, like a heavily loaded .44 Magnum or the .454 Casull, you have the power to punch through most shoulders and then get in that box if the animal is quartering toward you. Aim for the shoulder on the far side if the target is quartering away. Typically, when the shoulder is broken the animal more or less drops in its tracks.

Last, but surely not least, is our **personal protection.** Every gun we shoot makes a great deal of noise. In fact, every gun we shoot, including the .22 rimfires, will permanently damage our hearing unless we wear hearing protection for each shot. It's easy, too. Today there are electronic earplugs that shut off above 100 dB of noise and they'll amplify noises below 90 dB or so. If you don't want to spend the bucks for this high tech protection, then grab a good pair of hard-shell hearing muffs and use them in the field as well as at the range. It's even smarter to **use earplugs and good muffs** all the time. The point is that **permanent hearing damage, called tinnitus, is a tragedy that can easily be prevented.**

The same holds true for eye protection. **Get shooting glasses and wear them.** These big magnum handguns work at pressure levels usually associated with rifles. By design, a revolver features a gap between the barrel and cylinder and high pressure, high velocity things routinely escape through this gap. In the case of the 65,000 psi .454 Casull, this escaping gas is violent enough to remove fingers if one wraps his hand around or otherwise keeps it near the cylinder during a shot! So wear eye protection, too.

There's more to handgun hunting, as well. First and foremost, we have to **remember that we have 50 states and each state gov-**

erns hunters with a different set of rules. Here in North Dakota, where I live, to quote the 1997 Proclamation: "Handgun (pistol or revolver or single shot) cartridge cases under .40 caliber must be at least 1.285 inches in length and bullets must be at least .257 inches in diameter. Handgun cartridge cases of .40 caliber or larger must be at least .992 inches in length." Minnesota requires at least a .23 caliber "single projectile, soft point round, the case of which is no shorter than 1.285" again excepting the 10mm which features a case length of .95 inches. Wisconsin limits handgun big game hunters to the "three" magnums (.357, .41 and .44) "or any other handgun producing muzzle energy over 1,000 foot-pounds" and having a barrel length no less than 5-1/2 inches (measured from firing pin to muzzle). Wyoming wisely doesn't allow the use of a .357 Magnum and requires us to use a handgun which produces 500 foot-pounds of energy at 100 yards (with factory ammunition).

The point in all of this is this: **Check the regulations before you plan a hunt.** They change dramatically from state to state, and they change routinely, too. If you're traveling by commercial carrier, you've got more homework to do as well, and it goes without saying that if you're leaving the good old USA, you have even more homework. You can't hunt anything with a handgun in Canada.

Equipment recommendations generally hinge on what an individual shoots well, provided that the firearm is legal and capable of doing the job. Generally, any rifle cartridge over .25 caliber also works great in handguns, and they'll do fine in the field. Where revolvers are concerned, a single-action or double-action chambered for the .41 Magnum, .44 Magnum, .45 Colt or .454 Casull, of course, will do great in the field out to 100 yards, or to slightly longer distances in expert hands. Good factory ammunition is available for each of the above calibers.

Bullet style varies. Handgun bullets tend to expand poorly, and they impart little shock. The ace-in-the-hole we have is penetration. Any of our popular Magnum handguns will penetrate more than most high power rifles. **When handgun hunting, look to a well constructed, heavy bullet that will cut at least a full-caliber hole completely through the intended target.** I like Keith-style cast bullets; some of our best factory ammunition is loaded with similar projectiles. Stick with the heaviest recommended bullets for each caliber. The .41 Magnum was designed around a 210-grain bullet; it works great when so loaded. The .44 Magnum got its start with a 240-grain bullet; it works great in the field with bullets ranging from 240 to 300 grains or slightly more. The .45 Colt works great with bullets ranging from 250 to 320 or so grains, and the .454 Casull seems to work best with bullets in the same weight range.

Regarding bullet weight, we must remember that as mass goes up, velocity tends to go down. For hunting big game with a handgun, the load should produce at least 1,000 feet per second at the muzzle, and 1,200 fps is better.

Firearm type hinges on one's personal choice as well as on the regulations that govern our hunting activity. A revolver gets my nod most of the time, and it usually is a single action. That is personal choice, however. I've done quite a bit of hunting with double action guns, and they do a great job. The semi-autos chambered for similar rounds tend also to do a fine job in the field. When a gun produces good power and accuracy, it will do great in the field. It doesn't matter what the gun looks like, nor how it is equipped. The bottom line hinges on the hunter's ability to shoot the chosen equipment well and shoot it consistently, provided that the hunting arm chosen is legal and ethical in the first place.

That about does it. There's an exciting new world out there if you've not tried handgun hunting. You'll find that you will definitely work harder; you'll practice and study more. In the field, you'll work harder to get close enough to shoot, and sometimes you won't be successful. Still, that's why we call it hunting, not killing. The kill in reality only marks the end of the hunt most of the time, and the beginning of the utilization of some fine meat and beautiful hide. That's a wonderful renewable resource out there.

- Hearing and vision protection are safety essentials. Use them. It's only common sense.

- The author with a fine Wyoming antelope taken at long range with an XP-100 chambered for the 7mm-08. Photo by Lones W. Wigger Jr.

- The bolt action single shot handguns like this custom XP-100 chambered for the .17 Remington make 200 yard shots like this duck soup. The author's son Paul, shown here, is a member of the United States Army Marksmanship Pistol Team as well as the United States Shooting Team.

Handguns for Big Game

- Above. Dr. Andrew Kelley with 14-point buck scoring 170-6/8. He took it with a muzzleloader during Michigan's regular firearm season.

- Upper right. Red Friedrich with his black powder non-typical scoring 181-3/8 that he missed during the regular firearm season but didn't miss during the black powder season which followed. Knowing where to hunt, and getting a second chance the same year, can make the difference.

- The author with a 12-pointer with a nine-inch drop tine and heavy mass. The buck, taken during Saskatchewan's muzzleloader season, had a dressed weight of 235 pounds.

> Use what you learn during one hunting season for a payoff in a later season ...that same year.

by Richard Smith

Bag the Biggest Buck of Your Life With Black Powder

*T*here are a number of good reasons to hunt whitetails with black powder rifles:
• They can expand your hunting time, allowing you to participate in seasons reserved for those firearms.
• They can make you a better hunter by forcing you to concentrate on making the most of one shot.
• Deer hunting with a front loading rifle can also instill the frontier spirit in you, helping you appreciate the handicaps pioneer hunters might have faced when it came to securing venison.
• But the reason I like the most is that a muzzleloader can help you bag the biggest buck of your life. I used a muzzleloading rifle to collect the biggest whitetail I've ever taken, and I know at least four other Michigan residents who have done the same thing. There's a chance you can join us by following our examples.

Three of the four other Michigan residents who have taken their best bucks with muzzleloaders did so each of the last three years during the regular firearms season in southern counties. Gun hunters in the southern one-third of the state are restricted to using shotguns, muzzleloaders or handguns. Most deer hunters in that part of the state carry shotguns, but this threesome elected to use black powder rifles due to their accuracy and range advantage over shotguns. Their choice paid off in a big way.

Last fall was the third year in a row one of the highest scoring typical bucks bagged in Michigan during firearms season was taken with a muzzleloading rifle. Barry Boyes of Pinckney joined the ranks of gun deer hunters who chose the challenge, fun and accuracy of a front loader four years ago. It paid off handsomely for him on opening day of the 1996 season with a trophy 10-pointer from

Washtenaw County that had an official net score of 169 7/8.

That score puts the rack 1/8-of-an-inch shy of the coveted 170 necessary for entry in national records maintained by the Boone and Crockett Club, but Boyes is still happy with the deer, as any hunter in his right mind would be. The rack puts him in third place in all-time state records maintained by Commemorative Bucks of Michigan among typical black powder kills, behind the other typicals bagged in 1994 and 1995.

There actually isn't much difference in score between all three heads. Only two inches separates the first from the third. Dr. Andrew Kelley from Addison connected on a 14-pointer in Lenawee County with his Knight muzzleloader on the evening of November 19, 1994, that measured 170 6/8. Richard DeGrand of Ann Arbor was also using a modern muzzleloader made by Knight when he scored on a 12-pointer with an inch more antler than Kelley's deer in Washtenaw County on November 17, 1995.

Unlike Kelley and DeGrand, Boyes didn't shoot his book buck with a Knight rifle, but a Knight bullet was involved. His front loader of choice is the Thompson/Center Thunderhawk in .50 caliber. He has a 3x-9x Bushnell scope mounted on it. Before starting to hunt with the rifle in 1993, Barry said he tried round balls, buffalo bullets and a 260-grain lead bullet made by Knight. The Knight bullet performed best. He loads 90 grains of Pyrodex powder behind the saboted bullet.

Red Friedrich of Shingleton is another Michigan hunter who bagged his best buck with a muzzleloader. He did so during the state's special December black powder deer season, using a .50 caliber Thompson/Center Scout and a round ball. The whitetail he got had a non-typical 12-point rack that scored 181 3/8.

Michigan has an annual 10-day muzzleloader season that follows the regular firearms hunt. The season starts on the first Friday of December in the Upper Peninsula and begins on the second Friday of the month in the Lower Peninsula. No special license is required to participate in this hunt. Gun deer tags that are not filled during November remain valid for the black powder season.

Most states and many Canadian provinces now offer muzzleloader deer hunts, with some set during early fall and others as late season opportunities, so there are plenty of chances to expand your deer hunting time by hunting with a front loader. More on this later.

In Red's case, he first saw the buck during the regular gun season while hunting over bait and missed the deer with his centerfire rifle. He continued hunting the area with his muzzleloader after firearm season ended, hoping for another chance at the whitetail.

His persistence paid off. The 6½-year-old buck had a dressed weight of 170 pounds.

Red's buck presently ranks as the fourth highest scoring non-typical taken with a muzzleloader in Michigan. The state record non-typical black powder buck scores 185⅝. The 23-pointer was bagged by Robert Gendron in Hillsdale County during 1977. At the present time, no non-typical with antlers large enough to meet Boone and Crockett's minimum of 195 has been taken by a black powder hunter in Michigan, but I expect that to change in the near future as more hunters in the state try their luck with muzzleloaders.

Although the muzzleloader season gave Friedrich a second chance at his buck of a lifetime, **for many hunters, special black powder deer seasons offer them their first opportunity to see and shoot their biggest bucks.** The snow and cold weather common during December in Michigan, for example, often increases the vulnerability of bucks to hunters as the deer move from summer to winter range. Increased energy demands the cold weather puts on antlered whitetails, many of which have lost a significant amount of their fat reserves during the rut, makes these deer spend more time feeding, too.

The same factors also can play a role in big buck success during other late season hunts. Early fall muzzleloader seasons give black powder enthusiasts a chance at undisturbed whitetails when a maximum number of trophy animals are available. It was on such a hunt in Saskatchewan that I took my best whitetail. That province has an October black powder hunt.

Hunting during the last week of the province's muzzleloader season, I collected a heavy-beamed, non-typical 12-pointer with a nine-inch drop tine. The rack had a gross score of 174⁶⁄₈ and netted 165⁶⁄₈. The big-bodied whitetail had a dressed weight of 235 pounds, making it one of the heaviest deer I've shot.

I was hunting with a Knight Legend muzzleloader in .50 caliber when I got the trophy Canadian buck with a 125-yard shot. These modern in-line muzzleloaders are accurate and dependable, providing the best performance with saboted handgun bullets in either .44 or .45 caliber. I used a 240-grain semi-jacketed hollow point .44 caliber bullet out of my muzzleloader.

Manitoba has had a pre-firearm season muzzleloader hunt, for residents only, for a number of years. That hunt may open to non-residents in the future. If and when it does, it will provide some excellent big buck hunting opportunities for residents of the United States. I know this because bow deer season coincides with the latter part of the black powder hunt and while bowhunting in the province one year, I saw two amazing bucks that were out of bow range but which would have been a sure thing with a dependable muzzleloader. I'm positive one of the bucks would have qualified for Boone and Crockett Records.

There's nothing wrong with using a muzzleloader during regular firearm deer hunts in Canada like Richard DeGrand, Andrew Kelley and Barry Boyes did in Michigan. In fact, that's exactly what I did in Manitoba after failing to score on the trophy bucks while bowhunting. **The regular gun season opened the day after bow season ended, so I stuck around to hunt the same stand where I had seen the big bucks, but this time with my muzzleloader. It paid off.**

I hunted barely an hour on opening morning before shooting an 11-pointer that had a live weight of 250 pounds. I passed up a pair of eight-pointers before the bigger buck showed up. Several days later, another hunter shot a 160-class 10-pointer from the same stand — and it wasn't one of the big bucks I had seen earlier.

You can bag your biggest buck ever with a muzzleloader, just like those mentioned have, by taking advantage of the seasons in your home state and/or the hunts offered in other states and provinces. **Use what you learned in one season to make the black powder season pay off.** It's as simple as that. Most black powder rifles available today are user friendly and it's possible to master their use in a short period of time. The most important thing to do before trying to load and shoot one is to read thoroughly the owner's manual. It helps if you know an experienced muzzleloader shooter who can coach you.

Percussion cap muzzleloaders, rather than flintlocks, are the way to go for deer hunting. The most popular caliber muzzleloader for whitetail hunting is .50, but some hunters prefer .54 calibers. Front loading rifles in .45 caliber also are available and will do the job, but they tend to be on the light side for big deer.

Modern in-line muzzleloaders on which the hammer is directly in line with the cap and nipple, just like centerfire rifles, have advantages over side-hammer replicas. It's easier to keep powder and cap dry, reducing the chance of misfire. Cleaning in-lines also is easier than cleaning side-hammers because they are designed for easy removal of breech plugs, further reducing the odds of a misfire.

The fact that the guts of most in-lines can be quickly removed makes it easier to correct possible problems with them, too. If you forget to put powder in before a bullet, for instance, in-lines can be dismantled and the bullet pushed out. A special tool is required to remove a ball or bullet from a side-hammer gun.

In-line muzzleloaders are generally safer than side-hammers, too. Knights, for instance, have double safeties, reducing the chance they will discharge accidentally. They can be cocked with the safety on and they won't fire if the trigger is touched. Once a side-hammer is cocked, it can go off if the trigger is bumped.

   While waiting for whitetails from a stand with a side-hammer rifle, it's safer to have the gun uncocked until a deer is sighted. When the hammer is cocked, however, the clicking sound that's created could spook a deer. An option is to have the rifle cocked with no percussion cap in place. A cap can then be put on the nipple to prepare for a shot, but neither way is as convenient as using a rifle with a safety.

   As mentioned earlier, in-line rifles are designed for shooting mushrooming pistol or solid lead bullets with a plastic patch or sabot. The size and color of the sabot varies depending upon the caliber you're shooting as well as the type and caliber of bullet you choose. Bullets tend to be more accurate and perform better on deer than lead round balls. Side-hammer muzzleloaders were designed for shooting round balls.

   I started deer hunting with a side-hammer muzzleloader — a Thompson/Center Hawken — long before in-line black powder rifles were developed and enjoyed many successful hunts with it. I shot a dandy 11-point buck with that rifle during the December muzzleloader season one year that scored 129 $^6/_8$. Round balls were accurate out of that rifle, but what I disliked about using the lead balls is that too often they didn't generate much, if any, blood trail. That didn't pose a serious problem when hunting in snow, but without snow it easily could be a different story.

   Loading a muzzleloader is a simple process. All you do is pour a powder charge down the barrel, then seat a patched round ball or saboted bullet on top of it. The final step is capping the nipple.

   Either FFg black powder or Pyrodex can be used to charge muzzleloaders for deer hunting. I've used both with good success but prefer Pyrodex because it seems easier to clean. **As a rule of thumb, double the caliber of your rifle to determine a load to hunt with. For .50 calibers, 100 grains of powder, by volume, usually works for me. Ninety grains is standard for .45s and 110 grains for .54s.**

   However, after it's sighted in, it's a good idea to experiment with different loads when trying out a new muzzleloader. I know some black powder hunters who get the best accuracy out of their .50 calibers with 90 grains of powder. Try different bullets, like Barry Boyes did, to determine which gives the best performance in your rifle.

Black Powder Buck

Once you've done that, you're all set for the big bucks, as long as you keep your rifle clean and dry. **I've hunted whitetails with muzzleloaders for more than 20 years, and I've experienced only one misfire.** That came while hunting in the rain with a percussion cap on my side hammer rifle. The cap got wet. Once I replaced it with a dry cap, the rifle fired right away.

The reason I believe I've avoided more misfires is that I always thoroughly clean and dry my rifle at the end of each day I've fired it. The nipple, breech plug and hammer are all cleaned and dried, not just the barrel. I also use the best caps I can find to insure consistent ignition. CCIs have worked well for me. Hunters who don't properly care for their muzzleloaders can expect performance problems, because front loading rifles definitely take more care than centerfire guns.

Some black powder hunters make it a habit to discharge their rifle at the end of each day of hunting and start with a fresh load the next day. Based on my experience, that's a waste of powder and bullets. A better practice is to empty the rifle at the end of a hunt, so it can be cleaned and stored for the next season.

On an experimental basis, I've left my Knight rifles loaded more than a year and never had a problem with them firing. To avoid condensation from building up inside the barrel of your black powder rifle when it's loaded, always put it in a case when it is not in use. If there's a major difference in temperature between outside and inside, which is often the case during late seasons, keep the rifle outside in a safe place.

Whitetail hunting with a muzzleloader can be fun, challenging, rewarding. It can make you a better hunter and it can provide additional hunting opportunities. These firearms can also help you bag a buck of a lifetime. It worked for me and a number of other hunters I know. I hope it works for you, too!

> Everyone who hunts should learn these tracking skills . . .

by Tony Kemnitz

Inside the Track

Tracking a whitetail covers a wide range of skills that are learned over a period of time. In fact, skillful tracking is an age-old, time-tested part of food gathering, but **the real skills of tracking are largely forgotten today, a lost art.** Remember that our ancestors for over a million years survived by hunting, following game. Their lives depended on finding that game. We are "civilized" for but a second of geologic time and have many dormant skills which we have shut out in modern times, but which can be re-opened.

Everyone who hunts should learn these skills, for **our greatest responsibility is to recover a wounded deer or determine that it received only a superficial wound.** Tracking and trailing can be hard work, but it also is exciting, and when everything works out, you have the intense satisfaction of a job well done. You also will have learned more of the true meaning of patience and of thoroughness. This is NOT a job which can be hurried.

There is, however, **a "book" of details that most hunters don't learn, but which can help them unravel the most puzzling trails.** We're going to go into that "book" here. We'll study the animal itself – how it moves, what its mechanical movements are, the variety of impressions it leaves behind as it moves. These impressions simply are tracks, the writing of a story of what happens when something moves through the environment, the disturbances that "something" transfers to the earth as it moves. That is what tells the story. It is the signature of the animal that passed. **When we know why an animal moved, where it moved and what sign it left, then we can move to the next level – we'll know what to look for, where to look, and what to expect.**

However, to blindly follow impressions without understanding their significance could lead you astray. Many hunters consider themselves trackers because they find their deer by following blood drops alone, but what happens when this stops? Generally, the ani-

Inside the Track

mal is lost or found by accident through a grid search of the area.

Although it is commendable that there is an effort to locate the animal, many are lost because only part of the whole story was used in an attempt to locate the game. What we want to learn is why some hunters are more successful than others, what makes them more proficient at finding wounded game. I would like to address some of these issues and perhaps enhance your skills as a responsible hunter.

Pressure releases – the indication which remains after a hoof (or foot or boot, for that matter) presses on something and then is taken away — **are indicators of direction and movement.** There are all kinds of indicators – scuff marks, rolled pebbles, bent or broken grass, prints in dirt/mud/snow, etc. These indicators are only the tip of the iceberg, but since the track(s) and elements related to the track(s) tells the whole story, you just have to learn to read all of it.

Consider the normal forward movement of the walk. First we must identify the track as that of a deer. This may seem elementary here in whitetail country, but what if you're out west where there can be domestic sheep tracks, pronghorn tracks, etc.? Next, measurements are taken — width, length, stride and straddle. The placement of the feet in a walking pattern can determine the animal's gender for this indirect registrar diagonal walker. (See Figures 1, 2, 3, 4.)

For the novice I would suggest the following **equipment for field use:**
- One small magnifying glass
- A small tape measure or tracking stick
- Pencil and pocket-sized note pad for diagramming.

It also is helpful to take some popsicle sticks to mark each track. Stick them in the ground and you have easy-to-see indicators.

You can practice tracking, and that is a good thing. Begin in early summer. Find a soft medium, such as freshly cultivated corn or early wheat field where the plants are just beginning to grow. Then obtain permission from the property owner to go onto that field.

It should be noted that **lighting conditions are of extreme importance.** Early morning sun and late afternoon sun gives you the necessary light inflections to identify tracks easily. Shadows along the edges of the tracks gives them definition and makes them more visible. An overhead sun flattens things out and doesn't show details. This factor is important in good photography, too.

To begin actual tracking practice, you must start your search for tracks on your hands and knees. That's the only way you'll see the necessary details. Tracking is not done while bent from the waist

Figure 1-STRADDLE

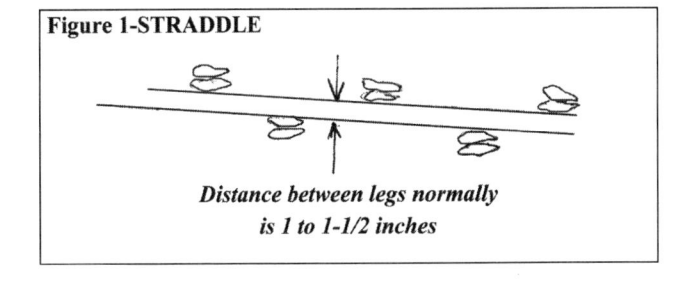

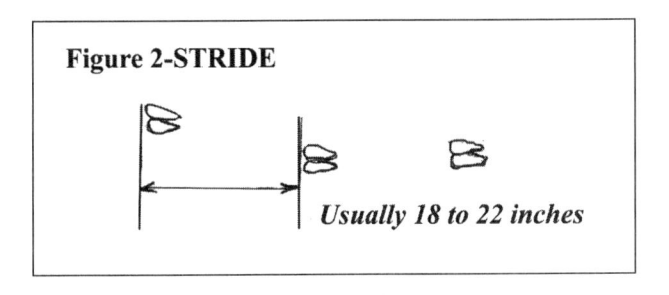

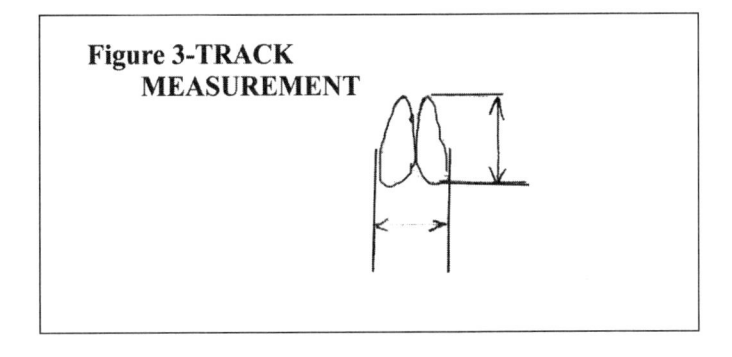

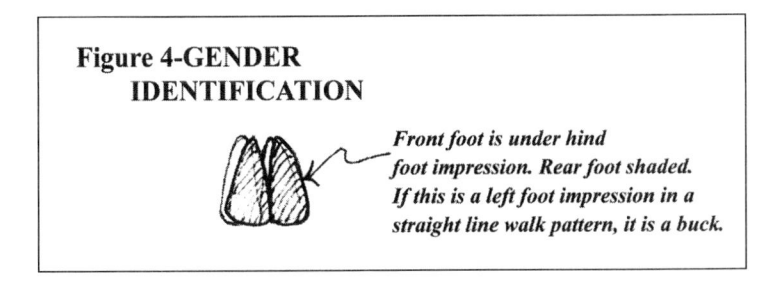

Distance between legs normally is 1 to 1-1/2 inches

Figure 2-STRIDE

Usually 18 to 22 inches

Figure 3-TRACK MEASUREMENT

Figure 4-GENDER IDENTIFICATION

Front foot is under hind foot impression. Rear foot shaded. If this is a left foot impression in a straight line walk pattern, it is a buck.

Inside the Track

until you have become extremely proficient. Even then there are times when the hands-and-knees position is necessary. Identify a deer track and its walk pattern and begin to take measurements and document them in your note pad.

Mark each track with a stick as you go along, and you will see a pattern forming — right foot, left foot, repeat. After placing seven to ten sticks, stand up and look at the bigger view. This gives you the opportunity to see if you missed any tracks and will better define the straddle of the animal for a more accurate measurement. If you stay crouched, you may be able to see other sign, such as bent grass or moisture knocked from grass and leaves, to indicate direction of travel, which can keep you going when finding actual tracks is difficult.

Be concerned first with the width and length of the track, then the stride, and finally the straddle. You will first notice there is a big difference in the size of tracks that you see, particularly if a doe is walking with her fawn. When you have marked fifteen to twenty tracks, stop and go back to the first tracks you observed and take out your magnifying glass. Make a close examination of the clearest impressions you can find, paying particular attention to how and where the front foot came down, whether it is a right or left foot, and then how the hind foot was placed on top of the front foot imprint. **The majority of the time, if it is a *doe*, you will find that the rear foot impression is on the *outside of the front foot impression*. If it is a *buck* deer, you will find the rear foot impression on the *inside of the front foot impression*.**

To go from here, examine each track more closely. (I like to imagine that I'm as small as an ant, and I am looking at the track from this perspective.) This will allow you to notice small details of this track which are particular only to this deer. If you were to look at the soles of the shoes worn by everyone in your household, you would find different wear patterns and marks in each. The same is true for animals. As you continue to the next track you have marked, you will see the similarities and come to recognize the small imperfections which are particular to this deer.

I strongly believe that when you are in the learning process of tracking, you should begin in this way, taking your time, being in a hands-and-knees position, getting close to the track and analyzing each one in a good, soft, clear print medium. You will be learning more than you realize just by relaxing and thinking only of the track and what it tells you. (This is an excellent time to teach kids. They like a mystery, and you're really trying to unravel a mystery.)

Now to the next details. If you have practiced the aforementioned exercises, you will begin to see other things in the tracks — a variation in the stride and straddle, foot placement on turns, stops and starts. We will go into this in more detail later. The tracks are then going to lead you out of the soft dirt and into the forested areas, perhaps grass, brush or pine duff. We still can continue.

You have, at this time, the stride of the animal and as long as this has not changed for some reason — sudden fright to make the gait change, for instance — you can measure to the next impression. This is a time to **relax and take your time.** Just sit for awhile and look at the vegetation in the direction of the next impression. Measure to where it should be and notice what changes have occurred in this area. You now won't be able to see the deep imprint because of the medium, but what you will see is how the grass or weeds were growing and how they have now been disturbed. Maybe where the foot was placed, there is a twig which is freshly broken, or the grass has been bruised or bent to a different angle. A slow, careful look will show you the entire outline across a leaf or in the harder dirt. Mark this print and go to the next one. Look for broken branches, twigs, or plants, even disturbed stones in gravel areas.

Remember to stay relaxed and unhurried. Look at the big picture, then focus in on the tiniest details. Look up to relax your vision, then back to where the track should be, and you will see it, because it is there.

We stop ourselves with preconceived ideas, such as, "can't track something on a hard surface". This is not true; everything that moves creates a disturbance on the surface it crosses, and with practice you will be able to see the disturbance, whether it is a track or a scuff, or whatever.

An exercise you can practice at home is fun and simple. Take your vacuum cleaner and vacuum the carpeting in straight lines. Then turn out all the lights and, using a flashlight, shine the light across the carpeting while lying with the side of your face on the carpet. See how easy it is to see your own tracks as well as the tracks of the vacuum. Move along into the kitchen or foyer area, with the house lights off, shining your flashlight horizontally across the floor see how many foot prints you can see on the tile or vinyl floor. You will be amazed, but there you are tracking across a hard surface. It gives you a new perspective on what you can and can not really see.

Go outside and walk across your lawn, then lie down with your light and look at your foot impressions. These exercises help you better grasp what your real capabilities are. They will open your mind to the fact that things which seem impossible really are just a lack of training, and a lack of awareness.

If you have a pet in the house, allow it to walk on the carpeting next to your tracks. Then do the exercise again and see how easily it is to track. Then go to the vinyl flooring and continue. You will gain confidence in your vision. **As your confidence grows, so will your tracking skills and tracking success, because you actually will be seeing what is there and you won't be stopped by preconceived ideas.**

To keep your skills and vision sharp, just look in your own yard. Look for sandy or soft areas where earthworms move, mice run and your friendly chipmunk lives. At first, you may have to use your magnifying glass to search these areas, but soon you will be tracking that chipmunk.

Don't be discouraged if you don't become a tracker overnight. Keep at it and it will come. Patience is the key.

From here, you will note that **more is going on in a track than just direction, gender and gait.** For each of these aspects there is significance that is shown by and in the track. Let's take gender first, because it is of interest in preseason scouting. Since we have explained the foot placement in the walk pattern, we realize that with a male the front quarters are larger in mass than the hind quarters; therefore, rear foot impressions are superimposed to the insides of the front feet; does, with larger mass in hind quarters, have their rear foot impressions superimposed to the outside of the front feet. However, that is not the only way to tell the difference between gender. The male also applies more pressure to the outside of his rear foot; this also helps make positive identification.

The mood of the animal also is shown in the tracks. For instance, if you see a change from a walk gait to a pace gait, this shows that is it is approaching another animal in which it is making a dominant expression. A pace gait is when both legs on the same side of the body move forward at the same time. The toes are placed down facing slightly toward the inside of the body, then twist to the outside and push off for the other side to go forward. It is a stiff-legged movement and leaves an undercut and mounding to the outside of the impression with an upside down rocker in the center. (See Figure #5.) This may be helpful in locating a dominant buck in your area.

They also like to show off during breeding season when they are moving, and they give an extra straight-leg forward push, making their feet come down at a slightly canted angle. (See Figure #6.) It is like a fast walk but not a trot. Their hind feet still are placed in the front foot impression.

Figure 5

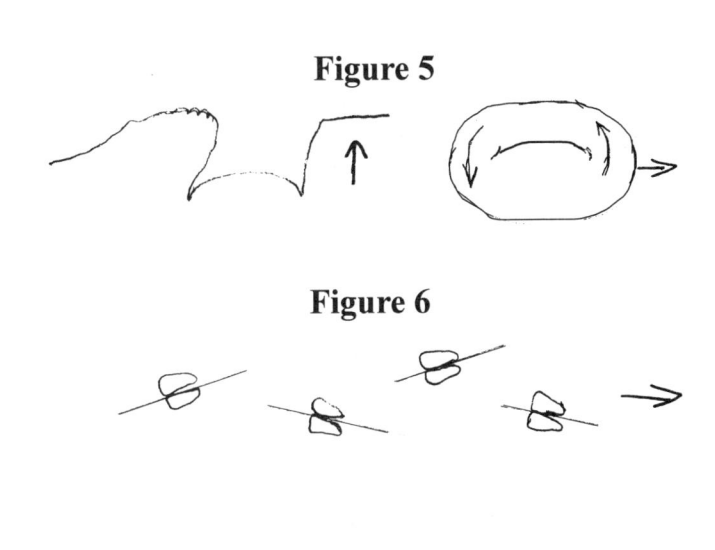

Figure 6

Figure 7

- *Figure 5 - Pace Gait (See page 56 for description)*
- *Figure 6 - Straight-leg Push (See page 56 for description)*
- *Figure 7 - Plume of Debris (See description below)*

All these indicators help you identify gender and what the animal is doing.

The other common gait pattern is the gallop. It is used for escape, either from another animal or when frightened. This is evidenced in both female and male deer. When making these track observations, you will then have to make note of direction, which is left by the impact of the foot onto the earth. Although you can't use your stride and straddle measurements at this time, you can take note of the individual markings and size of the foot. Since pressure is applied with greater force on the two toes of the foot, they will splay out, but this will not change the marks or wear patterns. This will help you stay on the same deer if you are following it.

Now for a matter of physics: For every action there is an equal and opposite reaction. This is very important. If an animal accelerates at a rapid pace, there will be a plume of debris to the rear of the foot impression. (See Figure #7.) You must watch the direction of the plume, because it will tell you the direction of the force exerted, thereby showing the direction of the animal.

* *Here's an effective tracking tool — a measuring stick with rubber O-rings. The O-rings can be used to mark track width, straddle, pace gait, etc.*

To better understand this concept, you can conduct experiments at home in a sand box or on a sandy beach. First smooth out an area and then run as fast as you can across it in a straight line. You must be accelerating as fast as you can as you go. This will leave behind the pluming, showing your direction of travel. Sit down and just look at these impressions for a few moments. Then do it again, but this time when you are about halfway through turn at a 30 degree angle away from the straight line. Now go back and observe the difference in the track. How did the plume move? In which direction? What happened to the bottom of the track? Which way was the toe pointed and where was the pressure exerted to make the change in direction? Was there a placement and then a twist with a plume opposite of the acceleration?

This exercise is one of the most useful as far as direction changes are concerned. **You will use these cues most often in the field just after you have shot your animal.** So take your time with your observations and make notes of the formations the imprints leave behind on acceleration and turns. Draw them in your notebook to better set them in your mind. Since this does not have to be done in the field, but right in your own back yard, it gives you more time to practice.

These cues are critical to learn if you have an animal that is not bleeding upon being shot and takes off, but you know you made a

hit. Such an animal won't run far if not pursued too quickly. It then will go into its walk pattern, depending on the extent of injury, and you then can establish the correct stride, straddle and size measurements, along with the individualist characteristics of this animal. Even if it goes among other animals, you will be able to follow it to retrieval.

There are many other clues inside of a track, all of which take time and observation to learn. The best tool is your own sand box or tracking box. You can do your own experiments on movement and see what happens in the track. Tom Brown Jr. has charted 85 pressure releases, but you don't have to know them all to be an accomplished tracker.

I believe that tracking and retrieving your game is as much a part of the sport as practicing with your hunting tool and knowing the safety rules. **Let's all be responsible to our planet and all the things which live upon it.**

I have read many books on tracking and find many to be useful. The best at this time is by T. Brown Jr. — "Tom Brown's Field Guide to Nature Observation and Tracking", published by Berkley Books, New York, in 1977. Check with a local book store for its availability. It may be out of print. If that's the case, you might want to check at used-book stores. There are field courses and seminars put on by myself and Medicine Hawk Wilderness Skills of Milwaukee in various parts of Wisconsin. I can be contacted for a schedule by calling (715)-358-3299.

Tony Kemnitz

At the age of nine, Tony Kemnitz got a job with the Scherbarth family near his southeastern Wisconsin home doing farm work. That family taught him and his brothers how to hunt, trap and read sign. At the age of 10 he ran a trap line on the Root River and small ponds in the area. Tony became a police officer in 1965 and began using his tracking skills at crime scene investigations. He's also used the reverse of that -- using body language and movement learned from watching deer communication and movement to help elicit confessions from suspects. He has been tracking instructor with Medicine Hawk Wilderness Skills and taught spring and fall classes to outdoor people and forensic tracking to sheriffs' deputies. He also has taught lost child locating to local fire department personnel.

Buck Fawn

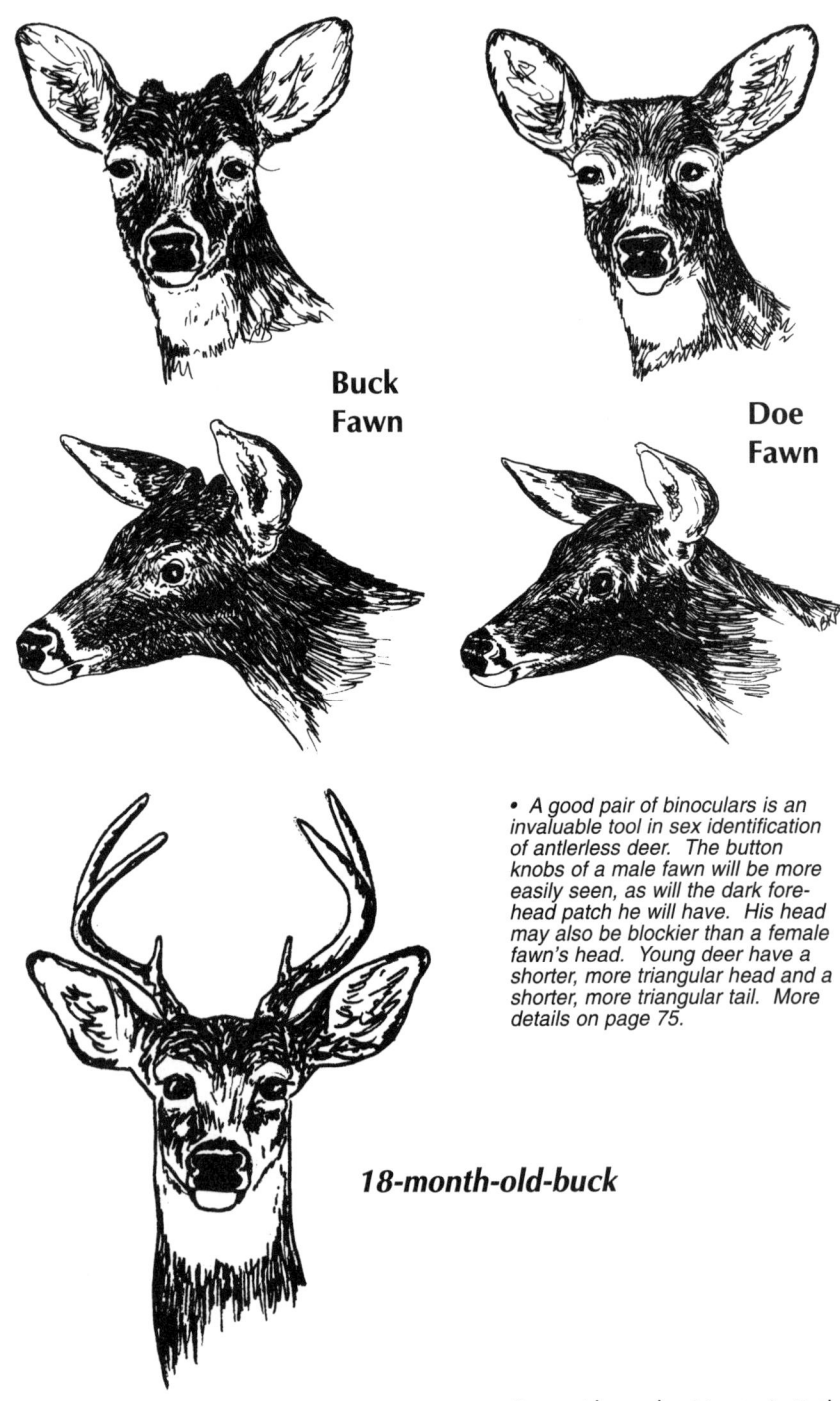

Doe Fawn

- A good pair of binoculars is an invaluable tool in sex identification of antlerless deer. The button knobs of a male fawn will be more easily seen, as will the dark forehead patch he will have. His head may also be blockier than a female fawn's head. Young deer have a shorter, more triangular head and a shorter, more triangular tail. More details on page 75.

18-month-old-buck

Steps Along the Hunter's Path

SECTION II:

IMPROVE YOUR HUNTING CONDITIONS

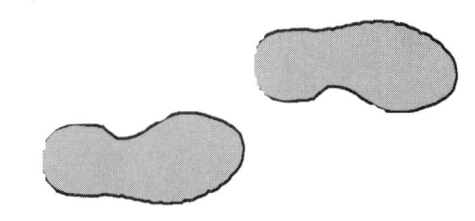

- A healthy bachelor group of bucks ranging in age from 18 months to 3-1/2 years.

- The author believes the best deer to harvest in a management program is the young doe. Not only does it need two years to become a solid producer, it does nothing but eat during that time.

> Want more bucks and better bucks, and more fat deer for your freezer? Here's how. There's nothing magical about it.

by John L. Sloan

A Clear Guide to Personal Deer Management Practices

*T*here is no single, simple solution to any problem involving whitetail deer. There is no one management technique that works for all areas or all habitats within an area. To manage a deer population effectively on a specific habitat, the management practice must be tailored to that specific habitat. To do this, the manager must thoroughly understand not only his goals but all of the repercussions that may result in his attempt to reach those goals. In truth, most whitetail management is done under the S-W-A-G principle....Scientific Wild-Ass Guess.

Perhaps this sounds confusing and complicated. It doesn't have to be, but a solid foundation of basic knowledge is a must if the management program is to work. Whenever possible, a trained professional *whitetail* biologist should be consulted before starting any management program.

Perhaps the place to start is by recognizing the symptoms of a problem and the possible or probable causes of that problem. Very often in a personal management program, a symptom of one problem is indicative of a greater problem. So let's begin by looking at some early indicators of a need for better management.

Recognizing the Symptoms

Early in 1996, I began to hear comments from hunters in various areas concerning a difficulty in patterning their deer rut. They spoke of an extended rut with rutting activity lasting far longer than they had experienced before. They spoke of a decrease in rubs and scrapes. They mentioned few sightings of bucks chasing does, little daytime activity and an apparent peak of the rut that was in December. Through 1997, the complaints became more frequent and more widespread. Occasionally a state agency even recognized that the rut was seeming to change. Was, or is, this a symptom of a problem?

In the early stages of this activity, probably this was more of a problem for the hunters than for the whitetail deer. But these, you see, are just symptoms of a greater problem. What could cause this type of rutting behavior?

Activity such as I have described above can be caused by unseasonably hot weather. It also can be caused by poor nutrition. But, by far, the largest and most likely cause is a severe imbalance in the buck/doe ratio of the deer herd and the age stratas of that herd. When the does outnumber the bucks by as much as 20-1 in some areas, a problem does indeed exist. These symptoms also can be caused by killing too many bucks at the wrong time of the season, and by the lack of a reasonable doe harvest. This can become a serious problem. Let me take you through a scenario that points out exactly how this may occur.

A mature doe in Anystate, USA, comes into her first estrous cycle on November 10 (all dates are arbitrary and vary from area to area). Long before that date, she has decided what buck will breed her. We now know this happens. Usually it is the dominant buck. That dominant buck may be only 18 months old, but he is dominant. On November 9, that buck is killed. It may take as long as 36 hours for the next buck(s) to assume the breeding duties of the dominant buck. During that 36 hours, the doe goes out of estrous.

Twenty-eight days pass and the mature doe now is in estrous again. It is now December 8. On this date the doe gets bred. Now 210 days pass and the doe gives birth to twin fawns — one doe, one buck. It is July 6. The fawns begin life a full month, perhaps more, behind the fawns born to does bred on their first cycle.

In November, the doe weans her fawns and enters her first estrous cycle in December. This is during what would normally be the second estrous cycle for most mature does. This mature doe is now locked into that December cycle unless she either aborts a fetus or goes barren for one year.

As for the fawns, probably the buck will be killed at 18 months. If not, who knows how long before he catches up to the early born bucks. Does he ever catch up? The doe fawn, in all probability, will enter her first estrous cycle in December of the following year.

If you multiply this scenario by several hundred or even thousand occurrences, you readily can see how that will affect the timing of the rut. It moves to a later peak period or becomes extended over two or three months as fawns are weaned at various times.

When bucks are killed before the first estrous cycle is complete and you have a herd that already is out of balance by sex, this is almost an inevitable occurrence. Here then is an explanation for the extended or hard-to-pattern rut.

Now let's look at what happens to a herd of deer that is badly out of balance. If there are many more does in heat than there are bucks to breed them, why would a buck need to rub or scrape? Why would he need to chase does? And again, in this situation, is it not likely that many of the does go unbred on the first cycle? Therefore, you have an extended rut.

Does this mean that many does actually go barren? No. In most areas, these does do get bred. That is why the numbers of deer are not in danger. But to some degree, that compounds the problem. And do we know the long term ramifications of this situation? No. It could be disastrous.

In a very simplified example, think about this. A doe has twins. For simplification, we assume the twins are born one male and one female. Now let us also assume that the normal lifespan of a deer is seven years.

If this is true, in seven years, all of the deer we had to begin with are dead. No matter how many bucks and how many does we had at the beginning of that seven year period, they are all dead. What if, for seven years, we harvest, (kill, bag, tag, whack), an equal number of male and female deer. Think about it. If they are born in an equal ratio and we kill them in an equal ratio and all the original deer are dead, do we not have an equally balanced herd?

That is an oversimplification and won't quite hold true. We would have to figure in the young does that have one fawn, and we have to figure in natural mortality. But can't you see the basis you have here for some simple, personal deer management practices.

Using just such a basis for a starting point, you find out what the fawn rate is for your area. You find out what the natural mortality rate is (usually a little higher for bucks). You estimate your current buck:doe ratio. You decide how many deer you want to kill, either to increase the herd population, hold it steady or decrease it. And then you set goals as to the quality of your herd.

By using just that formula you immediately can begin a personal management program. Let's assume, on your property, you have 100 deer —six bucks and 94 does. Your goal is to maintain a herd of about 100 deer, but you want a better balance between bucks and does and you'd like a better age strata. We'll also assume you have no nutritional problems. In the first two years of the management program, your goal is to bring the buck/doe ratio into better balance. After that, your goal is to maintain a balanced herd and a number of about 100 animals. Here is the rough starting point.

Multiply the number of does you have by the fawning rate for your area, (We are using 1.6). Divide that number by two and you know how many female and male fawns you have. From the total number of fawns and adult deer, subtract your mortality — all causes of death except hunting. (We use 25 percent.) What you have now is your huntable population, those deer surviving until hunting season. Now plan your harvest to fit your personal management goal.

Our goal is to maintain about 100 animals, balance the sex ratio and spread out the age strata. To do this, we kill 40 percent of our huntable population in each of the first two years. We divide that kill into 60 percent does and 40 percent bucks. In short, we kill 50 percent more does than bucks (60 / 40 = 1.5). That will reduce the wide disparity between sexes quickly. We do not, at this time, place any emphasis on age of the deer killed.

At the end of just one year, we have a carryover herd of 31 bucks and 82 does – a 1:2.6 sex ratio. In the beginning it was 1:15. We do the same in the second year and our carryover at the end of that year is 43 bucks and 66 does - a 1:1.5 buck:doe ratio - and we have 109 animals.

In the third year we maintain a 40 percent kill of the huntable population, but we now balance the kill at an equal number of bucks and does. At the end of the third year, we have 40 bucks and 57 does.

From the fourth year on, we decrease the kill to 30 percent and kill an equal number of each sex. After five years, we have a total of 98 animals - 45 bucks and 53 does. By adjusting our kill percentage, we control the herd size. Now we can get picky about the quality of our deer.

But do you want a buck:doe ratio of 1:1? If you do, keep in mind your natural mortality will go up. More competition leads to more fights, and that results in a higher mortality to bigger bucks. Is a 1:1 ratio possible in any situation other than behind a high fence? It is your call.

Now this is important. Except under the most ideal conditions, all of these figures are done by estimation. Few people actually know how many deer they have or in what ratio. Few people actually know what the carrying capacity of their land is. We depend on our observations and estimations. These may or may not be accurate. In many climates, the natural mortality may vary from year to year, and the fawning rate may vary. These must be taken into account. If herd numbers appear low, reduce the total harvest and reduce the doe harvest. The reverse is true for high herd numbers. A trained whitetail biologist is invaluable in these calculations.

Now let's look at the quality of your herd. What are your goals? What do you want that you can realistically expect to achieve? Much depends on how much land you have. If you have a large tract, say 5,000 acres or more, you can do a great deal. How much are you willing to spend? Quality or trophy management can get expensive when you consider supplemental feeding. What are the genetics in your area? Can you expect big, heavy bodied, massive racked bucks from the herd you have to start with?

What if you have 500 acres of hardwood timber with maybe a smattering of crop land? What can you do? Let's assume you own the land and can do whatever you wish with it. The first thought that comes to mind is, you are going to say, "No matter what I do, my neighbors will kill any buck they see." That is only partially valid. Sure, 500 acres can accommodate only so many deer. Sure, your deer cross the fence. But think about this: Any change in habitat will result in a change in habit. What can you do to attract, hold and support more deer on your 500 acres?

To begin with, you provide the best food source. You open up some timber land and fertilize the natural browse. It takes a chain saw and some fertilizer. Perhaps you clearcut some small areas and plant a winter/early spring forage crop. You simply manipulate your habitat to attract and hold more deer.

What bucks do you shoot? That is your call. Is eight points and 15 inches of spread a shooter buck to you? If so, shoot. Quite simply, if you allow enough bucks to reach two-plus years of age, you'll have a good supply of older bucks. Shoot them at 18 months, that's as old as they get. In the above samples, if you kill 30 bucks the first year, obviously most of them are either button bucks or spikes. That's the hedge against mistakes. You also have at least 31 that are going to be a minimum of 18 months the next year. You can figure at least 16 of them are going to reach two-plus years of age. That's 10 more than you had to start with.

Have trouble shooting enough does? Why not have a hunt for young people? Allow them to harvest only does. Invite friends, but allow them to shoot only does. Got a hunting club? New rule. You can't shoot a buck until you kill a doe...or two. What doe should you shoot? I believe that the best deer to harvest is the young doe, but I could be wrong. I believe the young doe is the best deer to shoot because she is the most expensive deer you have. For the first two years of her life, all she does is eat. Only then, generally, does she begin contributing to your deer herd. The incurred problem here, in following this crop-the-young-doe principle, is that too often it leads to shooting a button buck by mistake. Remember, a button buck is a buck, not an antlerless deer. Learn to recognize the small bucks by body type, not by antlers. It's your plan; you make up the rules.

By utilizing the information available to us, by taking advantage of the state wildlife department's biologists, by doing some thinking and planning and using a calculator and tools and materials that are all available to us, we can solve many of the deer herd problems on our land.

Once a symptom is noticed and the trouble diagnosed, it is not hard to form a plan of correction that can be implemented within the framework of the regulations for your area. It may take some help from other hunters. It may mean going a year or so without shooting a buck. It may mean changing the time of year you shoot bucks. But once you realize you have a problem, you can fix it.

Editor's Note: The information and calculations in this chapter are those of the author. They are to be used only as a guide or example. Always consult a certified whitetail biologist before starting any deer management program.

JOHN L. SLOAN

John L. Sloan has been hunting and studying whitetail deer more than 43 years. His articles have appeared in most of the major hunting magazines, and he has presented seminars at many of the top hunting shows in the country.

John's specialty has always been the understanding of what deer do and why and then presenting that in straightforward, common sense terms. It is his belief that the same formula can be used for whitetail management once the hunter (manager) understands some basic principles of whitetail biology.

John lives in Lebanon, Tennessee, and hunts across the United States and Canada. He is primarily a bowhunter but hunts some days each year with muzzleloader and centerfire rifle.

Basic Formula for Deer Herd Calculation

1. TOTAL DEER (prior to fawning):   BUCKS   DOES

2. Determine number of fawns:
   DOES
   multiplied by FAWN RATE
   FAWNS   (MALE   FEMALE)

3. TOTAL DEER: Bucks plus Does plus Fawns

4. Determine Huntable Population:
   TOTAL DEER
   multiplied by % NATURAL MORTALITY
   HUNTABLE POPULATION

5. Determine Percent of POPULATION TO BE HARVESTED

6. Determine Percent of
   DOES TO BE HARVESTED and BUCKS TO BE HARVESTED

7. Remaining Deer in Herd after Hunting Season:
   CARRYOVER TO NEXT YEAR

Plugging In Some Numbers.....

HERD CALCULATION — 1st YEAR

1. TOTAL DEER: 6 Bucks   94 Does

2. 94   DOES
   x 1.6 Fawn Rate
   150 FAWNS   (75 Male 75 Female)

3. 150 fawns plus 100 deer (6 Bucks, 94 Does) from start = 250 Total Deer

4. 250 Total Deer
   -62 Deer Lost to 25% Natural Mortality Rate
   188 Deer - HUNTABLE POPULATION

5. Percent of Population to be Harvested
   40% = 75 deer   (188 x .4 = 75.2)

6. Percent of Does to be Harvested   60% = 45 (75 x .6 = 45)
   Percent of Bucks to be Harvested   40% = 30 (75 x .4 = 30)

7. CARRYOVER TO NEXT YEAR:
   31 Bucks + 82 Does = 113 Total Deer

Personal Deer Management-Calculations

HERD CALCULATION – 2nd YEAR
1. TOTAL DEER: 31 Bucks   82 Does

2. 82   DOES
   x1.6 Fawn Rate
   131 FAWNS   (66 Male 65 Female)

3. 131 fawns plus 113 carryover deer (31 Bucks, 82 Does) = 244 Total Deer

4. 244 Total Deer
   -61 Deer Lost to 25% Natural Mortality Rate
   183 Deer - HUNTABLE POPULATION

5. Percent of Population to be Harvested
   40% =   73 deer   (183 x .4 = 73.2)

6. Percent of Does to be Harvested   60% = 44 (73 x .6 = 44)
   Percent of Bucks to be Harvested   40% = 29 (73 x .4 = 29)

7. CARRYOVER TO NEXT YEAR:
   43 Bucks + 66 Does = 109 Total Deer

In two years, you have come from a buck:doe ratio of 1:15 to a ratio of 1:1.5. Your herd has increased by 10 deer. Your buck population has increased from six to 43.

HERD CALCULATION – 3rd YEAR
1. TOTAL DEER: 43   Bucks   66   Does

2. 66   DOES
   x1.6 Fawn Rate
   106 FAWNS   (53 Male 53 Female)

3. 106 fawns plus 109 carryover deer (43 Bucks, 66 Does) = 215 Total Deer

4. 215 Total Deer
   -54 Deer Lost to 25% Natural Mortality Rate
   161 Deer - HUNTABLE POPULATION

5. Percent of Population to be Harvested
   40% =64 deer   (161 x .4 = 64.4)

6. Percent of Does to be Harvested   50% = 32 (64 x .5 = 32)
   Percent of Bucks to be Harvested   50% = 32 (64 x .5 = 32)

7. CARRYOVER TO NEXT YEAR:
   40 Bucks + 57 Does = 97 Total Deer

By the third year you maintain a 40 percent total harvest but balance the buck/doe kill, still maintaining a herd of about 100 deer.

HERD CALCULATION – 4th YEAR
1. TOTAL DEER: 40 Bucks   57 Does

2. 57 DOES
   x1.6 Fawn Rate
   91 FAWNS   (46 Male 45 Female)

3. 91 fawns plus 97 carryover deer (40 Bucks, 57 Does) = 188 Total Deer

4. 188 Total Deer
   -47 Deer Lost to 25% Natural Mortality Rate
   141 Deer - HUNTABLE POPULATION

5. Percent of Population to be Harvested
   30% = 42 deer (141 x .3 = 42)

6. Percent of Does to be Harvested   50% = 21 (42 x .5 = 21)
   Percent of Bucks to be Harvested   50% = 21 (42 x .5 = 21)

7. CARRYOVER TO NEXT YEAR:
   44 Bucks   55 Does = 99 Total Deer

The sex ratio is now 1:1.3. By the fourth year, you reduce the total harvest and balance the herd, still maintaining a herd of about 100 deer.

HERD CALCULATION – 5th YEAR
1. TOTAL DEER: 44 Bucks 55 Does

2. 55 DOES
   x1.6 Fawn Rate
   88 FAWNS   (44 Male 44 Female)

3. 88 fawns plus 99 carryover deer (44 Bucks, 55 Does) = 187 Total Deer

4. 187 Total Deer
   -47 Deer Lost to 25% Natural Mortality Rate
   140 Deer - HUNTABLE POPULATION

5. Percent of Population to be Harvested
   30% =   42 deer   (140 x .3 = 42)

6. Percent of Does to be Harvested   50% = 21 (42 x .5 = 21)
   Percent of Bucks to be Harvested   50% = 21 (42 x .5 = 21)

7. CARRYOVER TO NEXT YEAR:
   45 Bucks   53 Does = 98 Total Deer

The sex ratio is now 1:1.7 with a herd total of about 100 deer. From this point on, with slight adjustments, a harvest of 30 percent of the huntable population, equally divided between male and female animals, should maintain a healthy, well balanced herd. It is obvious that with 45 bucks and a kill of approximately 21, the age classes of all the deer – bucks and does – will also begin to balance.

Personal Deer Management-Calculations

Variables:
1) Harsh winter
2) Agricultural crop failure
3) Mast failure
4) Flood or drought (may or may not affect #2 or #3)
5) Bad weather during hunting season - reduced harvest

Notes:

1) Fawning Rate – 2-1/2-year-old does will likely have twins; 18-month-old does will likely have a single fawn; 7-month-old does will likely have a single fawn.

2) The 25% mortality rate is arbitrary. It is high for some areas, low for some areas. It will vary from year to year in some given areas, especially where winters can be harsh. Figure 50-50 ratio of males - females lost to natural mortality.

3) The harvest rate begins at 40% because of the terrible buck:doe imbalance in the herd. You obtain a quicker buck:doe balance with a higher early harvesting of does. In any year, you can manipulate these numbers through harvest to effect any change you want.

4) If you were to stop all harvesting, the worst ratio you could have, even in a severely unbalanced herd, after just one year would be a 1:2.25 buck:doe ratio, assuming 50:50 male:female natural mortality. But there also would be 260 deer in the habitat. Now you're looking at severe habitat deterioration. So you MUST hunt them to keep the herd in control and maintain optimum habitat. Proper harvest of the deer is the key.

For instance, in a herd of 100 bred does and zero bucks (they all were shot during hunting season, or all but one were shot and the last one was clobbered by a rural mail delivery vehicle, or whatever), use the same 1.6 fawning rate. Those 100 over-wintering does produce 160 fawns, of which 80 will be female and 80 will be male. This gives you a herd with 180 females and 80 males.

Take it one step further. Assume 25% natural mortality, resulting in 195 surviving deer (260 x .75 = 195). Of the 65 lost, figure 33 bucks and 32 does. Going into the fawning season, there is a herd of 148 females and 47 males. If the 148 females have a 1.6 fawning rate, there are 432 deer in the herd after only the second fawning season following the stopping of all hunting. This is why it is said, not facetiously, that deer breed like rabbits.

5) The closer you get to 1:1 ratio, the more mature bucks will be lost from natural mortality.

• Above. Fertilization of natural browse and mast trees may attract and hold more deer to a specific habitat.

• Left photo. A sex ratio of 1:1 can result in a higher mortality among larger bucks due to a greater number of violent encounters.

> **F**or PDM to work best, you MUST identify – and not harvest – button bucks. Give them a chance to grow up and become mature bucks.

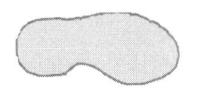

by Stan Potts

Personal Deer Management, Done Right,
is Like Having Your Cake and Eating It Too!

The term "quality deer management" has been around long enough that most hunters recognize the basic philosophy. However, there may be several definitions of Quality Deer Management (QDM), dependent upon each hunter's interpretation, personal frames of reference, and tagging preferences and goals. Many hunters confuse QDM with trophy deer management when, in fact, trophy deer management is actually a more intense version of QDM.

I would like to offer yet another version of deer management – **Personal Deer Management, a philosophy that involves selective hunting and harvesting.** This seems to be what most hunters are looking for today. QDM and PDM are not for everyone, but for those interested in big bucks, this type of deer management is appealing.

My definition of PDM involves a high harvest of does and protection of immature bucks. In that sense, I would like to stress the importance of protecting button bucks. What we are after is an improved buck:doe ratio, closer to 1:1. That is the primary goal of PDM.

In the spring when fawns are born, the ratio of those newborns is typically 1:1, one buck fawn for every doe fawn, or very near that even split. As these deer mature, the natural mortality for buck fawns often is greater than for their female counterparts. Therefore, we need to concentrate our harvesting efforts on does to balance this natural occurrence.

For those hunters who remember the days when a deer sighting was a rare event, it may be difficult to harvest does. However, I believe that you cannot harvest too many does in some of today's deer herd population levels. You really have to work hard on those does to reduce their numbers significantly, to the level where they should be.

In central Illinois there is a special deer management area with an outstanding track record in Quality Deer Management. The success of the QDM program at the Clinton Lake Special Archery Hunt has shown that in some situations an archery hunting program can hold deer numbers within the carrying capacity of quality habitat, improve buck:doe ratios and increase the number of quality bucks in the area.

This 2,000 acre tract of ground was overpopulated with deer and no hunting was allowed for 12-15 years. The deer population skyrocketed. As a result, Illinois Power and the Illinois Department of Natural Resources started a herd reduction program with quality in mind. Bringing the herd numbers under control, balancing buck to doe ratios and improving the number of upper age class bucks were all part of this program.

Plenty of people were skeptical that an archery program could achieve such goals. Yet, in fact, the Clinton Lake Special Archery Hunt turned out to be one of the most successful QDM programs in history. So let's look at some of the methods that helped this program succeed.

In the beginning, hunters were required to harvest an antlerless deer before they could hunt for an antlered buck. The area was well known for big bucks, due to the absence of hunting pressure. There was tremendous participation among hunters in the program, because the big bucks were an incentive to adhere to the rules.

Hunt coordinators soon realized that **the antlerless deer harvest requirement had a problem.** It did not protect button bucks. During the first couple of years, button bucks made up 30 to 40 percent of the antlerless harvest. Biologists and concerned deer hunters discussed this problem and decided to require hunters to harvest a female deer before being able to hunt an antlered buck. Button bucks were off limits. The decision by Ron Willmore, an Illinois Power biologist, showed their strong commitment to a successful QDM program.

There would be no penalty if a hunter accidentally harvested a button buck while doe hunting. Mistakes can and do happen. But now hunters began to be more careful. They began to practice selective harvest, or PDM, on a stricter level. Education became the key to keeping button bucks out of the harvest tally and giving them the chance to grow up. Every button buck saved by this decision had the potential to grow into a mature buck. We all know that mature bucks in Illinois are trophies in any state!

Once hunters educated themselves to identify button bucks, the percentage of these young bucks in the harvest fell to 12 to 15 percent. Of course, some may say that even one button buck harvested is too many. Yet, it takes time and commitment on the part of hunters to learn how to identify button bucks before they shoot. They learned to be absolutely sure that the deer before them was not a button buck. If they weren't sure, they did not shoot.

Of course, some mistakes were made. But the important factor is that the number of button bucks harvested was reduced. When a mistake was made and a button buck taken, the hunter simply tagged the buck and took it home or donated it to the Sportsmen Against Hunger program. Most returned to the woods with the conviction to be even more careful the next time around. Yes, a certain amount of peer pressure was applied, and education efforts were kept high. Taking the time to identify the button buck before shooting will produce the desired selective harvest results.

One of the most valuable tools in this type of hunting is a good pair of binoculars. When you get in this situation, try to examine the approaching deer for those button knobs. A button buck also will have a dark forehead patch just like a big buck. Even if you cannot see the buttons, you usually can see that darker patch of forehead hair. His head often is a little blockier, like an adult buck. Many times a button buck will behave differently from its female traveling companions. It often is the lead deer and seems oblivious to danger. It may spend time investigating everything in its path and not seem as cautious as the doe fawn or the big doe.

If a deer is alone, this can add to identification problems. An overall size comparison is not possible. So look for a shorter, triangular head, and a shorter, triangular tail. Both indicate a young deer.

The button buck is one of the easiest deer in the herd to harvest. Therefore, you need to look before you shoot when you are practicing Personal Deer Management.

Personal Deer Management (PDM) works well on private property, whether that is 200 acres or 1,000 acres. The larger the area, the more you will be able to affect the deer herd. There are several things to consider in a PDM program: Desired buck:doe ratio, carrying capacity of the habitat, amount and quality of food sources, desired herd size, natural mortality rate, which bucks to harvest, which bucks to let pass, how best to improve the numbers of quality bucks. These are not all the factors, but it is most of them.

Regarding buck harvest, in my opinion, an antler spread system (often called 'spread credit') is one of the best methods to follow. Spread credit seems to be the best way to identify quickly what to shoot and what not to shoot when you are buck hunting. This system protects immature branch-antlered bucks from harvest.

If a buck's antler spread is wider than his erect, outstretched ears ... shoot; if not, let this buck gain at least another year of antler growth. That's the usual dividing line. In the Midwest, if a buck's antler spread is not wider than its ears, the animal almost certainly is only 2-1/2 years old or less and would be considered an immature buck. Making a PDM rule that you will not shoot a buck whose antler spread is not "wider than its ears" will protect almost 100 percent of the 18-month old bucks and probably 75 percent of the 2-1/2 year old bucks. Protecting those young bucks creates a higher number of upper age class bucks to hunt. The greater the number of mature bucks available to hunt increases your chance of harvesting a big trophy whitetail.

If we can protect a buck from harvest until after it is 2-1/2 years of age, that buck won't have much trouble protecting itself afterward. Once it has survived three hunting seasons as a button buck, as a yearling buck and as a 2-1/2 year old, it becomes much more difficult to harvest. That buck can protect itself.

In my book, a 3-1/2 year old buck is mature. It is a smart cookie. Harvesting such a mature buck is difficult. It is just too tough to get within shooting range under shooting conditions.

People around the country are looking for that mature whitetail to hunt. Practicing PDM will help hunters in their quest for better numbers of this type of buck to hunt. Finding large concentrations of mature bucks in any section of the country may be rare, but with the advent of PDM, those numbers likely will improve.

In most states, harvest statistics show that 70 percent to 90 percent of the antlered harvest consists of 1-1/2 year old bucks, principally because the hunting pressure is so heavy. Few bucks get a chance to survive to maturity. With plenty of food and good genetics in most areas of the whitetail range, all these bucks need is the opportunity to grow older on the hoof instead of in someone's freezer. Once bucks reach maturity, a greater portion of the nutrients they take in can be used for antler development instead of body growth.

In some instances, the spread credit criterion may be challenged by a buck that doesn't fit the profile. What I mean is, occasionally a mature buck with huge 150-class antlers may have only a 13-inch spread. This buck would fall below the minimum antler criterion of "wider than his ears". In cases such as this, you simply must use common sense. Go ahead and harvest that buck!

The Illinois Department of Natural Resources has developed several Quality Deer Management areas. On many of these areas a criterion exists where the buck must have four or five points on a side before the hunter can harvest that particular deer. This criterion is better than no QDM at all, but it does not protect young bucks as well as the spread credit criterion.

In most of the Midwestern states, an 8- or 10-point buck could be 1-1/2 years old. Its rack may not even make the minimums for Pope and Young record books, yet under the four- or five-points-on-a-side criterion, this buck could be harvested. And don't forget about the monster eight-pointer that doesn't fit the five-points-on-a-side rule. The Boone and Crockett record book has a few eight-pointers that no hunter would pass up.

Nutrition in any PDM program is important. In the Midwest, adequate nutrition usually is not a problem. Some management programs do a lot of supplemental feeding and others do not. I believe that in the Midwest we are fortunate not to have to concern ourselves with supplemental feeding. The typical Midwestern habitat supplies deer with all the nutrition they require. There is plenty of browse, mast crops, and other food sources. Plenty of corn, soybeans and alfalfa for the average deer.

In today's mixture of deer management philosophies, many hunters have the mistaken impression that the number of Boone and Crockett-class bucks that occur in the wild will greatly increase. Not so. Boone and Crockett-class deer are incredibly rare, even on the most intensively managed properties. You would be better off to set your sights on harvesting a mature deer rather than holding out for a Boone and Crockett contender.

Any buck that is $3^1/_2$ years old or better is a trophy, in my mind. Even if you had 100 bucks that received all the nutrition they needed and were allowed to reach eight or ten years of age, you might only have one net Boone and Crockett buck out of the whole bunch. There may be several bucks which gross Boone and Crockett, but net B&C bucks are rare. A $5^1/_2$-year-old 140-class buck is just as cunning in his ability to elude you as is any B&C buck. That $5^{-1}/_2$ year old is a true trophy.

If you have realistic expectations for your Personal Deer Management program, you will have a much better chance of success. Many average hunters just hunt for the experience itself; they simply love the outdoors and hunting. A Personal Deer Management program is not what they are looking for. However, for an ever-increasing number of hunters, selective hunting is looked upon as the key to future big buck hunting opportunities, with the opportunity – and need – to harvest many female deer to get to that point. That produces great hunting experience, shot selection experience and great-tasting venison.

State game management agencies must take into account the opinions of all types of hunters when managing deer herds. They must consider the opinion of the hunter who wants the opportunity to see a deer and harvest a deer. They must balance their decisions between those hunters and others who prefer Quality Deer Management or Personal Deer Management. Providing different opportunities at various sites is one solution.

State game agencies provide the recreational hunting opportunities. It is a personal decision to practice any degree of Quality Deer Management. Some hunters choose not to, and others choose to implement a PDM philosophy. Whatever road you choose, selective or non-selective deer hunting, make sure all your hunts are quality ones.

STAN POTTS

Stan Potts works as a hunting consultant for Heartland Lodge in Pike County, Illinois. Stan's best bow-tagged buck is a net 195-5/8 score typical that ranks number two in Illinois. His best non-typical is a 21-point buck that nets 193-5/8. He has taken 13 whitetail bucks which meet Pope & Young record book minimum score.

Stan was recently featured on Mossy Oak's "Hunting the Country" television series on TNN. He also joined the Drury Outdoors team in filming two videos – Power Callin' and Dream Season. He is on the Pro-Staff of Browning Archery, Mossy Oak, Drury Outdoors and M.A.D. Calls. He also represents Muzzy Products, Toxonics and Easton Archery. For the past few years Stan has traveled the country presenting seminars on the techniques of hunting big whitetail bucks. He also has been featured in several magazine articles and books on whitetail hunters and whitetail hunting.

SECTION III:

WHITETAILS, WHITETAILS, WHITETAILS

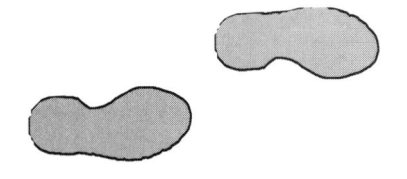

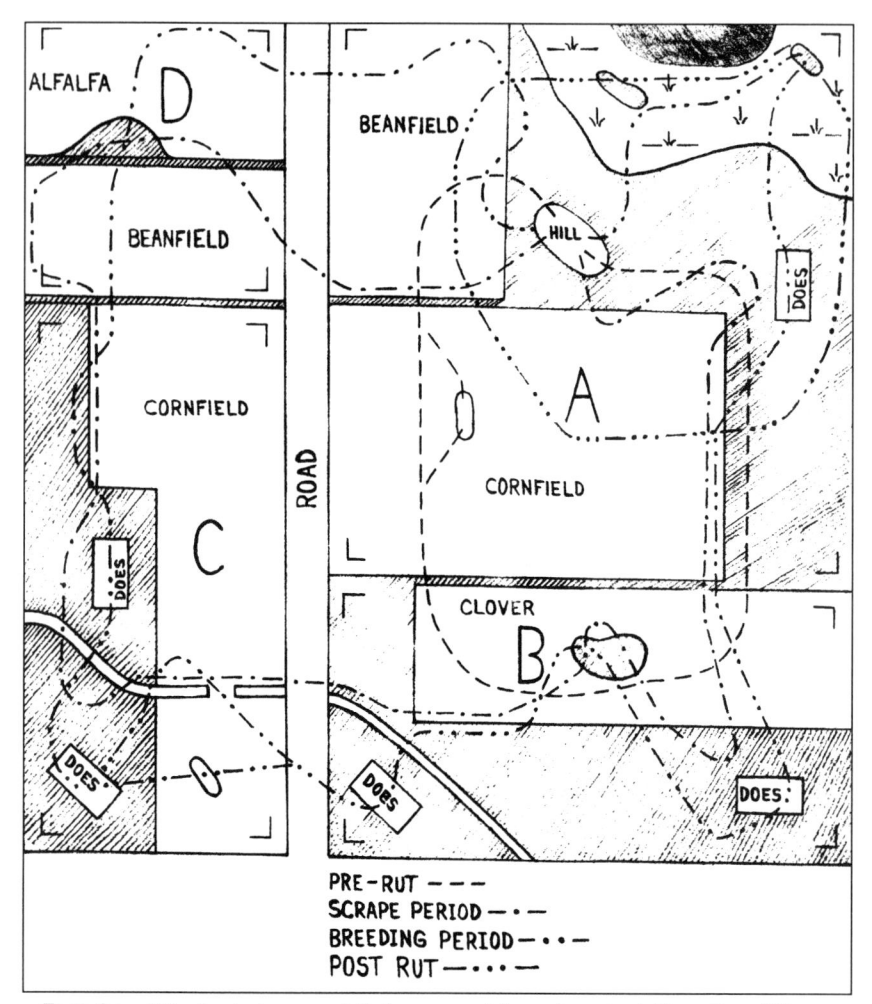

• Farm A could be hunted successfully from pre-rut through post-rut. Farm B could be hunted successfully from pre-rut through the breeding period of the rut. Farm C could be hunted successfully only during the scrape period and the breeding period of the rut. Farm D could be hunted successfully only during the breeding period of the rut. The article explains why. The shaded area indicates woods of varying thicknesses of cover; deer beds are in the thickest cover.

> The biggest mistake most hunters make is hunting all season from only one or two stand sites.

by Tony LaPratt

Are You Hunting A November Stand in October?

*T*hat title is a legitimate question, for very few stands are good all the time, from season opening to season closing. The best way to begin figuring out where you ought to stand at a given date on the calendar is to accept a couple of rules of common sense:

1) Have several stands ready for any given time period, so you will NOT overhunt any of them and will keep all of them fresh. The biggest mistake most hunters make is to spend the entire season hunting from only one or two stand locations.

2) Keep open eyes and an open mind. See what's there before you, instead of only what you want to see. This will keep you mentally flexible; you'll prepare better, adapt when you need to adapt, move when you need to move – and anticipate the necessary changes and moves, so you can be in the right place at the right time before the deer gets there. I have stands that are just for the first seven days of hunting season. Then I have stands for the scrape period of the rut and the breeding period of the rut, plus the post-rut.

3) Pay attention to details.

4) Prepare thoroughly.

5) Realize that deer change and adapt. Their movements (travel, feeding, bedding) are affected by changes in foliage cover, food sources, weather, hunting pressure and the stage of the rut. They're all important, but knowing the four stages of the rut – and how to deal with them — is most important. That's because nearly all strategies and deer movement revolve around the rut. All these factors – rut and the others – affect where you should hunt at any given date on the calendar.

Let's set the four rut periods as follows:

Pre-Rut   September 1 - October 15, or thereabouts

Scrape Period	Oct. 16 - November 5, or thereabouts
Breeding Period	November 6 - November 22, or thereabouts
Post Rut	November 23 - Whenever antlers are shed (varies from buck to buck)

These rut dates are for a herd which is in relatively good balance. If the balance is out of whack, these periods will be changed. For more on that, see the articles on Personal Deer Management by John Sloan and Stan Potts elsewhere in this book.

Here's an example of why it is so important to know the four stages of the rut.

A hunter called me and said "If you have big tracks and big buck rubs, rubs the size of a pop can or bigger, you have big bucks on your property. That's the sign I have, but I never see the bucks." He added that he is careful about his scent, and he watches the wind. He starts hunting from the first of October (the day Michigan's bowhunting season opens), four to five times a week.

I said I would talk to him and take a look at his property. When I got there, we walked the farm. I noticed several small doe bedding areas. Across the road was a lake with a big swamp around it. I said, "You have a Rut Farm".

"What do you mean?," he asked.

"Your big buck lives in your neighbor's swamp. He doesn't live on your farm. What you are doing wrong is hunting your farm in October like it should be hunted in November. In October, that buck isn't getting to your farm until late after dark. The buck keeps smelling you where you've walked back and forth from your stand. After a while, he has pinpointed your stand. By hunting him in October and scenting up the place, you have either made him nocturnal, or he will stay far away from your stand sites. He will still make scrapes and rubs on your farm, but most likely at night.

"This Fall, move your stand so he can't key on past experiences, and don't hunt it the month of October.

"Now, when November comes, when he ordinarily would come to your farm during daylight hours looking for does, that's exactly what he'll do."

That November, the third time he hunted the farm, he took a Pope and Young-class buck. Later, he took another nice buck. In his letter he said, "I had hunted the farm for eight years. I had never seen bucks on it before, but this year I took two nice bucks. Thank you for your time and my new hunting strategies."

That's not an isolated instance. So let's look at the changing situations through the four stages of the rut.

PRE-RUT

Pre-rut can be said to begin when bucks shed the velvet from their antlers. At that time, they will be much more interested in food than in does. They will have regular, predictable movement patterns from bedding to feeding and back to bedding areas, and those travels will be fairly short. This is the best time of the year to pinpoint core areas. (Greg Miller has more details on this in his Core Area article elsewhere in this book.)

Your best bet now to locate and pattern bucks is to check individual rubs and rub lines.

Your hunting efforts now include quite a bit of information gathering. For instance, mark as much information as you can on topographical maps and aerial maps, noting such things as food sources, bedding areas, trails, rub lines, even other hunters' stands and the places they park their vehicles and their routes to their stands. Aerial maps can be eye-openers; quite often the land does not lay as you believe it does. Also, you'll see things from this overhead perspective that you'll not see from ground level.

Now study your maps. Look for travel barriers, bottlenecks and structures, edges, changing timber or types of hiding cover, clearcuts and small clearings, beaver dams, creeks, swamps, points of ridges separated by swamp or clearing, wooded draws across from each other on opposite sides of an open ridgetop, and anywhere deer might move with the least amount of exposure.

This is like the old Yellow Pages statement – let your fingers do the walking. Here, with maps, you're doing a lot of scouting without walking. Of vital importance, maps provide information access to land you don't have permission to go on. They can help you scout without being there.

Later, when you're doing on-site scouting, you can look in the most likely places for large rubs worthy of your time and attention, and for a tree stand location. You can pinpoint major food sources, then backtrack trails to staging areas just outside bedding areas, and to bedding areas themselves.

Here's how to find and define a staging area. From any major food source area, follow a major runway back into the cover. At a certain point the main trail forks off into several smaller trails, which all just seem to disappear. This area may appear fairly open; at the very least, it will not be heavily brushy. This open area where the trails splinter and fade out – that is the staging area. If you hunt near there, you will see young bucks gathering there about an hour before dark, then begin their journey out to the major feeding area. Smarter bucks will begin ghosting into this staging area just about dark. There may or may not be shooting light. They will wait here until dark, then begin their movement to the major feeding area, or maybe not begin the movement. Keep in mind that mature bucks sometimes feed at out-of-the-way, secondary food sources. They're not going to expose themselves on an alfalfa field when they can do well back in the brush, browsing on twigs and eating some grass and picking up food here and there, safely under cover all the while.

During pre-rut, you'll be looking for a wide range of deer sign — rubs, trails, tracks, boundary scrapes (small scrapes made at the edges of their territories), and droppings. Take a close look at the droppings. Soft, greenish ones indicate alfalfa and rich grasses; harder, darker round ones are created by a more balanced fare. The type of pellet can tell you a bit about where they are or are not feeding.

Pre-rut Rubs

In general, rubs tell you more about a buck's size than do scrapes. I personally don't get fired up on scrapes, but I do when I find big rubs. There were big rubs in the area where I hunted almost all of the big bucks I've taken. The first rubs of the season usually are the dominant buck. He will rub small saplings and trees. This may give you clues for a pre-rut stand site. For the scrape period of the rut, I'm looking for bucks which rub high above the ground and on trees that are the diameter of a pop can or larger.

I have found that different bucks favor different species of trees. Some will show a preference for aspen, sassafras, cedars and so on.

Rubs can give you direction and travel patterns of the buck.. If the rubbed part is on the side of the tree facing the bedding area, the buck most likely made that rub in the evening on its way from the bedding area to the feeding area, as an example. A line of rubs, of course, indicate a line of travel. If you see rubs suddenly blossoming in an area, or two parallel lines of rubs, you have an area where bucks are calling each other bad names, so to speak. These all are more pieces to the puzzle. So take a minute to examine all rubs and mark them on your map, because they may lead you to a trophy book buck. I can't overemphasize the use of maps and marking details on them. You cannot remember everything, and sometimes patterns show up on paper that you had missed noticing until you marked enough details on the map.

When you see bucks in bachelor groups during this pre-rut period, expect to see them beginning to get aggressive toward each other. They're posturing and sparring, working out the pecking order of dominance. These aren't serious fights; not even close. As the days pass, the bucks will go their individual ways to their individual core areas. This is especially true of the older and larger bucks. They're most likely to be dominant.

The pre-rut period comes to a close when the bucks shift efforts away from feeding and toward increased rutting activity, principally the making of scrapes. The change happens gradually over a few days' time.

SCRAPING PERIOD

Along with increased scraping, the number of rubs begins to increase. Bucks, especially the younger ones, begin showing more interest in does than in feeding. They probably still will be on predictable travel patterns, but those patterns will be different, to allow for the increased scraping and rubbing activity. Check the scrapes and scrape lines, plus the rub lines, to try to figure out travel patterns. Now also is the time for you to home in on core area location, if you haven't already done so. This is important information to know right now.

Rubs

When the scrape period of the rut is on, hormones are flowing freely. Bucks now do some heavy duty rubbing, sometimes called breeding rubs. This is when you'll see shredded and mangled trees and brush. These rubs are distinguished from earlier rubs by their freshness and the increased extent of damage from the buck's growing aggression. They are most often found near scrape lines.

These rubs also give clues about antler characteristics. If a sapling several inches behind the rub tree is scarred or scraped, the buck likely has long tines. If the rubbed tree bark is shredded into tiny ribbons, the base of the buck's antlers are likely to be heavily burred. I also like to find pieces of small saplings one to two inches in diameter. Broken off by the buck thrusting his antlers into the saplings and twisting his head, these 12-inch to 24-inch pieces of sapling get my hunting blood boiling. The overall degree of damages are clues to the buck's size.

During this scraping period, bucks travel to areas of high interaction with other deer and make scrapes in these social hubs. They're playing to the doe groups. These are good stand locations. Does will go to fields at this time to feed, but bucks don't really like to and for the most part will not.

Breeding scrapes now come into existence, too, of course. These scrapes usually are oval and roughly 36 inches by 36 inches. Some are larger, others smaller. Approximately 4 to 4-1/2 feet above the scrape there almost always will be an overhanging limb, usually a half-inch or so in diameter. This limb will be broken and probably twisted, the result of the buck's efforts to leave scent on the limb. This scent usually is from his forehead or preorbital glands. It also may be from his saliva since he frequently will bite the small branches and pull them through his mouth.

An active breeding scrape will appear and smell fresh, with a musky smell.

Bucks also will deposit their scent on limbs known as licking branches which are not associated with scrapes. These licking branches appear to be an important form of scent communication. They are rare. I know of only two in the areas I hunt in southern Michigan. They are used consistently, from September on, by all the deer in an area, not just the bucks. This licking branch usually is a part of a scrape line series, and can be an excellent place to hunt.

One thing is for certain — the scraping period is the best time for antler rattling and calling. Bucks are on the prod but does aren't. That is, for the bucks, a frustrating situation and they would cordially like to beat the tar out of most anything, but especially something which looks and acts and smells like competition. More than one hunter, busily clearing some brush for a hot new stand, has been greeted by the sudden appearance of a curious buck.

Things are about to become even more intense, for this is the end of the scraping period. The breeding period now begins as does come into estrus.

BREEDING PERIOD

Bucks now are predominantly interested in does. Their travel is unpredictable; they will be anywhere and everywhere, at any time. Scrapes, rubs and most other deer sign isn't important now, but fresh tracks are, simply because that's the most recent place a deer has been and with luck it is still in the area. Staging areas and high interaction areas are hot-spots to set up now. To pattern bucks now, pay attention to the travel patterns of does. Don't worry if you push deer out of an area as you're moving through or to it, because other deer may be along shortly.

This segment of the rut really begins with the first major wave of does entering estrus and breeding. It occurs fairly suddenly, seemingly like someone shot off a starting gun, and at roughly the same time each year, unless there have been major changes in the make-up of the deer herd. True, some does come in heat earlier and some trail.

This major group of does, most of which are 2-1/2 years old and older, triggers truly amazing breeding activity and brings on what is generally called the peak of the rut.

Trophy bucks are now most vulnerable and most likely to act stupid and get your tag placed on them.

Your most important hunting strategy during the breeding period is to spend as much time as you can hunting, and hunt near doe concentrations. Major food sources are important, because doe groups usually are found near them. You now have a wide range of options – stillhunting, stand hunting, even rattling.

This period ends when most of the does have been bred and are no longer in estrus.

POST-RUT

The post-rut period starts when the two-week breeding period ends; the timing of the post-rut is dependent on when breeding first starts. The start of the scraping period can be determined by backing off two weeks from the start of the breeding period, and the post-rut can be timed by adding two weeks to the starting date of the breeding period. The breeding period is the key which times all four periods of the rut.

Breeding does not end after this first rush of hot does is past; about 26 to 28 days after peak rut the secondary rut begins. This second batch of does is much smaller in number and made up mostly of 1-1/2 year old does, along with any older does that did not conceive during the peak breeding period. This secondary rut, occurring during the post-rut period, is neither as important nor as visible as the first breeding cycle. A third minor breeding time often occurs when six-month-old female fawns enter estrus for the first time. Anywhere from 20 to 50 percent of these young females come in estrus at six months of age; in Michigan it's close to 50 percent.

For the most part, then, breeding activity gives way to feeding activity and resting. As this period progresses, bucks become more interested n food and physical recovery. Their pattern becomes more predictable in the latter portion of the period. Rubs and scrapes are not especially important as signs; bucks are exhausted and not paying much attention to them. Fresh running tracks, family units and food source locations are the most important signs and areas now, and your knowledge of core area locations becomes more valuable. Bucks become more nocturnal. This occurs for two reasons: 1) The results of too many recent contacts with humans – hunting pressure, and 2) there's no reason to get up and move around during the day and they are primarily nocturnal anyway. Nothing much will happen for a while. Bucks are getting back into their survival routines, jumpy and exhausted, feeling the effects of practically continuous and furious activity for the past few weeks. Nothing is better than a safe bedding area.

This recuperation time seems to take two to four weeks. As they recover, their daily routine changes. They move farther and farther from their core areas in search of quality food. Sometimes they leave their core area and relocate miles away near prime food sources.

Hunting is extremely difficult now. Mature bucks will be spooky and difficult to sneak up on. Hunt to the last legal minute of the day. You may find some activity by hunting the social hub areas of doe groups, catching a buck or bucks chasing the few does in heat. If you're looking for a big boy, go to the nastiest, thickest places and be prepared to work hard. If you're going to a stand, get in position before daylight so you're set before any buck in the area has a chance to move onto you.

If you want to force the issue, make something happen, you might want to slip ever so slowly through the thickets that are likely big buck bedding areas. This requires patience, patience and more patience. If the bucks move at all during legal hours, they'll move in the security of thick cover. A favorable wind and total quiet are essential. Hunting like this is a slow, tedious way to go. It can get your mainspring wound pretty tight.

I like to hunt this way. Three good things can come from this: 1) I may jump a buck and get a quick shot; 2) a buck may stand up upon hearing a slight noise or seeing an unidentifiable movement and hold momentarily for a shot, or 3) I may catch an unsuspecting buck loitering around in his bedding area. (This is how I've taken a couple of my best bucks. The best one scored 151-7/8.)

Another tactic to force movement is deer drives. There is no other time of year when deer drives are justified. There are times and situations during the post-rut period when deer mostly won't move unless you move them. Try to find bottlenecks or some physical feature to help funnel a buck your way. Things are going to be extremely tough in the post-rut, so use every advantage you can.

Then, right after season ends, it all begins again. This is a great time for scouting. The things I find now I put to good use next season. And remember ... make sure to mark everything on your maps.

For additional information on the rut and different hunting strategies, I recommend "Hunting Trophy Whitetails" by David Morris and "Hunting The Four Periods of the Rut" by Dick Idol.

> Here's why knowing core areas can give you better results than hunting the rut!

by Greg Miller

Buck Core Areas— Fact & Fiction

My largest bow-killed buck is a 202 3/8 gross non-typical. The 18-pointer was a mature animal, to be sure. That fact was impressed upon me many times throughout the two years I chased him. The buck displayed survival instincts the likes of which I'd never before encountered, and, believe me, I had chased my fair share of mature bucks prior to taking up pursuit of this non-typical.

My day in the sun finally came on a cold December afternoon. After effectively evading my most dedicated and disciplined attempts to ambush him, the big buck made an almost unbelievable and fatal mistake. With more than a half hour of legal shooting time remaining, he wandered out into a snow covered alfalfa field for a bite to eat. Eventually, his feeding efforts led him to within 15 yards of my stand site. The rest, as they say, is history.

I could cite many reasons why everything finally came together for me on that December afternoon in 1990. But the factor that contributed most to my success was my ultimate, total familiarity with the big buck's core area. Not only had I pretty much figured out the boundaries of that core area, but more important, I also had figured out when the buck would be there. This last bit of information was exactly what prompted me to be on my stand on the fateful day.

The benefits of gaining a thorough understanding of buck core areas has been made apparent to me many times in the years since I arrowed the non-typical. But another interesting fact also has become apparent during that same time. While there are many deer hunters who routinely use the term "buck core areas", a rather large percentage of these individuals have a mistaken impression of what the term really means.

In the past several years I've heard a broad range of descriptions for the term "buck core areas". Some of these descriptions were right on the money. But far more of them were way off the mark. Adding even more confusion to the core area issue is the fact that many of the totally inaccurate descriptions I've heard were being passed along by so-called trophy whitetail experts. I actually heard one of these experts tell a large seminar audience that core areas are those places where whitetail bucks take does during the rut. And while watching a hunting video recently, I heard another "expert" state that clusters of buck sign, i.e., concentrations of rubs and scrapes, are also known as core areas. Wrong in both cases!

Okay, so what is the simplest and most accurate definition of a core area? **Core areas are those places inhabited by whitetail bucks during non-breeding and/or non-stressful times.** During those times when they aren't chasing hot does or fighting to survive severe weather conditions, bucks will do the majority of their feeding, watering and traveling within the boundaries of an already established "home range". In my opinion, this is the most correct definition of a core area.

Almost all the truly successful trophy hunters I know understand the importance of becoming core area literate, but I've run into a major problem trying to convey that message to up-and-coming big buck hunters. Quite honestly, I get the impression that many couldn't care less about learning more about buck core areas. As one guy told me recently, "Yeah, I hunt the entire archery season, but I concentrate most of my attention on the rut. From what I've heard, big bucks abandon their core areas at this time of year. So why should I waste my time trying to learn more about core areas?"

Let me tell you why.

I must admit, for many years I harbored this same philosophy. While I did do some hunting at other times during the archery season, the majority of my efforts revolved around the rut. As I eventually discovered, however, when compared with the rest of the season, the rut was actually a short-lived thing. At most, I could count on getting seven days of the type of hectic daylight buck activity associated with this time of year. Worse, there was a good chance I might not even be in the woods during the "right" seven days, which meant the odds could be stacked against me even more. This approach meant I was neglecting better than two months of my home state's archery season.

As I learned more about core areas, I began to realize that there actually was a better time than the rut to try to ambush specific bucks. I knew that big bucks seldom got into predictable patterns, such as showing up at the same food source at the same time every day. However, I learned that there was a time during the archery season when mature deer became somewhat predictable. This somewhat predictable behavior occurred during the lengthy pre-rut period, when the bucks were hanging out in their established core areas.

Let's face facts here. You can run into all kinds of problems by waiting for the rut before setting up an ambush for a specific buck. To begin with, at this time of year you never know where that buck might be. I can, however, tell you one place he probably won't be, and that's somewhere within his core area. Just about all the mature bucks I've hunted over the years abandoned their core areas once the rut began. The urge to breed would lead these deer miles from their home ranges.

I remember one big buck in particular several years ago. On a frosty morning during the peak of the rut, a buddy of mine saw that buck two miles west of his established core area. The buck was seen again two days later. This time he was chasing a group of antlerless deer a mile east of his home turf. It's this type of unpredictable behavior that makes it tough to ambush a targeted buck, or any buck for that matter, during the rut. There is a better time.

It's entirely possible that some bucks may have several distinctly different core areas they'll use throughout the year. However, we as hunters are most interested in those core areas bucks inhabit during the open hunting season. I might add that, in many instances, these core areas actually are established during the early summer. If all conditions remain suitable, bucks will often remain within these same core areas until the rut begins.

It's also important to note that core area size can vary dramatically. Individual buck temperament seems to be somewhat of a factor in how much acreage a certain buck might include in his home turf. However, from what I've ascertained over the years, another factor has more bearing on core area size, and that is the location of suitable bedding cover in relation to the location of preferred foods. Quite simply, the closer a buck can bed to several primary feeding areas, the smaller his core area will be. Just the opposite is true for bucks that are forced to bed a long distance from preferred foods.

Farmland whitetails usually are able to find several preferred foods within a relatively small area, maybe a mile or less. On the other hand, it's not unusual for big woods deer to have to walk a mile or more to find just a couple of nutritional foods. For this reason, **big woods bucks almost always establish larger core areas**

- Spot-checking feed areas during the final weeks of summer is a great way to get actual sightings of big bucks. These sighting also can help you pinpoint the exact location of buck core areas.

- The location of preferred foods plays a significant role in just how large an area might be encompassed within a buck's core area.

- The only time mature bucks get into something remotely resembling predictable patterns is during the pre-rut period. At no other time during the season will they relate so strongly to their rub lines and scrape lines.

92   Steps Along the Hunter's Path

than their farmland relatives.

As stated, most big bucks establish their basic core areas at some point during the early summer. These deer become homebodies, staying pretty much within the boundaries of their core areas through the rest of the summer and then right on through the entire pre-rut period. It's this last bit of information that can prove to be beneficial to bowhunters especially.

Remember those big, velvet-antlered bucks you were seeing with regularity during the last few weeks of summer? No doubt you also remember that those deer suddenly disappeared right before the opening of archery season. Like a lot of other deer hunters, your initial reaction was probably that the bucks had pulled up stakes and moved to other areas. I doubt that was the case, however. In fact, there's a better than average chance those big deer were still in the immediate vicinity. Even more important, they already had supplied you with the information you needed to pinpoint the location of their core areas.

Although you might believe otherwise, a buck's feeding preferences really don't change all that much from late summer to the late pre-rut period. So if you routinely see a couple of big bucks feeding in a certain alfalfa field in late August or early September, you can just about bet those bucks will still be somewhere close by in early October. In other words, they will still be residing within their core area!

This is the time of year when whitetail bucks start displaying that somewhat predictable behavior I spoke of earlier. Put simply, at no other time during the season will they be relating so strongly to their rub-lines and scrape-lines. Granted, trying to figure out exactly which rub-line and/or scrape-line a buck you're hunting will visit on a given day is guess work at best. However, you at least have the assurance of knowing that the buck is still in the area. And if he's in the area, there's every possibility he might stroll by within bow range. (As opposed to the rut, when he could be chasing a hot doe miles from your stand sites.)

There are those rare exceptions when a big buck might suddenly abandon his core area during the middle of the pre-rut. Several factors could cause such behavior. It could be that the deer is having repeated confrontations with a bigger, more dominant buck(s). It's also possible that a preferred food source has come into season a good distance away. But the number-one reason why big bucks suddenly relocate at this time of year is because of repeated human intrusions. In other words, because of intense hunting pressure.

Unfortunately, there's no real gauge for just how much pressure it takes to drive big bucks out of their established core areas. Some of the big bucks I've hunted in the past were being subjected to a tremendous amount of hunting pressure. Yet these deer stayed put in their core areas throughout the pre-rut. On the other hand, I've also hunted a number of big bucks that wouldn't tolerate even a small amount of hunting pressure. They relocated to completely different areas after only a couple encounters with humans.

I've repeatedly mentioned the fact that gaining an understanding of core areas will make you a better hunter during non-rut times. That also includes the late-season, which is December for my home state. Big bucks often will return to their core areas once breeding is finished. Of more interest to bowhunters, these deer will once again start using the same travel routes they used throughout the lengthy pre-rut.

The non-typical I mentioned at the beginning of this piece was arrowed during the late archery season. Four years after taking that deer, I ambushed another Pope & Young-class buck during the late season. Both of those bucks had quickly vacated their core areas the minute the rut kicked into high gear, but they both returned when the breeding ritual came to an end. Interestingly, I shot those bucks while sitting on stand sites I also had hunted from during the pre-rut.

If I've learned one thing over the years, it's that you'll stand a much better chance of harvesting a mature buck once you discover where that animal is feeding, where he is bedding and the routes he's using to reach his destinations. Having a thorough knowledge of buck core areas can be a tremendous asset to your trophy whitetail hunting schemes!

GREG MILLER

Greg Miller is a hard-core deer hunter from northwestern Wisconsin. He has consistently taken large whitetail bucks with gun and bow for more than 30 years across most of North America. Many of Greg's bucks have been taken from public forest and farmlands. Because of this, he feels well qualified to explain techniques that will work for other deer hunters. Greg writes for several hunting magazines and is the author of two books on whitetail deer hunting.

> **R**ugged jungle-like cover beside water often is overlooked. It shouldn't be; that's where more and larger bucks hide.

by Les Davenport

Take the Water Trail to Deer Hunting Success

Many wallhanger whitetails live out their lives in impenetrable cover along watersheds. They avoid average hunters by using water and dense vegetation as human barriers. Let's analyze the habits and terrain tendencies of these Sultan trophies as we review pre- and post-season scouting, stand placement, and equipment.

If you're looking for a magic formula with little work involved, this topic isn't for you. The objective here is to open your eyes to a high-odds approach to harvesting trophy bucks. Effectively hunting near a stream or lake requires more effort than garden-variety hunters are willing to muster; that's why mature bucks find wetland areas so alluring.

If, however, you invite a true challenge for the upcoming season, let me walk you through some watery steps to success.

Numerous animal tracks covered my old footprints along the sandy river bank near the launch point. I climbed into the canoe and paddled downstream to the mouth of a smaller tributary that flowed through the heart of a dense river bottom thicket. More than one shooter buck called this water's-edge jungle home.

Having visited the wooded region for more than 20 years, it had become evident that increased hunting pressure was changing the bedding haunts of mature bucks. Less human encroachment in years past allowed bucks a more free-roaming lifestyle during daylight. They had commonly bedded in accessible areas close to a primary food source. This is rarely the case today.

Many buckless outings in successive seasons forced me to change from a same-old-spot-along-the-field hunting plan to a move-and-watch-and-move-again strategy. Earning a close encounter meant locating an unbothered bedding area and intercepting bucks as ebbing light triggered their activity. This new hunting scenario pushed me deeper into the forest valleys. Ultimately, I found myself closer to the river and farther from an ever-increasing stir of fellow hunters.

The aluminum skiff slid onto a sandbar formed by the lesser tributary. After beaching, I uncased and once-overed my Browning Explorer before tiptoeing up the smaller stream's soft edge. The hike was short, only 200 yards. At 2:05 p.m. I climbed aboard a portable tree stand placed two days earlier along a bedding exit trail.

It was late October and slightly sultry for good pre-rut activity. Or so I thought. Bucks had grown winter's hollow hair and now weighed their heaviest. They weren't eager to travel far to a food source or toward the core of does until evening cool-down.

It's a no-brainer to say mature, hunted deer survive by learning their pursuers' habits. In my opinion, **we are more often patterned by them than vice versa.** They easily make associations that cost us success, and they have a nose that knows where we've been. For example, the arrival of a truck too near a stand site puts deer on alert. When followed by human scent drifting through the woods, deer waste no time fleeing the hunter's arena. Thereafter, only the truck clatter or headlights arriving at the scene is needed to route deer from harm's way.

Reaching the riverside bedding area by canoe was a first for me in those early years. It required considerably more effort than my initial river approaches of hiking a quarter-mile of bordering woods. The combo walk-in and paddling exercise from an opposing direction tallied three times that distance. However, the merit of silently floating down the current to a high-odds stand site made the task seem worthwhile. A direct woodland entry had always alerted whitetails to my presence. Vehicle noise, popping twigs, hundreds of feet of potential to-and-fro human ground scent, and spooking bedded deer, increased the chance of 'association' and lessened the likelihood of scoring a P&Y-class buck.

Though unsuccessful in terms of tagging a deer, this pioneer canoe outing ended as a most memorable hunt. Five bucks were seen, two of them rival giants that dueled till long after dark. The sound of hammering antlers while I paddled upstream by starlight won't be forgotten. I later took a 164-score 5x5 on the opposite side of the river from my initial stand placement.

We, as hunters, tend to push male deer into seeking water barriers and head-high cover. These "walls" deter our daytime interference. Though we often create hunter-wariness in deer, mature

bucks are also reclusive and loungers by nature, especially during non-rut periods. Bucks store their year's energy for breeding season. They're not unlike old bull cattle that rest most of the year under a shade tree in hot weather or in a sunny spot during cold, usually distancing themselves from cows and calves.

While scouting pre-rut over the last decade, I've found countless beds inside dense vegetation along rivers, creeks and lakes. **Willow stands, nettle and horseweed thickets, and multiflora rose mazes are favorite cover for Midwestern watershed wallhangers.** A walk-in-from-the-road hunter has no chance of surprising these hideaway bucks. They'll hold tight or avoid head-on confrontation by quietly exiting along or across a stream or lake. Water-smart whitetails feel so protected from intrusion that it's evident from ground impressions that they rest on their sides with heads against the earth for long periods. The same bedding sites often repeat from year to year.

Bushwhacking Sultan bucks near water entails three primary ingredients – proper equipment, ample scouting, and the patience of a teacher in a schoolroom of fourth-grade boys. Achieving two without the third seldom adds to success. Here's some thought-provoking advice on each.

Shallow creeks and rivers or ones with sparse river-bank vegetation can be walked quietly. It's also possible to hike the edge of some lake shores. If the distance is great and weather warm, however, carry in your outer clothing to avoid sweating. Moisture from sweat evaporates and goes airborne to whitetail noses. Evaporating sweat lowers body temperature, which is undesirable once you're on stand. Though many hunters use backpacks for carrying in extra clothing, a pull-string turkey bag with back straps is quieter and easier to stash.

A plastic or fiberglass canoe or kayak is your best bet for lightness and a stealthy approach in a stream that cannot be waded. Though expensive (about $400), the Number One choice in this hunter's book is a Sportsmen plastic kayak. It is approximately 12 feet long and weighs about 55 pounds. Too many accidental aluminum 'thunks' convinced me to buy one of these non-metallic stream machines. With one seat removed, a lucky hunter easily can board and paddle out a 200-pound-plus animal in this wide-body kayak (though you may need to return for your hunting buddy). Most of the weight in a kayak balances at water level. This design makes it less prone to roll than a canoe. Regardless of choice, wear a lifejacket while you're paddling in and paddling out. This is a smart safety move, and if you should dump it also lets you begin grabbing instantly for gear that isn't tied to the canoe or kayak without worrying about your own safety quite as much.

Opt for a more seaworthy boat in rivers and lakes known to whitecap in windy weather. Employ an outboard if a stand site is too far for oars. Cut the engine well before reaching your destination and use an electric trolling motor or oars to cruise soundlessly to shore. Leave a visible note on the boat stating that you're hunting nearby. This prevents conservation officers or the Coast Guard from suspecting trouble. Always tell your spouse or a close friend where you're hunting and when you'll return.

Hip boots or chest waders hidden near a crossing saves carrying them in each time. Store these items inside an army surplus duffel bag. The canvas prevents squirrels and other rodents from chewing holes in them. Unnoticed holes in waders don't go unnoticed long in the water and are a chilling experience. Store those bagged boots on high ground so an overnight gully-washer won't sweep them away if that type of storm occurs in your area.

Pre-season scouting in a new area entails locating and mapping the approaches to dense water-side cover. Bucks rarely stay in these low spots until insects disappear and hunters reappear. Once hunting pressure has begun, trails and bedding-area rubs materialize along primary ridges and near water crossings. It's then a matter of selecting a prime ambush in an area you already know how to reach quietly. In addition to a quiet approach, rivers offer an excellent no-scent feature for deer hunters most of the rut. Odor is somewhat contained when a human passes over cool or cold water. It won't rise to the higher shelf of warmer air, which is especially good when primary ridges overlook a river. Scent does not lift and disburse to the noses of bucks bedding along the incline of a paralleling river slope. Rather, it wicks away with the air current.

Exercising patience for this style of hunting may be the toughest bridge to cross. Hunting in a valley is risky business before temperatures reach freezing. Fog, rain and temperate weather detains human odor from rising. Add a slight wind to any of these conditions and hunter scent disbursement looks more like a mushroom than a cone. This makes it ultra-important to know exactly where deer exit and enter a bedding area. An advantageous wind for approach and stand placement is crucial. You'll reduce your chances of success tenfold by allowing a wise buck to smell you just one time.

Scouting and patience go hand in hand. Having narrowed the field to a promising buck haunt, place your stand where multiple trails or water crossings can be watched, possibly on an overlook-

ing ridge. **Your objective for three or more outings is to watch deer movement.** Determine most-used funnels, best stand placements and approach with regard to wind, optimal shooting lanes for quartering-away shots, and most important, when deer move and where they stage before deciding the coast is clear. Don't crowd in for the kill after seeing a good buck once. Allow time to figure him out before moving in to close quarters. Be patient and you'll dramatically improve your chances to own him the first day you camp on his backdoor.

Post-Season Scouting Really Pays Here

Wetland bedding areas repeat from year to year, giving serious post-season scouters an advantage for the upcoming season. Put on some brush-buster coveralls and investigate river- or lake-side thickets and weed patches. Look for deer-size depressions in the weeds and travel corridors to these concealed resting spots. To attempt this during hunting season could permanently relocate bucks for the year.

Some of the best daytime lairs for mature bucks are found in dense patches of 400 square feet or less – 20 feet by 20 feet. Seasoned whitetails particularly favor dry, slightly raised knobs surrounded by marshy stands of small softwoods. These are tough places to set up; there often are few sizable trees for portables and rarely shooting lanes of any width. Consider a ground blind in this situation. Plan your best approach and blind placement in accordance with predominant wind during post-season when bucks are camping next to food sources. They will rarely return to these areas for bedding until persistent hunting pressure begins next season.

Construct the ground blind and clear shooting lanes two to three weeks prior to opening day. Do not destroy the terrain's aesthetics by cutting shooting lanes that look like logging clearcuts. Don't use the new ambush site until telltale sign appears – bedding rubs, heavy tracks at water crossing, and escalated trail use.

Peninsulas Can Be Great

Midwestern Army Corps of Engineers impoundments typically form many peninsulas. These are some of the best buck magnets in North America, particularly if they provide southern exposure. Undergrowth is commonly dense on south-facing shorelines. Deer locate a body-size opening in the brush and soak up the sun's rays

Water Trail Hunting

throughout the day. Inland vegetation on a south-facing peninsula also blocks severe northern wind.

Set up on a buck's inland pathway and make sure your approach and exit is downwind. Converging fronts generate wind gusts that swirl in a lake cove and adorn a peninsula with hunter scent. Hunt peninsulas when there is no wind or a favorable constant wind.

• *The dream still lives. These 5x5 sheds were found in western Illinois in 1996. Given an inside spread of only 20 inches, they would have a net score of 206-plus inches. Something like that taken with a bow would be a new world record.*

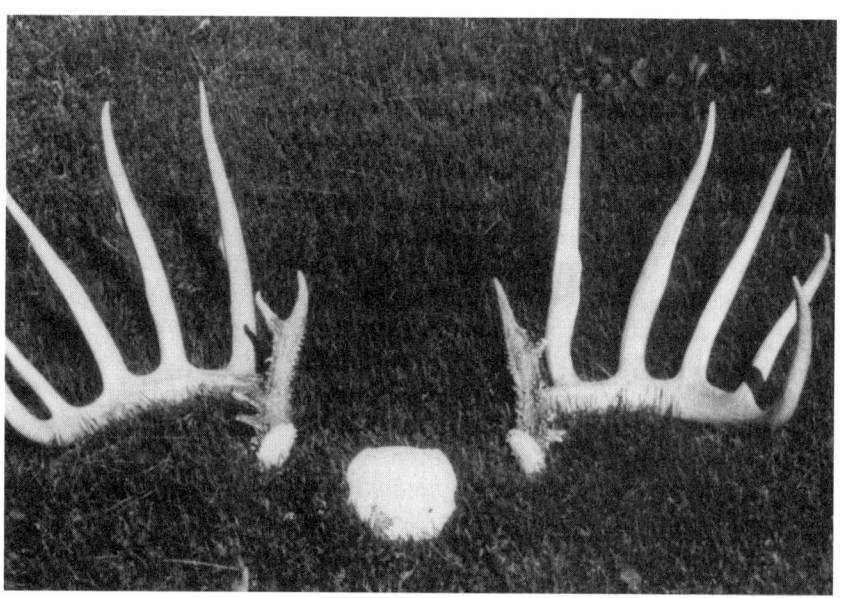

> Consistently harvesting exceptional whitetails requires meticulous attention to detail and unbreakable patience.

by Les Davenport

Harvesting the Exceptional Buck

A three-to four-year-old male whitetail surviving in a pressured hunting area surely is an exception. He's learned us better than we have learned him, and he's adopted travel patterns and bedding haunts that avoid human interference. A distant glimpse of tall tines at twilight, a shredded sapling, a ground paw, or a deep hoof print may be the extent of a mature buck's known existence. He could teach an Army Ranger a thing or two about stealth reconnaissance.

Bucks of this age typically carry a minimum Pope and Young (P&Y) set of antlers (125 inches net) in regions where good genetics and nutrition reign. Most Boone and Crockett (B&C) qualifiers (170 inches net) have lived through at least four seasons of dodging hunters. Though there is a degree of good fortune needed to harvest a trophy whitetail, "luck" is most often the result of homework. "I was just lucky," is a modest cliché spoken by hunters who fertilize the seed of luck with time, and effort, thought and a willingness to change or adapt tactics as needed.

The best advice that could be offered a would-be trophy hunter is "don't hunt an area where you see no trophy deer during daylight hours". Lots of trails, rubs and scrapes with no sightings mean only two things: 1) mature bucks have discovered your ambush or 2) they do not visit the area until after sundown. It is especially true in Midwestern farm country that mature bucks travel great distances to bed in one place by day and feed in another by night.

Over-hunting a particular stand site before peak rut is a major flaw in many deer hunters' game plans. Here is one example of how a deer season can get off to a bad start. A bowhunter arrives on-stand at 2:00 p.m. and observes several does, fawns and a couple of two-year-old bucks before dark. His bow is lowered just as a dandy 5x5 decides to exit a brushy thicket from behind. The bowhunter has no idea of the deer's presence as he climbs down the tree. The deer senses an out-of-place movement or noise and eases downwind for a whiff.

Once the bowhunter's scent is pegged, the buck invariably starts his next few exits from the thicket by scenting the downwind area of that stand site. If the deer's senses are alerted by the bowhunter a second time in the same spot, the buck begins a pattern of checking downwind of the site before attending to business. Frequent detection of a hunter creates a habit that wary old whitetails may repeat the next bow season.

Use several stand sites and move often in early pre-rut. Be content to locate travel patterns that connect bedding areas to food sources. These are where primary scrapes and aggressive rubs show first. Do not crowd or over-hunt a buck's core area during the first stages of pre-rut. Early- to mid-October's thermometer ranges widely and causes inconsistent movement in older-class bucks. A hunter can be pegged easily during early pre-rut when bucks appear from any direction, any time of day.

Radical temperature changes mean shifting and gusting wind, a whitetail's best friend. Hunters commonly set up a stand for a west or northwest wind and use this site regardless what the day's forecast warns. Once a mature buck pinpoints a hunter's ambush, odds of harvesting him in that area decrease tenfold.

A hunter should strive to be downwind of deer movement. This is a no-brainer statement, but not always possible to accomplish. Therefore, it's crucial to depress and mask human scent. Opinions vary greatly on how to accomplish this task. The best method, however, is using pure deer urine on scent-free clothing. It took three decades of frustrating trial and error to reach this conclusion.

First there was the apple. Deer love'em! Smash one on the ground and saturate the bottom of your boot with apple juice. Your woodland entry trail could not be detected by deer (and maybe they'd follow the pleasant scent right to your tree stand). Not! Deer seem to know that apples do not saunter through the woods. Most mature does and bucks that crossed the sweet smell were instantly distrustful of the ambling odor.

Next on my list of things to try was fox urine. Apply a dab on the bottom of the boots and your entry trail would become that of a little red woodland canine. If a yearling smelled it, the young animal most frequently looked about briefly, then wagged its tail and moved ahead. A second-year buck was curious enough to track me to a tree where it smelled human scent from my gloves on a tree peg. It bolted pronto! Thinking this was the magic potion, I then began rubbing fox urine on my gloves.

The end determination on fox urine: About 70 percent of mature does and nicely racked bucks about-faced upon smelling it and eased yonder. This made me wonder how many deer on my far backtrail veered off before being spotted. Skunk scent offered the same results, except my wife also shunned me. I stopped using non-deer animal scents.

Animal cover scents are rarely pure. Many are watered-down and mixed with preservatives. Whitetails encounter foxes, skunks and other woodland critters every day. Mature deer, in my opinion, go on alert at the smell of diluted and polluted imitations of animal urine. Many older whitetails, too, have previously made the hunter/animal scent connection and may become suspicious when crossing even a true fox trail.

Non-odor cover scents that supposedly depress human smell are also voodoo in my book. Hunters who claim success with these probably bathed with unscented soap and habitually wear de-scented clothing. Many of these water-based scent depressants do just the opposite, wicking human odors into the air. Airborne moisture acts as a transportation medium, carrying odor particles to a deer's nose. Depressant-type cover scents evaporate as a hunter heads for the stand. Human odors start drifting during the evaporating process and alert deer to hunter arrival.

Wash yourself with unscented soap and avoid sweating on the walk-in. Also, wash clothing articles (including boots and liners) with unscented soap and store them where it's scent-free. Your days in the woods will be more eventful, in the right way.

I'm convinced from years of personal experiments that deer can not identify animal urine types without the association of other specific animal odors. Let me explain. All animal urine, human included, is made of the same organic components — 95 percent water and a five percent mixture of complex solids (urea, hippuric and uric acid, sulfuric and phosphoric acid, ammonia, calcium, magnesium, creatine, sodium and potassium chloride, and more). An animal's urine takes on singular identity only after other individual bodily odors remain near or mixed in its urine. A buck deer, for instance, splashes urine off the tarsal glands on the inside of its hind legs to denote individualism.

Regardless of which deer urine you get, don't store it from one year to the next. Use it fresh.

Rut is closing in. You found where does are feeding and saw a dandy buck twice there at twilight. You know the direction he's coming from. Now is the time to make your move.

Quietly walk the targeted area in mid-day and look for aggressive rubs and primary scrapes. Aggressive rubs appear on large saplings and small trees. Antler strikes are deeper into the bark and small trees nearby may be broken or twisted. Primary scrapes usually are found within 100 yards of an aggressive rub and vice versa.

A primary scrape is not always large in diameter. The key element when locating this scrape type is an aggressively torn overhanging branch (or licking limb). Eighty-five percent of all ground paws by male whitetails are made under a hanging branch. Those that are found near a buck's central breeding ground (or hub scrape) show more assertive biting, tearing and twisting of vegetation.

After finding what you believe to be a primary scrape, determine the closest ambush spot in regard to predominant wind. This site must also offer a hunter entry and exit path that will not cross the buck's incoming trail. Set up your stand and be as scent-free about the operation as possible. Alter little of the immediate vegetation for shooting lanes. Wait 24 hours before hunting the stand. This is in case you have left some detectable scent or made a noise heard by a nearby but out of sight buck.

Approaching a scrape hunt-site before daylight often alerts the deer being hunted. It's best to wait until first light and make the walk-in slowly and without a light. Once stationed in the stand, do not leave until day's end. Odds increase greatly when a hunter's mind-set is patience. Do not let rain or snow be a deterrent. Bucks freshen scrapes more regularly during these conditions. When natural movement is slow, a primary scrape site is an excellent spot for mock rattling and grunting.

If there is no result after three outings, you'll need to **tease the buck into a daylight appearance.** Put several drops of buck urine in the scrape and on the overhanging branches as you leave the site on the third evening. Continue to do so each additional outing. Always freshen the bottom of your boots with deer urine before entering the area of the scrape. If there's still no result, you're probably hunting a line scrape hit only at night, or does have come in estrus and the buck is attending to procreation.

Harvesting exceptional bucks is a constant chess match. **Hunters who desire to close the gap between luck and skill must practice evasion of the whitetail's nose and apply extreme patience until a buck's vulnerability brings him to the right spot at the right time ... for you.**

Odor-Free Washing & Storage

Spending lots of money at your local sports shop for unscented laundry soap? If so, visit the nearest grocery store. They, too, carry unscented soaps in liquid and granular form. Grocery store soap is much less expensive per ounce than are sport brands. Use only enough soap to break down body oils that have wicked through clothing. One-half the recommended measurement is plenty.

Store hunting clothing in a scent-free area. This does not include a garage or basement. Both of these homerooms allow house odors to infiltrate them. Hanging clothes in an open-air porch works well. Many successful hunters store clothing in a cedar-filled, de-scented canvas bag. This works great if cedar trees are native in your hunting area. Use vegetation that is native to the area you're hunting.

Be careful storing clothes in a plastic garbage bag; some plastics have a strong resin odor which will find its way into your clothing. (And some plastic garbage bags also are treated on the inside with an insecticide. All the more reason NOT to use them for hunting clothes storage.)

Smelly boots and liners cause more hunters to get caught by whitetails than any other article of clothing. Liners are not flushed of foot odor often enough, and boots pick up foreign smells from anywhere they're worn (gas station, restaurant, etc.). It's best not to wear de-scented boots until you're ready to leave a vehicle for the woods. Keep them in a canvas duffel and put them on when you park your vehicle.

Wash your headgear regularly, too. We lose 47-48 percent of our body heat from our neck and head. Our head and neck are thus likely to perspire more than other areas. That leads to a buildup of human odors in any head garment not washed frequently. Yet, how many times do we see or hear of the favorite hunting hat ... can't be without it ... it's the good-luck charm, etc. If that good luck charm isn't washed, it's just like a bad odor wick, with all the heat from our head broadcasting human odor into the air.

Change Tactics For The Rut

Bucks temporarily abandon a primary scrape when does begin estrus. This is the time to change tactics and hunt funnels and doe-visited food plots. Between breeding periods, however, bucks re-open and again tend scrapes. Watch for pawing that signifies new activity.

If the buck tending a primary scrape has not been seen, aggressive rubs tell a hunter much about the configuration of that buck's rack. Long, deep strikes often denote a male whitetail with good tine length and a tight rack. Finely shredded bark is the signature of a wide-antler buck that has learned to tear with its brow tines and pedicel beading.

LES DAVENPORT

Illinois bowman Les Davenport, whose admitted passion is pursuing big whitetails, also has hunted various species across North and South America. He believes that involving youth in deer hunting and tutoring good ethics is essential for protecting our sport.

Practicing what he preaches, Les first involved his son Monte in deer hunting. Monte had taken 17 deer with the bow before graduating from West Point Military Academy. He's now an Army captain on Korea's DMZ, and in pursuit of Asian deer and ringneck pheasants with recurve.

A freelance writer/photographer and active member of the Outdoor Writers Association of America (OWAA) and the Association of Great Lake Outdoor Writers (AGLOW), Les is a contributing staff member to *BOWHUNTER* magazine. He also has been published in *Deer and Deer Hunting, North American Whitetail, Whitetail Strategies, Buckmasters* and more.

You will understand from Les' seminars how whitetail hunting has changed over the last two decades. Though deer hunters have grown more knowledgeable, so have deer. This is especially true of mature bucks. Years of trial and error have taught this veteran whitetailer many intricacies about outfoxing the species. He hopes his school-of-hard-knocks lessons will increase your trophy success.

- *Upper left and above. These Illinois bucks are the result of completed homework, and the good fortune to help be in the right place at the right time, and then do everything right.*

- *To close the gap between luck and skill, and put yourself in this position, nullify the whitetail's nose and be patient, patient, patient. A tip: Lots of trails, rubs and scrapes with no sightings means that mature bucks have discovered your ambush or they do not visit the area until after sundown. Read more about this in "Are You Hunting A November Stand in October", page 81.*

Exceptional Bucks

- *A successful hunter takes a look back over the big country which produced this fine eight-point buck.*

- *Close-up of an essential tool for big country – a compass. Wearing one on your wrist keeps it easily and quickly available for checking. For more information on hunting big country most effectively, see "Topo Maps, Compasses and GPS", page 3.*

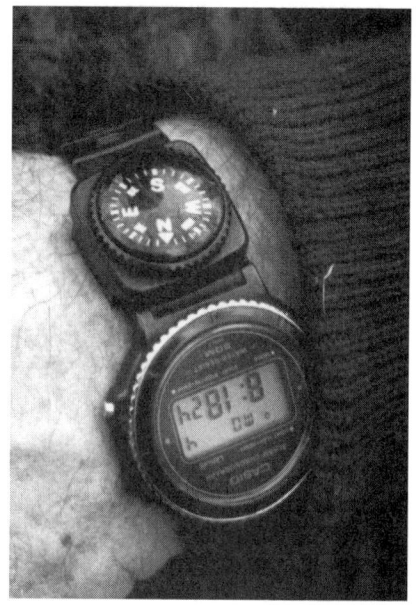

> **I**solate the places deer live and travel; the country won't seem so big. Then look for funnels, funnels and more funnels.

by Richard P. Smith

Finding Big Country Bucks

*H*unting big country bucks is tough. There are no shortcuts. You won't see many deer. The sheer size of the roadless tracts can be unsettling.

So why do it? There are advantages to hunting deer that aren't subjected to the heavy pressure common in most other areas. There are big bucks in those woods, and only parts of those big woods are deer habitat, so don't be intimidated. **Bucks here aren't pressured; they get a chance to grow up. They behave like undisturbed whitetails are supposed to, often being as active during hours of daylight as after dark,** rather than becoming primarily nocturnal like those in heavily hunted habitat.

Collecting one is a challenge. There's tremendous satisfaction in meeting that challenge. In fact, it can be a satisfying experience to take any buck from big country. Knowing the big ones are there, even if you don't see them, adds to the attractiveness of hunting big country. There's a sense of freedom which comes from low hunting pressure in big country. You develop and test your woodsmanship; it's good to be someplace you can key off topo maps and compass readings instead of roads and other orange coats.

It takes time and effort to put tags on bucks that inhabit unbroken woodlands. Hunters who are unwilling or unable to devote serious effort to getting acquainted with woodland whitetails are handicapped right from the start.

Big country deer hunters also have to be willing to accept the fact that, in most cases, they are not going to see a lot of whitetails. It's possible to spend entire days in the woods without seeing a single deer. If you see five whitetails between sunrise and sunset it's a good day, and you're doing excellent on days when as many as 10 are sighted. There simply are not as many deer in large woodlands with few roads as there are in farm country or a mixture of woods and fields.

Deer densities seldom exceed 20 per square mile in wilderness areas and are usually closer to 10 or fewer per square mile. There are a lot of places for 10 to 20 whitetails to hide in a square mile of woodland, even though not all of it is habitat. Finding their preferred hangouts can be tough, but it's far from impossible.

Wilderness areas usually don't have a lot of whitetails, but they also normally do NOT have a lot of hunters, at least in the more remote locations, which adds to the appeal of hunting big country.

Light hunting pressure and the presence of plenty of escape cover is why big woods produce big bucks. Whitetails are able to live long enough to start reaching their full antler development and body size potential. Bucks usually grow their best racks between $5^1/_2$ and $7^1/_2$ years of age. Few antlered whitetails live to see their fifth birthday in farm country. The odds of reaching and exceeding that age favor woodland bucks.

As an example, consider the ultimate big country buck that Louis Roy from L'anse, Michigan, bagged not far from his home. Expansive woodlands surround this small Upper Peninsula community and there is plenty of rugged terrain that is tough to get into. The massive twelve-pointer came from such a place. The antlers scored 184 $^7/_8$, easily surpassing the 170 minimum required for entry of typical antlers in Boone and Crockett records.

The rack from that buck presently ranks as the third largest ever taken in Michigan among typicals, according to Commemorative Bucks of Michigan, the state's big game record keeper. That whitetail was aged at $5^1/_2$. The deer's body was big, too. It dressed out at 228 pounds.

How much would you be willing to work to bag a buck like that? How much time would you be willing to spend? If your answer to both questions are "lots," you have the makings of a big country buck hunter. After more than 30 years of enjoying big country deer hunting and being consistently successful at it, I have had plenty of exposure to what it takes to score on bucks that live in large blocks of wooded terrain.

Keep in mind that not all bucks from big country that are $5^1/_2$ or older will score as high as the one Louis Roy got. That's why his is ranked number three in the state. Stuart Bennett from Marquette got a ten-pointer that was the same age and it scored 151$^6/_8$. An eleven-pointer I tagged tallied 148$^2/_8$. Some bucks with that many years behind them may only measure in the 120s, but even so, whitetails of that caliber are the type most hunters would be proud of. I certainly am.

As mentioned earlier, taking any big country buck can be satisfying. Roy's buck represents the upper end of what big country hunters can expect. I also mentioned Louis' exceptional whitetail because how and where he got it, as well as what prompted him to hunt where he did, help illustrate how to isolate spots likely to produce bucks in big country.

The site where Louis got his book buck is four miles from the nearest road passable with a conventional 4X4 vehicle. Although the country is wild, it's not a designated wilderness area, so he was able to use a four-wheeler to reach his blind, traveling an overgrown logging trail to reach it. (No wheeled vehicles of any type, including bicycles, can be used in designated wilderness areas.) Some states have laws restricting where and when ATVs such as four-wheelers can be used during hunting seasons in big country that isn't designated wilderness, so be sure to check local regulations before using one.

Louis said he found the spot, **consisting of a saddle in a ridge,** the year before he got the once-in-a-lifetime buck. Saddles like that one frequently funnel deer through them because they represent the easiest route from one side of a ridge to the other. On top of that, whitetails that use saddles are less visible than those which walk over the top of a ridge. A runway worn in the saddle, from repeated use by deer, confirmed that it was a good place to ambush a buck. What made this location especially appealing to deer is that the trail through the saddle connected swamps on both sides of the ridge.

While grouse hunting in the vicinity of the saddle the following year, Louis saw sign that renewed his interest in the spot. There was a large circular patch of trampled ground where two bucks had fought. The battle ground confirmed there were at least two bucks in the area and Louis knew they were probably both mature animals, because young bucks seldom tear up the turf like it had been.

He put his ground blind on top of a 30-foot rock bluff on one side of the saddle. That gave him a good view of the saddle as well as part of the ridge beyond it. The other side of the saddle had a gradual uphill slope, and the hardwood trees on that slope provided good visibility.

Roy didn't have to wait long for action on opening day of gun season. At 8:05 a.m. a six-pointer walked downhill into the saddle opposite his blind. It obviously wasn't one of the whitetails that had

- Scouting big country in the spring can be productive. You'll still be able to see scrapes like this before the soil dries out. Good time to scout new areas and really look them over.

- Snow can be a boon in big country. Not only can you see deer better, you can get on a track and stick with it.

- Louis Roy, left, with his big country Boone & Crockett buck scoring 184-7/8.

112 Steps Along the Hunter's Path

fought, but with a two-buck bag limit in effect, he decided to take the deer.

Heavy rain on the second day of the season almost discouraged Louis from hunting, but it's a good thing it didn't. Rain gear helped keep him dry during the four-mile ATV ride to his blind in predawn darkness. The Booner appeared in the saddle about the same time the smaller buck showed up the morning before, and the big boy wasn't wasting any time traveling from one swamp to the other.

"I didn't have time to think, just react," Louis said. "I saw him, grabbed the gun and shot him. The buck dropped right there, and then I started shaking all over."

He had good reason to shake, as any hunter does who bags a trophy buck. To experience the same kind of thrill, you have to find the spots. It doesn't have to be a saddle in a ridge four miles from the nearest road. After all, there aren't many areas of whitetail country in the United States where it's possible to go four miles in one direction without hitting another road.

You want to find a location or locations where there is regular deer activity, based on sign. If you can isolate spots frequented by bucks, especially a big one, that's even better. **Types of terrain and habitat where I've had good luck on bucks in big woods besides saddles in ridges are along swamp edges, on islands of upland habitat surrounded by swamp, in swamps and marshes and other thick cover that offers similar refuge to whitetails, and in funnels or bottlenecks created by beaver ponds and inland lakes.**

Bucks often use beaver dams as crossings. The water that backs up behind those dams frequently funnels deer around, along or between them. Narrow patches of woods between a pair of lakes are perfect deer funnels, too. The terrain around lakes such as hills, valleys and peninsulas also help channel deer around them. **In country with large hills or mountains, deer, and especially bucks, frequent the higher elevations.**

Here's where much of the necessary work comes in for consistent success hunting bucks in big country. Scouting, scouting and more scouting is the key to finding spots, like those mentioned above, which have the most deer or buck activity. The more area you look at, the better your chances of happening upon that hot spot like Louis Roy found. The idea is not simply to find one site with a well used deer trail or buck sign. The objective is to find as many centers of deer activity as possible, compare their potential and select the spot that looks the best for hunting.

Maps can be extremely helpful during the initial stages of scout-

ing. **They can be more than helpful; they can be critical because they are just about the only thing that can jump-start your scouting success and thus your hunting success.** County or grid maps, plat and topographic maps can be useful in helping to select big country or wilderness areas you will be most interested in hunting. County maps, usually available in book form for entire states, normally are color coded to show public versus privately owned land. The largest blocks of rugged, roadless woods are often public property, generally owned by county, state or federal governments.

Corporations own large tracts of woodlands in some cases. Plat maps, which usually come in book form by county, will show who owns what. In Michigan, all corporate lands listed under the Commercial Forest Act are open to hunting. The act provides for lower property taxes in exchange for public access to the property for recreational use. Plat maps for Michigan show which parcels are listed under the act. The information is also available from Department of Natural Resources offices.

Look for blocks of roadless terrain when examining maps for tracts to hunt. Roadless areas of five square miles or more are ideal, but parcels encompassing one square mile or less also offer good hunting if the terrain is rugged, the habitat is thick or the land has some other feature that would tend to discourage most hunters from penetrating it. A river with no bridge, a wet marsh or a steep ridge may be enough to limit access and reduce hunting pressure on some parcels of land. A pair of chest waders, a canoe or boat may be all it takes to reach big country bucks that most other hunters aren't willing to spend the effort to try for.

Once you've decided on a tract or two of land you're interested in, go over topographic maps to pick possible stand sites. Note features of interest for further investigation when you visit the location, and that's the next important step. There's no better way to assess the potential of a new area for deer hunting than actually to go there and hike the habitat. I usually check out the tract's perimeter first, taking note of points of access that will put me closest to locations I'm most interested in scouting.

Few maps are current. Many are five or more years old. New roads may have been constructed since the map was made, which is possible in areas where logging is an important part of the economy. Beaver ponds appear and disappear on an annual basis.

Spring is an excellent time to scout new terrain, especially in snow country. Do so as soon as possible after the snow is gone. Deer sign such as trails, antler rubs and scrapes made the previous fall still will be clearly visible until new vegetation starts growing. It's also possible to find antlers shed by bucks that survived hunting season. Visibility is excellent at this time of year due to the absence of screening vegetation.

Keep an eye out for antler rubs on full-fledged trees and concentrations of scrapes, in addition to well used runways. Large rubs are a sure sign at least one mature buck is in the vicinity. Areas which show sign of rubbing last fall and earlier falls are particularly interesting. Concentrations of scrapes will mark prime breeding areas used by local bucks.

Take note of signs of other hunting activity at the same time you're monitoring clues about deer activity. If other hunters are already hunting spots you're interested in, keep looking until you find sites that are as good as or better that haven't been hunted. Explore as much territory as possible.

Remember that the further you get away from roads and trails, the chances of competition are reduced. It may take a hike of two or three miles. One of my best big country stands is three miles from where I park my vehicle. That's where I got the 11-pointer scoring $148^{2}/_{8}$ and a pair of eight-pointers.

It's essential to carry a compass while scouting and to know how to use it. Carry a topo map with you and mark it with possible stand sites, and with feeding areas, deer trails, etc. Always take a reading when leaving a road or trail, noting which direction you will be walking and remembering that you will have to head in the opposite direction to return to the same point of access. Navigating cross country while scouting will increase your familiarity with the terrain and reduce the chances that you will get turned around or lost when hunting.

While scouting, you also want to notice if there are potential food sources which may concentrate whitetails during the fall. Are there oak, beech or other mast producing trees? Are there apple trees or secluded openings where deer can graze or browse on preferred plants?

All fruit and nut trees don't produce food annually, so if you scout during the spring, a trip to the area later in the year will be necessary to make a final determination the types of natural foods available and where they are. If you are unable to scout a location during spring, fall is next best. (Did anyone say grouse hunting?) Even when I scout in spring, I like to re-evaluate an area during fall before finally deciding where to hunt, based on current signs of deer and hunter activity. Sometimes things change dramatically between spring and fall; if you don't make a final, pre-hunt reconnaissance you can be caught off guard.

Don't expect to familiarize yourself with every nook and cranny of a huge tract of land in one year. Do the best you can the first year and expand from there in the future, trying to scout new sections every year. After five years, you should have a good handle on how deer use the big country you're hunting. That's how long it took Louis Roy to find the saddle where he killed his Booner. He tagged the big buck in his sixth year of hunting the block.

As I stated at the beginning, there are no shortcuts to bagging big country bucks. **Although stand hunting is a proven tactic for connecting on big woods bucks, so is stillhunting and snow tracking. Some hunters combine the techniques and others spend most of their time on one of them. I can assure you there is no better way to learn the habits of a mature buck than to spend a day following his tracks in the snow. Even if you don't see the whitetail, the effort is an education that can help you pinpoint future ambush sites where a shot may be possible.**

Always be on the alert when walking in big country during shooting hours. A shot at a big buck can come at any time, usually when you least expect it.

On the same day that Louis got his B&C buck, Howard Musick from Oxford got a whitetail in the same class from the same county. He was hiking to a remote location and got too warm after walking a mile, so he stopped to cool down. A doe crossed a logging road about 50 yards ahead of him not long after he stopped, so he decided to wait longer on the chance a buck was following. Sure enough! A huge 10-pointer appeared on the doe's trail about 30 minutes later and he dropped it, eliminating the need to walk further. The rack scored $170^{3}/_{8}$.

If you have to walk a long distance to reach your hunting area, dress as light as possible for the trip or take layers off as you go. A backpack is ideal for carrying extra clothes during the hike as well as for stowing snacks and lunch. **There's no better way to score on big country bucks than to spend all day where the deer are.** I've shot more bucks in the boonies during midday hours than I have early or late in the day. The hours between 10:00 a.m. and 2:00 p.m. are tops for seeing bucks in the wilderness, especially when the rut is on.

Woods don't get much bigger than they are in parts of Canada. While on a hunt in Manitoba one November with Buddy Chudy's Mantagao Outfitters, I saw three rack bucks between noon and 1:00

p.m. on opening day of gun season. Two of them had small eight- and ten-point racks and were probably 2½-year-old animals. The third one was a gorgeous 10-pointer that I guessed would have scored 130 to 135.

I could have shot any of those bucks but passed them up to wait for a bigger one. He came along the following morning at 8:30. The heavy-beamed 12-pointer had a live weight of 245 pounds. The rack had a gross score of 140.

The best way to hunt big country is to camp as close as possible to where you plan to hunt, as I did when I hunted with Buddy. Such an arrangement reduces the amount of walking necessary to reach stands, reduces worry about being late to get to where you want to hunt. Camping nearby also maximizes the amount of sleep you can get, increasing the chances you will be rested and alert when that big buck comes along.

There's nothing easy about connecting on bucks in big country, but if you pay your dues in time and effort and are willing to accept the fact you're probably not going to see a lot of deer, the work can eventually pay off. If you're in the right place, you don't have to see a lot of deer, just one. Ask Louis Roy and Howard Musick. They know.

RICHARD P. SMITH

Richard P. Smith is an award-winning outdoor writer and photographer living in Marquette, Michigan. He has hunted and studied whitetails and black bear more than 30 years. One of his most recent honors was receipt of the 1997 Ben East Prize from the Michigan United Conservation Clubs (MUCC) for conservation journalism about bear management. He also received the "Outdoor Journalist of the Year" award from the Flint MI chapter of Safari Club International in 1997.

Smith has written 14 books and hundreds of magazine articles, specializing in all types of hunting, but especially whitetails and black bear. He writes a regional report on the Upper Peninsula of Michigan for *Michigan Out-of-Doors* magazine and contributes to *Michigan Sportsman* and *Woods-N-Water News*. His writing and photography appear regularly in national outdoor and hunting magazines.

The titles of his most popular books about deer hunting are Stand Hunting For Whitetails, Tracking Wounded Deer, Deer Hunting / 2nd Edition, Great Michigan Deer Tales. He's also written four editions of Michigan Big Game Records. The books he's written about bears include Hunting Trophy Black Bear and Understanding Michigan Black Bear.

Big Country Bucks

- Rattling can work on big bucks like these when the herd's sex ratio is close to 1:1 because there will be more competition for does.

- The author and a mature buck he rattled in and took with bow and arrow.

> Rattling isn't a magic elixir; it's another effective tool in your mixed bag of hunting skills.

by M. R. James

To Rattle Up Bucks ...Easy Does It!

Let's get one thing clear here at the outset. I'm not a whitetail antler-rattling expert. I'm simply a veteran deer hunter with nearly four decades of bowhunting experience who employs a wide variety of time-tested techniques to fill my tags season after season. And I know that what works for me can work for almost anyone. So if you want to add some extra spice to your own deer hunting adventures, try rattling up a rutting whitetail. Following are no-nonsense answers to commonly asked questions about using "horns" to lure whitetail bucks within bow range:

Does rattling really work? Not always. In fact, more often than not deer won't respond. But rattling can work at certain times of year and all you need is a positive attitude, a bit of hand-eye coordination, some basic know-how combined with the knowledge of when to rattle and when to leave the "horns" hanging.

First, realize that rattling isn't a magic formula or a shortcut to deer hunting success. It's merely an effective hunting tool which can complement any deer hunters bag of tricks.

Second, realize that rattling is nothing more than simulating the sounds bucks make with their antlers when they spar or fight. And when do bucks fight? When they're establishing breeding rights during the annual rut. So does it make sense to expect to bring bucks on the run anytime you bang a set of antlers together during the deer season. No!

Third, I'm convinced that timing is more important than technique. So is location, buck:doe ratio and hunting pressure. More about this later.

So what do I need to rattle up a buck? Something that makes the necessary noise, opportunity and a bit of luck. Time was when any old set of deer antlers – often taped at the bases and joined by a cord

– was basic. Now there are look-alike synthetic antlers, rattle systems and rattle bags. Personally, while I prefer to use real antlers, I've used all kinds of rattling devices with good success.

Are there advantages and disadvantages between real antlers and the various manmade rattling products? Yes. Rattle bags and systems are easier to carry and climb with. They're also easy to use with a minimum amount of movement. The sound is good but typically doesn't carry as far as the real thing or the synthetic "horns". And if the cloth rattle bag and wooden dowels get wet on damp days, forget trying to rattle. Also, they don't work well for simulating the sounds bucks make while rubbing antlers on brush or trees.

Lightweight synthetic antlers sound more authentic and fit together well for convenient carrying to and from a deer stand (but they do take up more space and you'll need a daypack or backpack for toting them). They're not adversely affected by wet weather and typically don't have the same knuckle-busting or skin-scraping capacity of the real thing, either.

Real antlers, despite their bulk and inconvenience in carrying and climbing, are my favorite. I generally use a perfectly matched four-by-four rack that would score in the 130s. Whatever your personal choice, I urge you to experiment and pick what you like best. Self-confidence is an important part of rattling.

If I choose the real thing, can't I avoid nicks and gouges to my fingers and hands by sawing off the brow tines and sharp antler points? Yes, but I believe that's unnecessary, for a couple of reasons. First, the rattling style I recommend is largely nonviolent, so you won't be banging the antlers together. Second, I prefer to be able to click and tick the antler tips together as real deer do when they're sparring. I can't get the same sounds I want when I use antlers that have been modified by saws and files. Besides, I'm usually wearing gloves and have yet to mash a finger or lose any skin.

Do I need to treat rattling antlers to preserve them? Some hunters wipe linseed oil on their rattling antlers from time to time. I don't bother and haven't noticed any difference in tonal quality over the years.

So exactly how do you go about rattling bucks? If it's a morning hunt, I always wait until legal shooting time before rattling. It doesn't do any good to rattle in the dark and have a buck come close when you can't shoot him. On midday and afternoon stands, I usually wait 20 to 30 minutes after settling in before picking up the antlers.

Before I rattle, I typically begin with a few soft grunts from my deer call. After waiting a minute or two, I'll next scrape a convenient limb or tree trunk as if a buck is racking it. Finally, I'll click the antler tips together like two bucks beginning to spar.

I've heard experts say you should always begin by banging the rack together with a loud, attention-getting clack. Deer aren't bighorn rams. They can't back off and run at each other, forcefully banging heads and antlers together. While some deer fights are certainly serious, more often than not the bucks I've watched fight begin by meshing their antlers – rather carefully sometimes. Their "fight" is often more of a pushing and shoving match than a pitched battle.

In big, open country where you want sound to carry long distances, exaggerating the sounds of the fight may be necessary. But in woodlots, river or creek bottoms and brushy haunts where most whitetails are found and hunted, I personally see no need to recreate the Battle of Gettysburg with rattling antlers. Under normal circumstances, I'll take a low key approach to rattling any day of the week. It sure works for me.

Okay, what do you do next? I mentally picture what two sparring bucks would do. After clicking the antler tips together, I'll mesh the points and create a clatter of sorts for 10 to 15 seconds. Then I separate the antlers, pause for a five-count as if the two bucks are warily circling, and I bring the rack together again, clattering and grinding for 20 to 30 seconds before pausing again. After perhaps 10 seconds of silence, I repeat the entire rattling sequence, gradually increasing the intensity of the fight (without ever separating the two sides of my rattle "horns"). Finally, I end with a few light clicks of the antler tips, hang up the antlers, pick up my bow and sit back to watch and listen. On occasion I add a couple of grunts to cap things off; but after rattling, movements should be kept to a minimum since any approaching buck is on the lookout for another deer. If nothing happens, I repeat the entire sequence half an hour to 45 minutes later.

Does rattling really bring bucks on the run? It can, but I've seen it happen only a few times. Most often I'll catch a movement as the buck walks in to check things out. On occasion I've heard or seen an unseen buck racking a tree or bush nearby. Such whitetails may slip in or circle a stand, moving downwind to catch scent of the combatants. You need to be alert to any sights or sounds which mean a buck is nearby and moving closer.

When's the best time to rattle? Crisp, quiet days are ideal. For my money, I'll take the whitetail pre-rut period. Although I've rattled up bucks as early as late October, I don't usually get serious about packing my rattling antlers along until early November. While the exact time of the rut varies across our continent's vast whitetail range, you'd be well advised to focus your rattling efforts during the week or two ahead of the rut's peak in your home hunting area.

Don't expect rattling miracles if you have to hunt pressured deer or deer country with few mature bucks. Areas with good buck:doe ratios are best; however, even here deer can be educated by over-rattling.

Remember, too, bucks already paired with does would much rather make love than fight. They rarely pay any attention to antler-rattling ploys; however, lone bucks may check out these simulated sparring matches. So be prepared.

What's an ideal stand location? I like a tree stand with trimmed shooting lanes and a good view of the surrounding area. It's true a good level position allows you to add realism to your rattling sequence, namely thumping the ground with your boots or antlers bases to simulate a buck stamping its forefeet, and racking trees and brush. Approaching deer are looking for any movements at eye level and they can quickly zero in on you as you try to draw your bow.

The buddy system works well, with the rattler on the ground and a shooter in a nearby tree stand. Deer can pinpoint the exact source of the "fight" and are looking for movements in the brush. With an approaching buck's attention on the rattler, an elevated bowhunter can draw and shoot without detection.

Note: Safety is always a concern for hunters with rattling antlers, especially on public lands where firearms are legal during the bow season and vice versa. And any camo-clad hunter, partially concealed by brush and pretending to be a deer, is asking for trouble. It's best to wear blaze orange when rattling from ground level. (I don't think twice about wearing blaze orange in the deer woods since my experiences with countless animals have convinced me it's movement, not the color of my clothing, that most often alerts nearby game.)

But you've got to move to rattle and to shoot a bow. Right? Right. And that's what is so challenging and exciting about luring a buck within good range and remaining undetected long enough to slip an arrow into his vitals. That's why wearing gloves and a camo face mask is always a good idea.

Do you use scents and decoys when rattling? Yes and no. I often use a doe-in-heat scent near my stand when bowhunting the rut. Masking scents and attracting scents can help, but they're not some magic elixir. Like rattling "horns," scents are merely another tool to be used by hunters – intelligently and in moderation. I've not had much experience using decoys; however, I know several serious hunters who swear by them and I see no reason why they can't be effective (keeping in mind the need to be safety conscious at all times decoys are in use, of course).

Are there other times to try rattling? Yes. I've turned distant deer my way simply by clacking my antlers together to get their attention. Try it yourself. Also, whitetails can be curious animals and sometimes respond to the sounds of sparring bucks, even if it's not during the prime pre-rut period. Don't overlook the post-rut late season, either.

Will what works where you hunt really work for me where I live? Deer don't recognize state lines or other such boundaries. Rattling works, period! Wherever these deer are found, they can be rattled in. If you're not pursuing antler-rattling opportunities where you hunt, you're missing out on a lot of excitement.

M. R. JAMES

M. R. James is the founder/editor-in-chief of *Bowhunter* magazine. A lifelong hunter and an active bowhunter since the early 1960s, James took his first Pope and Young record book animal – a whitetail deer – in 1963. Over the years he's also collected trophy-class mule deer, black bear, pronghorn, elk, caribou, mountain lion, moose, mountain goat and sheep, along with a variety of other game. James has been responsible for the editorial content of *Bowhunter* since the magazine was founded in 1972. The author of hundreds of national magazine articles, he also has written four books and co-edited/written several others. He is a former newspaper editor, high school teacher and coach, college instructor and industrial editor. James was editor of the Pope and Young Club's first record book and the Club's fourth record book. He is first vice president, director, senior member and official measurer of the Pope and Young Club; advisor to the National Bowhunter Education Foundation; co-chairman of the Wildlife Legislative Fund of American Bowhunter Defense Coalition; regular/life member of the Professional Bowhunters Society; member of the bowhunting advisory council of *North American Hunter* magazine; member of the Outdoor Writers Association of America, and a member of more than a dozen state and provincial bowhunting clubs and organizations.

- *Only you can decide when and if to take a shot, but a lot of learning goes into that decision making. Study these photos and then read the author's advice regarding where to shoot and the importance of picking a spot.*

124　　　　　　　　　　　　　　　　　　Steps Along the Hunter's Path

You owe it to the game, to yourself and to hunting.

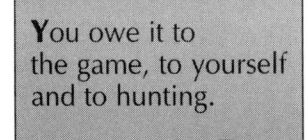

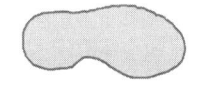

by M. R. James

Give It Your Best Shot

Knowing when and where to shoot is critical to any hunter's success. But there's much more to it than the obvious take-the-first-good-shot-you-get and hit'em-in-the-boiler-room advice you'll hear wherever deer hunters gather. Frankly, unless you understand – and accept – a few basic facts about yourself, your gear and the animals you hunt, chances are good you'll end each season making excuses about why your freezer is as bare as Ma Hubbard's cupboard.

Shooting Facts

Knowing when to release your arrow is somewhat learned, somewhat instinctive. It's based on your hunting tackle, your shooting ability, your hunting experience, your target's position and distance as well as your personal ethics. Therefore, only one person – you – can decide if and when to take any shot.

Sure it's easy – and tempting – to blame your hunting tackle for failing you at the moment of truth. But more often than not it's human error – not mechanical failure – that leaves most hunters shaking their head in disgust after blowing a shot.

Shooting at live game is much different from shooting at even the most realistic targets. Animals react to scent, movement and noise; targets don't. Mix in the heart-drumming excitement caused by the sudden sight of big antlers – when your hands tremble, your knees quake and your breathing becomes ragged as you gasp for air – and you've got the makings of an in-the-field disaster. Keeping your cool in pressure-packed hunting situations is the key to unlocking the door to consistent hunting success. This is true for all hunters, but it's even more critical for bowhunters who must get much closer to wary game before taking the shot.

Speaking of bowhunting, every hunter who heads for the deer woods with a simple stick and string – or a more complex modern bow with its wheels, cables and complement of composite or metal arrows – should realize that even the fastest, flattest-shooting hunting bow is still a short-range tool when compared to slug-loaded shotguns and muzzleloading rifles. **Getting close to game, remaining undetected and making a well-placed shot are mandatory for bowhunting mastery,** and it's a good idea when you're using any of the other hunting tools, too.

Big game animals have no appreciation for proper shooting form. In fact, it seems they often appear unexpectedly and present shots that would challenge a circus contortionist. That's why it's wise for you to **learn to shoot effectively and accurately from a variety of body positions – standing, sitting, crouching and kneeling.** Savvy bowhunters also do a lot of practicing at unknown distances in a variety of wooded and open terrain, shooting uphill and down. Practice doesn't make perfect; perfect practice makes perfect!

Shaving-sharp broadhead-tipped arrows kill by penetrating the animal's body cavity and creating massive hemorrhage or organ failure. Remember, hunting heads lack the shocking and stopping power of bullets. They're also more easily deflected by even the smallest of leaves and tiny twigs – or stopped completely by heavy bones. This means it's essential that you have clear shooting lanes and at least a working knowledge of big game anatomy before releasing an arrow.

Even at point-blank ranges, it's easy for an excited bowhunter to miss badly. "Pick a spot" is sage advice. Shooting at an entire animal is a sure-fire formula for failure.

Arrow-hit animals rarely drop on the spot – or within sight. Even mortally wounded game can cover considerable ground before dropping, a fact that often necessitates following a blood trail to recover the animal. Patience and a keen eye come in handy at this point because simply hitting an animal is not enough. Unless you are able to track and retrieve wounded game, you cannot consider your hunt a success.

The key to recovery begins with a sharp broadhead and well-placed shot. If you see or hear the animal drop and know it's dead, following up within minutes of the shot is perfectly proper. At other times a slow and easy approach may be the best approach. Pressuring wounded game can, at times, delay recovery – or make it impossible.

Quietly waiting 30 to 60 minutes after a shot is a common bowhunting practice, depending on the weather conditions and point of impact. For example, if rain or snow threatens to obliterate the blood trail, don't delay the recovery process. But never pursue paunch-hit animals for at least six to eight hours – or even longer. Weakening game will often bed nearby; however, injured animals hearing unnatural noises or immediate sounds of pursuit may crash away in blind panic.

Finally, never abandon the search until the animal has been recovered and tagged – or you are convinced that the hit was non-vital and the injured animal will recover completely.

Where To Shoot

If learning when to shoot is the first step in improving your personal growth and ultimate success as a bowhunter, knowing where to place your razor-sharp broadheads is the second – and perhaps most important – stride you can take along your hunting path.

The double-lung hit is bowhunting's most deadly shot. A well-placed, sharp broadhead through the chest collapses the lungs and creates massive blood loss. This result is a short blood trail and quick, humane kill. That's why the best, most successful bowhunters always aim for the chest area when an animal is standing broadside or quartering slightly away. Frankly, it's impossible to overemphasize the importance of proper shot placement. Here's a brief look at shots to take – and to pass up – in the deer woods.

Head and Neck Shots: While such shots may be deadly for gun hunters, stopping game in its tracks, they're among the worst any bowhunter can take. Sure, if a broadhead penetrates the spinal column or brain cavity, the animal is instantly dead or dying. The same is true if a sharp hunting head luckily cuts the windpipe or carotid artery. But the skull is mainly arrow-deflecting or broadhead-stopping bone. The neck is mostly muscle. Aiming at either spot is most likely to result in a wounded, unrecovered animal – and a black mark against bowhunting. Resist the temptation to try such shots.

Rump Shots: Rump shots are risky and should be avoided under most circumstances. While any broadhead that cuts the femoral artery has delivered a fatal hit, that tiny target which runs along the inside of each back leg is never an ideal aiming point. Miss it by a mere fraction of an inch and it's likely you'll simply bury your broadhead in the animal's hip or leg bone, leaving the arrow flagging from the animal's rump as it bounds away.

A few ground-level bowhunters have taken game by driving an arrow lengthwise through an animal's body as it stands facing away from them. While this can prove deadly on small-bodied game – providing a bow generates enough energy to push an arrow from an entry point beneath the tail into or through the chest cavity – these shots are always iffy. The patient hunter who waits and takes a chest shot is going to recover more game than the slapdash arrow-slinger.

Frontal Shots: Head-on shots can be lethal provided the broadhead's sharp blades penetrate into the vitals. But under most hunting conditions these are risky shots you should always avoid. With an animal facing you at ground-level, chances are good it is going to see you draw your bow or release an arrow. If you don't think he's capable of moving before your arrow arrives, you're dead wrong. Remember, even a perfectly aimed arrow can be well off target when a big game animal instantly reacts to imminent danger.

Running Shots: Even with plenty of practice on moving targets, hitting running game in an exact spot is difficult and often involves more luck than skill. While a handful of mostly instinctive shooters are adept at making killing shots time after time, few bowhunters should ever shoot at running game. Too many things can go wrong.

Walking Shots: Slow-moving animals passing close by your stand offer better possibilities than running game; however, stationary targets are best of all. A grunt, soft whistle or even the spoken word "whoa" can stop game in its tracks long enough for a killing shot to be made—if you're already at full draw, ready to release.

Broadside and Quartering Shots: Broadside is best, providing the animal's front leg is forward, fully exposing the lung area. As mentioned earlier, a double-lung hit is bowhunting's most desirable and deadly shot. For the best results – short blood trails and easily recovered animals – place your shaving-sharp broadheads through both lungs. Always! Just make a conscious effort to avoid the shoulder and send your shot through the animal's chest. It's a large target and if the shaft flies true you'll soon be tagging your trophy. And even if you're slightly off target – hitting a bit back or a little low – chances are good you'll get a lethal liver hit or slice the heart or cut a major artery.

If an animal is quartering slightly away, a deadly double-lung hit is easy. Hold for an exact spot just below an imaginary line dissecting the animal's body when you're both on the same level. Always try to envision sending your broadhead on a diagonal path completely through both lungs into the opposite shoulder. If you're in an elevated perch, simply hold low unless the animal is standing directly beneath you.

Front-quartering shots are much riskier. An arrow hitting just behind the shoulder will likely result in a gut-shot animal. Generally, it's best to be patient and wait for the approaching animal to turn, offering you a broadside or quartering-away shot.

In the end, the final choices about when and where to shoot are yours and yours alone. Whatever you decide, remember that there's no substitute for shooting experience.

> Control/elimination of your scent must be the foundation on which you build all other parts of your hunting effort. Here's how...

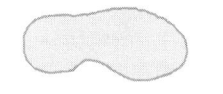

by Tony LaPratt

Hunting Pressured Bucks

*E*veryone knows that a "pressured" buck means one that has been or is being disturbed in its daily patterns (moving, feeding and bedding), but sometimes the pressure concept is thought of only as hunting pressure. That's too narrow a frame of reference. A buck can be pressured as a result of small game hunters, wood cutters or loggers, or farmers moving about through their field and/or woodlot chores. Most of the times, though, it's the hunter that pressures the buck, either during scouting and/or hunting efforts. We're talking here real pressure – the type of pressure deer get in southern Michigan farmland. Bowhunting pressure is heavy (more than 300,000 bowhunters in the state) and firearms pressure is heavy (nearly a million hunters). More and more of them are hunting southern Michigan. There is a lot of woodlot deer hunting here, and everything is intensified in woodlots.

The application of pressure can result in three main reactions. The buck may move to heavier cover on the same piece of property; it may move to another piece of property; or it may go nocturnal. Plus, you put all its senses on high alert. When any one of these happen, the odds of tagging that buck go down dramatically. However, if you know how to make pressure work for you, you can turn this negative into a positive.

A lot of times, the manner in which you disturb the buck has the largest influence in making it feel pressured. For instance, when you're small game hunting, try to stay away from buck bedding areas. If you have to go into the woods, for scouting or to move a stand, for instance, try to do it in the middle of the day and make a lot of noise when you're heading into the woods. This gives the buck plenty of time to sneak out, making him feel he has outsmarted you. You have disturbed him, but only momentarily, and he can deal with that. He feels as if he is in control. That deer will return soon and learn more about you when you leave the woods by smelling where you have walked.

You don't want that buck to jump up right in front of you and run away. You don't want to come upon him unannounced, so to speak. That's when he will feel pressured and will lose confidence in the safety of the area you kicked him out of.

A trophy buck has three defenses – hearing, sight and smell. He can hear you, and you still have a chance; he can see you and you still have a chance; he smells you and you have no chance! Body scent is the most important. If a trophy buck smells you, it is all over. It is that simple. So don't let him smell you, or minimize your scent so much that he thinks you're farther away than you are and thus will be of less concern to him.

Here is the detailed routine I follow to help control or eliminate my scent. Am I overdoing it? I don't think so. This attention to details is necessary if you're going to be consistently successful fooling any good buck, and especially a pressured buck.

1) Always take a shower before I go hunting…body and hair.

2) Use hunter-oriented scent removing hair and body soap.

3) Scrub with a rough wash cloth to remove all dead skin cells. Dead skin cells, together with heat and moisture, create body odor.

4) When I get out of the shower, I use a body shield gel all over. I even put it in my hair.

5) I wash my hunting clothes in hunter's clothes wash, then hang them outside to dry.

6) When the clothes are dry, I hang them in my greenhouse (I'm a vegetable grower) where the air moves through them all the time but keeps them dry. If you don't have a place like this, put them in a plastic bag and store them outside the house somewhere where no odors or only natural-to-the-area odors will be.

7) I get dressed in my greenhouse for hunting. When it's hot, I carry my hunting clothes in a backpack and don't get dressed until I'm at my tree strand.

8) Start to my stand early enough that I don't need to hurry. This is especially important in hot weather. If I think I'm going to start to sweat, I stop for a minute to cool off.

9) Plus, I will spray my self with scent shield's eliminate human scent spray.

10) My hunting boots are for hunting only; I don't use them for anything else. They don't go to gas stations or party stores … only the woods. That's it. So clean them regularly and keep them

sprayed with the eliminator spray, plus I spray all my hunting equipment regularly. In short, if it goes to the woods with me, I clean it and spray it.

11) Keep your vehicle clean. I spray the pedals to keep out all unnecessary odors.

12) It's actually better to have a separate pair of boots for driving. Store your hunting boots in a plastic bag and put them on – outside your vehicle – when you park your vehicle.

No, I'm not done yet. There's quite a bit more...

13) I also use the carbon-impregnated scent locking suit. It works great. It is a suit you put under your camouflage clothes. It traps human scent and keeps it from the deer. You must use the headnet to be totally effective. This is important. I wouldn't went to go in the woods without it. I know it has helped me out numerous times, and that little extra was all I needed. If you use it, I believe your opportunities will increase.

Remember ... a trophy buck will second-guess his hearing and even his sight, but he never second-guesses his nose! If you are laughing at all of this, I'll put it simply – this separates the men from the boys in the woods.

Control/elimination of your scent must be the foundation on which you build all other parts of your hunting effort. You can be the best shot in the world or have the best camouflage. You can be a master rattler or caller. You can be an excellent stand hunter or still hunter. You also can have the best places to hunt. But if a trophy buck smells you, the hunt is over. I tell you all of this so it will truly sink in, because you will never be a true master deer hunter until you understand and believe. This is the most important part of the lesson.

Stand Placements

I always look at topographical maps and my working map when considering stand placements. My working map really is more of a notebook. In it I keep aerial photos of each of the places I hunt, scouting notes, hunting notes, highlights of articles I've read ... anything I think is of value in helping me hunt big bucks more effectively. It's my bible.

I like to cover as much area as possible per stand, as many deer runs as possible. There's no sense setting up a stand on one trail when, with a bit more scouting, you ought to be able to find a place from which you can watch an intersection of a couple of trails. There might also be other goodies nearby to sweeten the area — scrapes, rub lines, funnels, licking branches, etc.

You must ask yourself whether you can get to the stand without spooking deer in the area. This is extremely important. You must NOT go through bedding areas, and try to avoid major feeding areas. Deer are like a coon dog. They pattern you. After three or four times of following your scent line out of a particular area, they will avoid that area. When you're going to or from your stand, don't take the easiest, shortest, most direct route every time. Vary it. You may need to go the long way around to get to your stand, but do it. Keep the area – the hunting area and the approaches – fresh. Have several stand locations, and use them. Too much of any human presence in an area is pressure a buck doesn't like.

Sometimes you can't use the same trail getting into your stand as you do leaving it. Sometimes, on sensitive stand sites (primarily a stand with 75-100 yards of a bedding area), I rake all paths to my stands. I'll do this in January or early spring, removing dead branches so there will be no possibility of loud noises when I use the trail the next season. Then I'll check them in the summer to be sure they're still clean.

You must ask yourself what period of the rut is the stand for. Is it for the pre-rut? Scrape period of the rut? The breeding period of the rut? Or the post-breeding period of the rut? A stand may cover only one period of the rut or it may cover two and maybe, but rarely, all of them. **Bucks change their behavior quite a bit from one period of the rut to another; this is why it is extremely important to know the four stages of the rut and what is happening in each stage.**

The stand must be comfortable and quiet. I like to position my tree stands 20 feet off the ground. This is high, I know, but deer don't pick me up at that height and there are less scent problems at that height. At lower heights, everything you do had better be right on the money, but you can get away with a lot at 20 feet. I haven't had a problem with double-lung hits, because I set my stands 20 yards off the trail. This gives me a better angle for a double-lung hit. Twenty yards off the trail also means there is less tension – less tension on your part and less tension for the deer to pick up on – and less noise concern. Yes, at 20 feet, safety has to be a concern. It becomes part of your routine.

I like ground blinds to be roomy and well camouflaged with native material. The roominess is necessary so I can draw my bow or raise my rifle without touching anything. I like to sit all day; the roominess allows space for my pack and lets me stretch my legs once in a while. I like to use pine branches as part of the natural material because they're thick. If I have to use dead materials, I'll make the weave thicker and then in the fall add some green stuff to freshen it up. Usually, though, my ground blinds look like brush piles with a shooting hole in them.

The best time to put up a stand is January through April. This goes for gun blinds also. You should cut all shooting lanes and paths leading to stand locations then, too. This time is best because all the signs from the last hunting season are right in front of you – bedding areas, other hunters' stand locations, etc. In addition, at this time you can clearly see the lay of the land.

I make my shooting lanes three feet wide. They are noticeable, but deer cross them without acting concerned. In fact, every once in a while one will stop right in the shooting lane to look around. I appreciate that, especially when the deer stopping has large antlers. I cut the brush low, at least down to knee height. If I know I will be hunting the area for several years, I'll cut the brush right to the ground. I cut out just enough to have a clear shooting lane; I do not make it look like a landing strip. I've noticed that deer react differently to wider strips, such as those made by bush hogs. The deer will stop on the edge of such a wide swath, inspect it, then jump across. That's not what I want.

What if you need to put up a stand during deer season? Most experts tell you to be quiet. I disagree. **I make as much noise as possible when I have to put up a tree stand during hunting season.** If I sneak into the woods and come upon the deer, he jumps up and bolts away. Now he is scared because I got inside his safety zone. Now he doesn't feel safe in that particular spot. But if I slam the truck door and whistle a tune, that buck slips away and thinks he has outsmarted me. He retains his confidence in that area and doesn't feel pressured. So I put up the stand, doing the necessary work of creating shooting lanes and access lanes to the stand. Then when I come to hunt it, I make no noise. I'll wait two to three days for my scent to clear before hunting from such a new stand.

You can funnel deer to your stand easily with brush, a fallen tree, snow fence, or some other barrier. At fence crossings, you can add a strand of wire to discourage deer in one location and lower wire in another place to increase usage. If you are not using these tactics you are missing some important opportunities.

Make a check list of all the above items each time you are going to put up a stand. If you do this, your success rate will truly go up.

How big is a safe area? It can vary greatly. A safe areas can be a little pothole in a big field, or it can be a thousand acres. I personally have taken a couple of trophy bucks in that little pothole that always gets overlooked in hunting season. On my farm, for example, I have about five acres of good, safe areas; five spots of about one acre each. That's not much area, but I have seen nearly 50 deer in those five acres at one time. Eight were bucks. It was unreal. On our other farm, we once watched 13 bucks run into a safe area in one day. My best friend Chris shot an eight-pointer that scored over 140 that was going into that safe area. Last year, I shot a 10-pointer sneaking back into that same safe area. It scored 13-15/8. In 1988, hunting a safe area on my farm, I shot a 13-pointer that scored 150-1/8. The very next day I shot an eight-pointer that looked almost as big.

What, exactly, is a safe area? It's any place of zero human intrusion – no scouting, no walking through, no nothing. And no human scent. It is a sanctuary that doesn't get hunted and is difficult for humans to get to. That's where big bucks hide when the hunting season starts. Bucks and does from miles around will go to these places, go to where the brush is thick, or where there's no hunting allowed, or miles from a road, or a small, dry hummock in the middle of a wet swamp. I've even known of deer to run into a wet swamp and simply stand in a foot-and-a-half of water – just stand there – until the hunters went away.

Most of the time there's not adequate food in a safe area, so the deer must leave the safe area to feed. Most of that movement is at night. Most safe areas are not really good bedding areas either, but the deer stay there anyway because they feel safe from hunters. Conversely, most bedding areas aren't safe areas because hunters can and do walk right through them.

Now, if you already have a safe area on your hunting land, I can show you how to hunt it without destroying it. You must put your stands on the trails leading to the safe areas. Plus you must get to your stands without disturbing the deer. You must have those prepared trails and ready stands. Your scent cannot blow through the safe area. Deer cannot be permitted to sense your presence.

Look at the map of my hunting land. Notice the stand locations, and the trails approaching my stands. Note where the safe areas are, and how I avoid as many deer trails as possible.

How to hunt a pressured buck in his safe area? All of this goes back to careful preparation and attention to details. Hunt the perimeter of the safe area. Cut shooting lanes into the safe area. Try to use the wind in your favor whenever possible. Control body scent. Have proper stand placement. Be quiet going to and from a stand. The smaller the area, the more important each of these elements becomes. They are crucial.

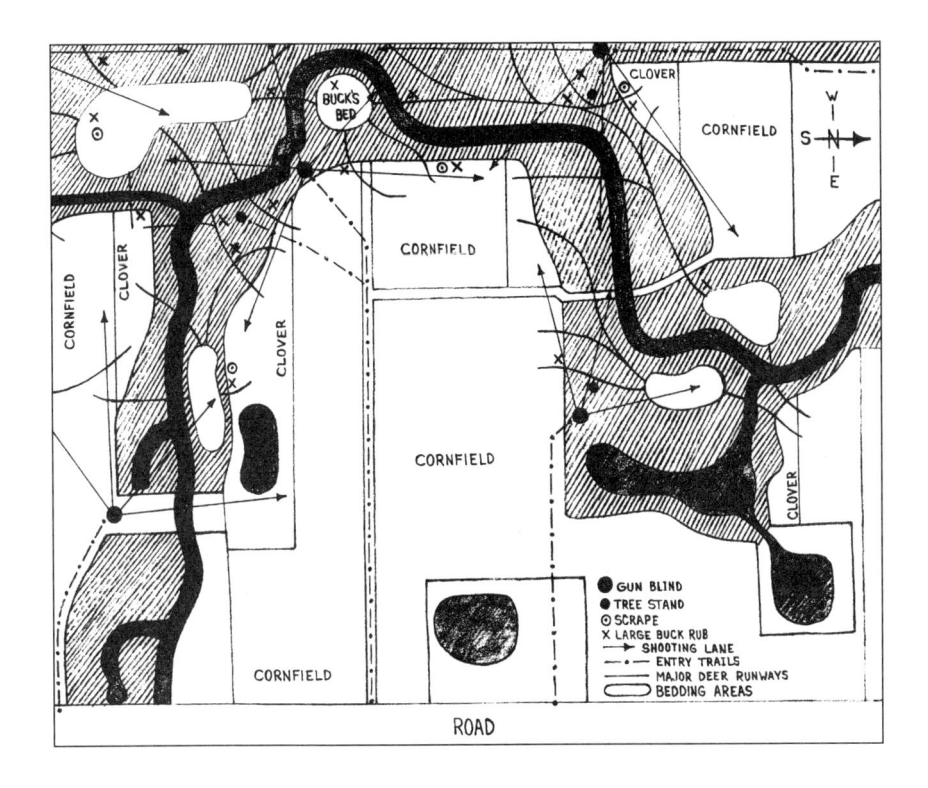

TONY LAPRATT

Tony LaPratt, a resident of southern Michigan, specializes in big whitetail bucks of the urban and farmland areas, where hunting pressure is high. He's taken record-class bucks with shotgun, bow-and-arrow and muzzleloader. Tony relies on year-round scouting, herd management, buck rubs and other signs, plus proper stand placement, for his consistent success. He believes that in some ways farmland whitetails are more wary than their woodland counterparts because of their constant and somewhat conflicting contact with man, but they're easier to locate due to their limited habitat (unless the corn hasn't been harvested). He is a late season specialist. All his trophy bucks have come later in the season, when pressure is less and the hunting is tougher.

SECTION IV:

THE GREAT FEATHERED BIRD

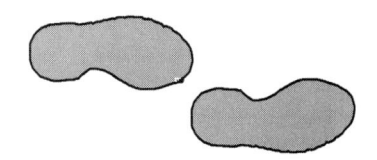

• *Roosting trees usually consist of large poplar, oak or tall pines. Rivers are important because they provide a water source, large roosting trees on their banks and cool, shaded areas along the water when the sun gets hot. Photo by Bob Lollo.*

> **N**o matter how good you are, you can NEVER ignore the basics. "Dance with him what bring you."

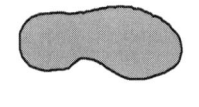

by Greg Abbas

Turkey Hunting Basics
...Building Blocks for Success

I have found through the years of guiding for and hunting the wild turkey that success at all levels of this fine sport starts with the basics. Everything else you learn builds on that foundation. You never stop going back to the sound basics that worked in the past. Therefore, to be consistently successful it is important to learn and understand these basics ... then apply them right.

There is no substitute for good turkey scouting. This always has been the most important key to success for me. Too many would-be turkey hunters put too much emphasis on their calling practice and skills and not nearly enough on scouting. To know where to scout, I look for areas that provide the basic survival needs for the turkey – food, water and sleeping areas.

The wild turkey diet consists of mast (mostly acorns), any farm crop, grass and insects. Therefore, I look in oak forests, farm fields and clearings. If I find a farm field surrounded by oaks, there is a good chance I will see turkeys and turkey sign.

Rivers are important to turkeys because they provide a water source, large roosting trees on their banks and cool shaded areas along their bottoms when the sun gets hot. Roosting trees usually consist of large poplar, oak and tall pines. Roost trees are often found along river edges, ridge tops and sometimes farm field edges. Turkeys often roost in the same areas day after day if not disturbed.

Once I have found an area that has the turkey's basic needs, I look for their tracks, droppings, dropped feathers, scratchings and dusting bowls. It sounds like a lot to do, but it's not.

Looking for tracks is my main concern. They can usually be found on most any backwoods road. Tracks tell me about the daily travel routine of the turkey. Tracks also tell me how many gobblers and hens are in the group and sometimes can help me estimate what time they pass through a given area. The track of the gobbler is approximately five inches from tip of front toe to tip of back toe, whereas the hen's track is little more than half that size.

Turkeys are birds of habit that usually follow the same routine day after day unless disturbed. With this in mind, I've come up with a way to determine the approximate time they travel through a given area. I usually go into an area in the evening and smooth out the turkey tracks. I'll return the next morning at 10 a.m. If I see a fresh set of tracks, that indicates the birds came through before 10 a.m. To narrow it down more, I'll repeat the process and come back at 8 a.m. the next day. If there are no tracks, I now know they come through between sun-up and 8 a.m.

The droppings of the wild turkey can be found anywhere the birds frequent. Droppings are distinct between gobbler and hen. The droppings of the gobbler are J-shaped and approximately two inches long, while hen droppings are the shape and size of popcorn. Feathers are another sign. Turkeys lose feathers as they fly up to the roost. Most often found are wing feathers which are the black and white barred feathers used on traditional arrows. When I find a couple of wing feathers in the same area, I start to look for a concentration of droppings, too. This usually indicates a roosting site.

Scratchings usually can be found in oak forests. They are made when the turkey scratches it's feet on the ground to move the leaves to find food. Scratchings are V-shaped and important for two reasons: 1) They tell me where the birds spend a lot of time and, 2) by following the point of the "V" I can determine the direction the flock travels and also can follow it back to the roost.

Last, dusting bowls are a good place to find birds in the late morning and early afternoon. The bowls can be 12 to 24 inches wide and three to six inches deep, found anywhere in sandy soil. Turkeys use them to cool off and dust their feathers when the sun gets warm. This is a good place to sit and wait for birds late morning and early afternoon.

You may need a call or two before you go out. Without question, the simplest and most effective call is the push-button call. By pushing the button you can make the basic calls, such as the yelp, cluck and purr. Since this call takes very little movement and only one finger to operate, I recommend it to hunters of all skill levels. Generally, wooden calls produce better sounds than plastic. Adjustable push-button calls work best because they allow you to adjust tone and volume. Push-button calls are a good mid to short range call. I also recommend taking a box call in the woods with you. This gives you a louder long distance call for the windy days of spring. Mouth diaphragm calls are popular because they take no movement. However, they require a little practice. For the beginner, I recommend starting with an easy-to-blow single reed diaphragm of any brand. I called in my first gobbler with one of these. Because both hands must be used on slate calls, I use them when calling for someone else. Some are excellent wet weather calls, especially with acrylic strikers that are water resistant and thus function when wet. Most wood and plastic strikers will not perform in wet weather.

If there is one sound you need to master, it is the yelp. It's an "I love you" type call to the gobbler. I use it 90 percent of the time. There are many more sounds that the turkey makes which you will probably learn and use as you advance, but the yelp is the call most often used by hunters of all skill levels. It is important to remember to call only loud enough to reach the gobbler. If you call too loud, nine times out of ten he will hold up out of gun range. As he closes the distance, call less and call quiet.

When you make contact with a gobbler for the first time, set up by a large enough tree to break your outline. If there are two hunters, you may consider using the buddy system where one person does the calling 30 to 40 yards behind the shooter. Thus, if the gobbler happens to hold up 60 yards from the caller, it already is well within gun range for the hunter. This method often is used on my guided hunts with deadly results.

When setting up on roosted birds before daylight, I set up about 80 yards from the roost. When the tom starts gobbling, that is my cue to start calling. I call very little, with soft yelps at this point. I just want the gobbler to know that there is a lonely hen nearby. If you over-call, he may stay on the roost, gobble longer and attract a real hen or another hunter. Either case is bad news. Once the gobbler is on the ground, I try to excite that bird by giving excited yelps and a few cutts, which are telling that gobbler "I want you now!" I call less and less as he approaches. Once I can see him, I cluck and purr just enough to keep him coming. Clucks and purrs are contentment type sounds the turkey makes when it is feeding. If he is coming in on course, I won't call at all. When he enters gun range and goes behind a tree, I move my gun if needed and will be ready for the shot as he comes out. The hope is that it will mean a sure turkey Thanksgiving dinner.

- *Turkeys are birds of habit and usually follow the same routine day after day unless disturbed. Use this knowledge and the advice on page 140 to determine specific times they will be in certain places. Look along fields, especially those bordering oak woods, because these will be preferred turkey feeding areas. Photo by Bob Lollo.*

GREG ABBAS

Greg Abbas is a five-time Michigan state turkey calling champion, a professional turkey hunting guide with a 91% success rate and a game call manufacturer (A-Way Hunting Products). He currently holds the state record typical turkey taken with a bow and has the most record-book entries taken with a bow. He has hunted turkeys throughout the United States. Also a skilled deer hunter and caller, he has three trophy whitetails in the Commemorative Bucks of Michigan record books.

- You must be on the same elevation as the gobbler, or on a higher elevation, for him to respond to your call. This also prevents him from circling above you and sneaking in from behind. Photo by Karen Lollo.

- When gobblers are fighting for hens, top photo, you'll hear plenty of gobbling, cutting and fighting purrs, accompanied by flapping wings. Photo by Bob Lollo.
- Above, the author with his big New York State gobbler.

- Hens normally fly down and go to the gobbler. Our hunting efforts usually are counter to this, which just goes to show you that when love is involved, sense goes out the window. Photo by Karen Lollo.

> One of this country's most successful turkey hunters spells out the basics everyone must follow.

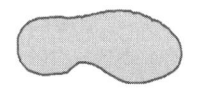

by Bob Clark

To Hunt Wild Turkeys Successfully....

To hunt wild turkeys successfully, it is important that you know what makes wild turkeys do the things they do and why they do them. To call a wild turkey into shotgun or bow range, you need to know what each turkey call means and sounds like, and have some ability to imitate each turkey sound. You need to know why turkeys make certain calls in the spring and almost abandon them in the fall. Turkey hunting is a sport, not a competition, and once you have a thorough knowledge of the wild turkey, you can then begin to learn the art of turkey hunting.

To understand the wild turkey, let us begin with the life cycle of this magnificent bird and take you through a year in the life of the wild turkey.

Normally, throughout the year – and this applies to the four primary sub-species of wild turkey in America, the Eastern, Merriams, Osceola and Rio Grande – there are three groups:

1) flocks and birds of the year,
2) young gobblers,
3) old gobblers.

Young jakes want to be part of any group. **Old gobblers, usually about two years old or more, normally live throughout the year in groups of two to five and do not want to be part of any other group.** This group is the smartest and toughest of all the turkey groups; the gobblers do little talking and rely more on visual contact than vocal contact. Young jakes, on the other hand, make lots of sounds, normally half-hearted yelps, putts and clucks, and start to develop both their yelps and gobbles. The jakes have a distinctive yelp, as it takes more than a year to develop a clean, clear yelp. You often will hear the hoarse sound that indicates their presence.

Throughout America, starting in December in Alabama, for

example, but later further north, these three groups start coming together to begin the breeding cycle. The breeding cycle takes place about two months in advance of the spring gobbler season so that the females will be fertilized and after this, the males, or at least some of them, are surplus and available for hunting. This management tool protects the species and keeps their numbers in balance.

Spring gobbler season begins in mid-March in Alabama, Georgia, Florida and South Carolina; several of these states have a six bird limit. As you move north, spring gobbler seasons are set in states like Tennessee and Kentucky, as well as in our western states, in mid-April. As we continue to move up the country to Ohio, Pennsylvania, Wisconsin, New York and others, seasons open in late April or early May. Naturally, spring gobbler seasons in states close to the Canadian border wrap up in late May. Spring gobbler seasons are set for the time the biologists think the hens will have mated, laid 14 eggs and be on their nest.

In all these states and with all the sub-species, the same procedure takes place. Hens move into areas that provide cover and water and seek out nesting areas. Gobblers, on the other hand, follow the hens to their select areas and begin the elimination procedure basically to see which gobbler is left standing, so to speak. The winner of these fights earns the right to be the boss gobbler for this season and dominates and conducts all the breeding. It should be noted here that only one gobbler – the strongest – wins the right to do the breeding, and the hens honor him by mating only with him.

During this elimination process, hunters visiting the forests and fields will hear lots of gobbling, cutting and fighting purrs. The fighting purr sound is loud and accompanied by the flapping of wings and continuous purring. To make this sound, you can use two push-button calls, mouth calls or the calling device which I prefer and can control – a slate call. During this period, the hens select their nesting site and await the gobbling of the dominant gobbler.

As the sun starts to rise, the small birds of the forest begin to wake up and make their sounds. A crow or two may begin with the caw caw, or a barred owl may join in with its "Who cooks for you? Who cooks for you'allllllll?" All at once, everything seems to stop, the woods become silent and then, usually from a point off a ridge or in the woods next to a flat field or stream, we hear a gobble gobble, or more gobbles. With this, the boss gobbler has announced his location and unlike the hunting of a gobbler, where we ask them to come to us, the hens will fly down, giving out with a cackling sound, their mating sound for "I hear you and am on my way", and sometimes run or fly/glide several miles to the gobbler.

The mating sounds or fly-down cackle starts with a few clucks or putts as she literally gets awake and the very fast yelps, very fast yelpyelpyelpyelp, with more staccato than any of the other turkey sounds. She hits the ground, clucks and putts and tucks her wings and goes directly to the gobbler.

It is during this period that the hens kick out of their group or flock the one-year-old males (jakes).

The process of breeding takes about 18 seconds and a few or many hens might be waiting their turn to be fertilized for this day. The hens go to the gobbler every day or every other day over a two month period, lay one egg at a time until they have 14 eggs in their nest. At this point, the hens cease going to the gobbler and devote their energy and life to the development of their young. During this nesting period the hen is bonding with each chick in its egg, and she is passing on the sound of her own voice to them. She purrs, clucks, putts, yelps and teaches each of them the key sound that they must understand and immediately obey if they are to survive. This sound is the danger "pert pert pert". The easiest way to explain this danger sound is to take the soft sounding putt and raise it to a higher level of sound. The basic difference between a walk-around putt and a danger pert is the speed and shrillness of the sound. The hen will use this sound as any danger appears.

One day on the side of a ridge, looking over a small valley, I saw a large hawk swoop toward a flock of young turkeys. The hen immediately gave a pert-pert-pert and each chick immediately pressed itself down motionless on the ground or moved under brush cover and pinned itself to the ground. After some time, the hawk left and the hen gave an assembly call – yelp, yelp, yelp, yelp, yelp – to call her young together. They went on with their feeding, heading for a water hole.

During the breeding cycle, the hens are fertilized; even if they lose their nest, they do not need a gobbler again after the first nesting to reproduce another clutch of eggs. Sometime during the spring gobbler season, hens will hatch their eggs, but depending on the length of your particular spring gobbler season, most of them will still be incubating their eggs. This is when gobblers become frustrated, because hens will not come to them and they now go looking for hens.

Normal Spring Gobbler Hunt

At dawn, you are on the top of a ridge or near a field or stream where you have heard or seen wild turkey gobblers. As the sun peeks over the land, an old gobbler sounds off. You now have a starting point. **The first rule of the hunt is to be above or on the same elevation as the gobbler you hear.** If you're below it, it tends to circle you. You don't want to give the gobbler an opportunity to hide someplace where he can see you but you can't see him. That's the first thing a smart gobbler will try to do. A smart gobbler feels most comfortable when he can approach in thick cover. He will feel comfortable enough to approach in areas of less than thick cover, but that's probably not his 'druthers.

It's where you sit; your position is everything. Therefore, the second action you should take is to find that position, preferably an area that a gobbler will feel comfortable walking through.

Find a large tree, if available in this area, that you can use to cover your backside and that will break up your image. Now make sure your shotgun is loaded, your face mask is on, gloves are in place, nothing shiny is visible, and you have selected your best turkey calling device. Which one is this? The call that you can best use and deliver the sounds that you may need to present.

It is now time to present your first call. Hopefully, your gobbler has been gobbling while you have taken the necessary steps to begin your hunt. If you have an aggressively gobbling gobbler, present him with an aggressive series of cutts or cackles. I prefer just to present loud, clean, sharp yelps. If you have a gobbler that gobbles very little, then present an aggressive first call and totally stop your calling. Above all, do not call to a gobbler on the roost (still in the tree) more than two times. This is the most important part of your hunt. The more you call to a gobbler on the roost, the more he might gobble but stay up in the tree.

Present your opening call or calls (two) and if he answers, he knows exactly where you are even if you never make another call. You might have a better chance to kill him now than if you call too much. When he flies down, he may drop to your left or right. No matter from which direction he drops down, the second mistake most first-time turkey hunters make is by not moving or facing the direction you last heard the gobbler on the ground.

From this point on, I will not call to the gobbler unless he gobbles to me. If he makes one gobble, I answer with one call. If he gobbles a lot as he moves toward me, I tend to answer him more often but not every time or even every other time. You have to feel this experience to know when to answer and when to shut up. Remember this, if you ever have a doubt, call less or not at all.

As the gobbler approaches you, move only your eyes, and if you have to move your gun or your body to a better position, never … I repeat, never ... move unless the gobbler's head is behind a tree or other obstruction, and even this may not be appropriate.

If you have patterned your shotgun, you will know what shot pattern you have with the gun in your hands, up to 40 yards. If you have sighted in your shotgun at 25 yards and 40 yards, and your shotgun shell places 10-12 shot in the brain, not just the head, and 10-20 shots in the vertebra, not just the neck, you should be able to take many gobblers.

First Time Mistakes

On opening day, you hear several gobblers sound off. You wait till fly-down and make a soft series of yelps. Several gobblers reply but don't head your way. Why not?

- Your first mistake may have been your position. If you were not on their elevation or above them, this may have caused them not to respond. If you didn't get in position until after fly-down time (and none of us know when this time will be), or you did not take an aggressive approach to the gobblers in hand, or another hunter or a hen may have taken charge of your gobblers ... each can be a mistake. You may save the morning by having patience and waiting. If the gobblers shut down, you may be in a silent gobbler area, which is an entirely new hunt.

- On opening day, you have located a gobbler and, at dawn, he gobbles but attracts another hunter who is moving toward your gobbler. You try to out-call the intruder. This can be a dangerous situation; do not try to call this gobbler at this time. Your own safety is your first concern right now. I will throw a loud danger pert-pert and sit quietly. If I see the hunter, I will produce a blaze orange hat and yell to him that I am a hunter. The danger pert will shut down the gobbler. Maybe it will sit quietly, and maybe your intruder will lose patience and leave. The gobbler, when ready, may let you know where he is and when he is ready to go, but don't count on it.

- In your area, the gobblers have a lot of pre-season calling pressure and by opening day already are call-shy. You have tried all kinds of calling and nothing works. How do you start hunting these spooky gobblers?

You first need to know whether birds are still in the area. Once you are convinced they are, you now are dealing with a silent gobbler or group of silent gobblers. These gobblers may or may not give you one gobble, but assuming that they do not, do the following:

Set up high on the ridge in mountain country or inside the woods off fields and streams in flatter country and let the day begin. If no gobbler gobbles, present a series of loud yelps or loud cackles and be prepared to sit quietly for hours. If you have faith, move only your eyes, do very little calling on this type of gobbler, your chances of taking him will be better than you think.

Spring gobbler hunting is a fascinating and wonderful experience. We have just scratched the surface regarding this unique species. Learn as much about spring gobbler hunting as you can. First of all, find a friend who has hunted wild turkeys and get the friend's help and advice. Attend turkey hunting seminars and take notes. Do not be afraid to walk up after a program and ask specific questions you might not feel comfortable asking in front of the group.

Turkey hunting is fun, but it's also serious, and it can be a dangerous sport if someone does not play by the rules. Always be aware of what is around you and assume that anything that moves could be another person. As a turkey hunter, never try to sneak up on a wild turkey. Their eyes and ears are ten times better than ours. If they could smell, I doubt we would kill any of them without a rifle. Never stop learning all you can about wild turkeys. Take notes on your hunts and try to recall different situations, especially the successful ones. This knowledge can improve your days afield. Like anything, but unlike most, just about the time you feel you know all there is to know about spring gobblers, one will teach you a new trick.

BOB CLARK

Bob Clark is an award winning author and a member of the Pennsylvania Wild Turkey Hunters Hall of Fame. He has taken 205 gobblers in 37 states and is an American Wild Turkey Society Certified Turkey Calling Judge. He has presented turkey hunting seminars, which include big game and forest habitat management, for all wildlife for the past 30 years.

Bob is the author of four books. In 1996 he teamed up with Alex Zidock Jr to produce the video "Bob Clark's Wild Turkey Primer".

Clark is one of the founders and past president of the Pennsylvania State Chapter of the National Wild Turkey Federation (NWTF), past national vice president of the NWTF, founder of the American Wild Turkey Society in Pennsylvania, and retired executive director of the Pennsylvania Forestry Association.

In 1995 he took the third largest Eastern species of American wild turkey ever taken in New York State, with spurs nearly two inches long.

He has been a big game guide in Colorado, South Dakota and Wyoming for deer and elk, and a bear guide in Canada.

> **Y**our first priority when you go into the turkey woods is to locate a gobbler. Elementary, but not always easy.

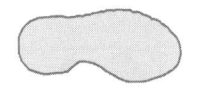

by Gary Sefton

Locating Techniques for Spring Gobblers

*T*he two most important tactical problems confronting a turkey hunter when he enters the woods are location and location. Just like the old real estate motto. You want to know the gobblers' location and where you should be to take advantage of his location. My Georgia turkey hunting buddy, Dr. Frank Catrett, likes to say, **"It's not how you call, it's where you get."** **The very best place to get is between the turkey and where he wants to be.** The right place. To get this done, you first need to locate the gobbler. Turkeys are accommodating about this in the spring, since they are more than willing to sing out in response to a variety of different sounds, proudly announcing their exact location to any and all who might be interested. If you can make him gobble, you have a small foot in the door.

To best understand how to make turkeys gobble, you need to **know WHY turkeys gobble.** The two most basic reasons are: 1) because they want to, a communicative sound, and 2) because they can't help it, an involuntary or "shock" gobble. They gobble on purpose as a summoning call to hens in the spring, and to reassemble their bachelor groups in the fall. They gobble, I believe, as an audible territorial marker and also because they can. The wild turkey gobble is my favorite sound in the world and the sweetest music any turkey hunter can hear.

The involuntary or "shock" gobble is the preferred initial response for the spring turkey hunter. You want the turkey to give away his position without you giving away your own. The "shock" gobble is automatic and involuntary, almost like a sneeze. Turkeys don't seem to know they did it and don't seem to know or care what caused it. When gobblers hear turkey sounds, they become alert and pinpoint the location of the sounds. They may decide to investigate your calling without announcing their intentions, so you're better off if you can locate the bird with a non-turkey sound, get in

Locating Techniques

position, set up, and then try to call him in.

The sounds that trigger involuntary responses from turkeys are many and varied, ranging from owl hoots to thunder and almost anything in between. There are differing opinions as to why turkeys respond to these sounds, with some explanations as concise as "they just naturally want to gobble at those sounds" to others claiming they are chastising and/or challenging their natural enemies.

The most consistent locator I've come across mimics the sound of a peacock. What does a turkey know about a peacock? I have a theory that makes common and biological sense. Turkey gobblers in the spring are "wired" to the eyeballs with testosterone and other hormones, not to mention the urgency and pent-up emotions that are the result of a whole year of abstinence. I believe one would gobble I if you poked him with a sharp stick if you could do it without him seeing you. They are poised to respond, but they can't respond to everything or they wouldn't get anything done but gobbling. Anything that can hear as well as a turkey must have some kind of an audio-filtering system to sort out the sounds that occur naturally in their environment. Each and every sound has a unique shape or frequency, and the turkey's audio-filter will allow only sounds that are of the proper shape or frequency to penetrate the filter and trigger a response. Some of the sounds that trigger shock gobbles fall within the frequency range of the turkey's natural voice, while others are very abrupt or piercing. The crows, owls, squirrels, etc., that stimulate responses are probably within the natural voice category, while thunder, sirens, peacocks and other abrupt and/or piercing sounds cover a broad range of frequencies that overpower the audio-filter and trigger a response that is the result of "stimulation over-load".

Whatever the reason, if you can get a turkey to gobble before daylight, the earlier the better, the odds are not necessarily in your favor but they are better.

Any of the sounds that make turkeys "shock" gobble can be used to locate turkeys in the spring. The barred owl hoot is a great locator, as is the crow call. A wide variety of ingenious devices are commercially available to reproduce these sounds, some better than others. Use your own judgment as to what you think sounds best. crow and owl sounds are most effective at first light while the turkeys are still on the roost, but they can stimulate gobbles at any time of the day.

Get to an elevated position, if possible, before first light and make the "Who cooks, who cooks, who cooks for you all (y'all, if you're in the South) sound on your owl hooter or with your natural voice if you're so inclined. If there is a gobbler within hearing, he'll gobble at your owl hoots – if he wants to. Don't be discouraged if he doesn't gobble at your first call sequence. Wait five minutes and try again. Turkeys seem to have an internal clock that tells them when it's time to start gobbling – "after the first redbird sings", the late Ben Lee used to say, especially when you're using locators that fall in the natural voice frequencies.

Time and positioning are about the same with a crow call, but you want to **be aggressive with your crow call.** Imitate a crow chasing a hawk or an owl. Put some growl and squall into your calling; turkeys usually don't gobble at plain crow caws. It's to your advantage to get a gobbler to sing out as early as possible since the darker it is the closer you can get without him seeing you. Early in the spring when the gobblers are roosted with hens, the closer the better. Just be sure they can't see you.

The abrupt or piercing "stimulation over-load" calls such as the peacock, the coyote howl or the predator scream are more likely to trigger an earlier response.

If the turkey doesn't respond, you haven't done any harm with any locator call you might want to try. Turkeys don't respond negatively to locator sounds. If you know the gobbler is there, but he's not talking, he's seen your or something else on the ground that made him hush. If he gobbles in the tree but won't gobble after he flies down, it usually means he can see one or more hens. That presents a new set of problems.

Wild turkey gobblers are some of the most single-minded creatures on earth when it comes to courting. When he gets all puffed up trying to grin down a good-looking hen, about the only thing he can hear is thunder. He is so intent on winning her favors he just plain doesn't pay attention to anything else. You really have to jar him to make him gobble, and the "stimulation over-load" locators are your best bet in that situation. He may get together with hens when he first flies down and stay with them all day, so don't be afraid to try your piercing locators at any time of the day. You won't do any harm, and you just might do some good.

If you haven't done any good locating with non-turkey sounds, try some turkey sounds. One of my favorite locating techniques employing actual turkey sounds involves putting together long strings of loud, lost hen yelps on a slate or glass call. The difference between lost hen yelps and plain yelps is in the volume, inflection and the number of yelps. Where plain yelps are just five or six yelps of equal volume and intensity, I've heard and documented on video a lost hen yelping 60 or more times without stopping. I won't do 60 yelps, but I may do 25 or 30 loud yelps in a sequence. By inflection, I mean there is a pleading quality to the yelps – "I'm lost! Somebody come get me!" Lost hen yelps serve a dual purpose. A gobbler will respond to any hen yelp — he doesn't care if she's lost or not, and other hens will respond to lost hen yelps out of sympathy for a flock mate. If I can get a turkey to gobble at a hen yelp, I have a good chance of getting him in close since that is a communicative response and he obviously is looking for company. If I can get a hen to yelp in response to my yelps, there's a good chance any tom that's close to her will gobble at her yelping. He can ignore my calling from a distance, but when the current object of his affection, the one he's all puffed up about, helps right in his ear, he can't stand it. He'll gobble. Even if he doesn't gobble, I can strike up a conversation with a hen and possibly get her to investigate my calling. If she does, he'll be right behind her.

Cutting on a box call can sometimes make a turkey gobble when all else fails, especially on those too far away to hear lost yelping.

One word of caution – **when you use turkey sounds to locate turkeys, get set up before you start calling, just like you would if you knew a gobbler was close by.** If you don't, it is inevitable at some point in time you'll call up a turkey that you're totally unprepared for and when you do you'll surely run him off, and he'll be the last turkey you'll see for the rest of the day. There also is the possibility that your calling will attract another hunter, and you'll be much safer sitting still in an encounter with another hunter than you would be walking around sounding like a turkey. If you don't get a response in an area after you've tried everything, tray a new area.

If I'm not successful with the turkey I call to before fly down time, I usually will move on in hopes of finding another gobbling turkey. I like to get on a ridge or a high place, sit down by a wide tree, put on my face mask and gloves, then try a series of different locating techniques until I'm satisfied there are no gobblers in the area. I'll start with crow and owl sounds, then try the stimulation overload sounds, then lost yelps, then cutting on a box call. I'll usually spend 45 minutes or an hour at a good location. When I'm satisfied there are no gobblers within hearing, I'll move a quarter of a mile or so and I'll do it all over again. I'll continue to move and call and move and call until I run out of time or properly. I've had good luck with gobblers that answer between 9 a.m. and 3 p.m., since they usually are away from their hens and eager for company. I try to keep that in mind when the morning begins to drag on. Patience and persistence have killed more turkeys than all the calls put together.

Your first priority when you go into the turkey woods is to locate a gobbling bird. Once that is accomplished, the game will play itself out according to your skills and abilities versus the turkeys' innate paranoia and natural born luck. (Not that they drive me crazy or anything.) There are no magic bullets or secret tricks. If you can get him to gobble, you're in the game. You won't always win, but you'll be glad you got to play.

• *Turkeys will drive you crazy, but their gobble will get your blood boiling. And when it all comes together.....*

• Friction calls are easy to work and produce wonderfully natural sounds. With slate calls, you must hold the striker at the proper angle and maintain contact with the striker on the surface of the call, then hold the pot so your hand doesn't muffle the sound. Top photo by Karen Lollo.

Want calling ease and calling accuracy?

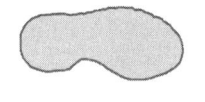

by Gary Sefton

Pterodactyl Pturkey Ptalk
Pfriction Turkey Calling Pfacts and Pfundamentals

Not long after the first Pterodactyl learned to gobble and evolved into a turkey, primitive man developed a taste for turkey breast and evolved into a turkey hunter. It didn't take primitive man long to figure out the advantages of being able to attract turkeys close enough to inflict a mortal wound with a thrown rock. When a caveman was attacked by a lovesick gobbler as he tried to scratch some graffiti on a rock wall with a sharp stick, an idea sparked in his prehistoric brain and friction turkey calls were born out of coincidence and necessity. Or something like that. I'm not sure how it started, but friction turkey calls have been around for a long time.

A friction turkey call is characterized as any device that involves rubbing two different surfaces together to create a sound. A vast array of implements and devices fall into this category including scratch boxes, hinged lid boxes, push-pin boxes, slate and peg, glass and peg, aluminum, carbon, and any combination of the aforementioned and on and on. Every one of these devices has been pondered on and pounded on and prayed over and perspired on for one ultimate purpose – to sound like a turkey. More precisely, a hen turkey, a yelping hen turkey. And even the sorriest of the lot does a decent job of it. Some of the old calls have yet to be improved on, while some of the newer models which blend computer technology with space age materials are simply amazing.

Friction calls are easy to use. You can be tone deaf, with no sense of rhythm and post-nasal drip, and still be able to call turkeys with a box or a slate call. A little dexterity won't do any harm, but it isn't necessary. **Anyone can call turkeys with almost any of the friction devices, the main reason being, you only have to learn to make one sound – the yelp.** Most friction calls make yelps to perfection with a minimum of technique and effort.

If I could make only one turkey sound, it would be the yelp. Most of the turkeys that are called in using cutts and cackles and clucks and purrs could have just as easily been called with yelps. That's not to say friction calls are limited to yelps. I think a good slate or glass call is the most versatile call available when accuracy is part of the equation.

I know you're feeling better about yourself now that you know you can call turkeys, so I'll take it one step farther and tell you how to operate some of these wonderful friction calls.

Hen yelps are two-note sounds. The first note is a high-pitched "kee" sound that abruptly breaks over into a "youk" sound. Kee-youk, kee-youk, etc. (They don't do the "etc." sound.) Friction calls employ increased pressure or different angles of contact to produce the "kee" sound. As the pressure is decreased or the angle is changed, the "youk" kicks in.

The push-in or push-button call clearly illustrates the mechanics of friction calls; you should be able to master it with no trouble. It is one of the most clever turkey calling devices on the market, and it is e-a-s-y to play. I mean, if you can fog up a mirror you can yelp on a push-button call. You just push the button. How hard is that? To yelp three times, push the button three times. If you can't call on a push-button, you have no business walking around in the woods with a loaded shotgun. There are a lot of push-button calls on the market, some better than others. Try them out and choose the one that sounds like a turkey. The good ones sound exactly like a turkey. Since push-button calls are so easy to use, requiring absolutely no technique, if you continue to use them after your first year of hunting you will be considered a bottom-feeding wimp and a tourist by your hunting buddies. I wouldn't be caught dead with one of them in my pocket, but they *will* call turkeys.

A good step up in the friction call food chain is the hinged lid box call, another ingenious design featuring a resonating box with a paddle or lid attached at one end in a hinge arrangement so the lid or paddle can be used to stroke the edge of the box with some degree of consistency. Good box calls make beautiful turkey music, especially yelps and clucks. They are also capable of producing more volume than other calls, so they are great for long range calling.

Box calls require a little more technique than push-button calls, but the basic yelps are easy. The trick to playing box calls is in realizing the paddle makes a sound going only in one direction, so there is never a need to lift the paddle off the surface of the box. The general tendency is to raise the paddle after each stroke, and that's where you get the squeaks and squawks that are the result of improper angles. Just let the lid rest lightly on one side of the box and shuffle it back and forth. Good box callers use more finesse, but we're just talking about calling turkeys, and yelps are all you need. With just a little practice, you should be able to make good clucks and cutts as well.

Here again, there are literally hundreds of box call manufacturers, some ordinary, some good, and some great. Most of the major call companies make decent box calls for around $25. There are a few 'master' call makers left, like Albert Paul, Neil Cost and Doug Camp, who still make Stradivarius-grade box calls, but these custom boxes can be expensive. You have to use your own judgment. If it sounds good to you, it will work; turkeys aren't that particular.

Box calls can be operated within the confines of a plastic bag (bread bags are just the right size) without adversely affecting the tone or volume, so they will work in the rain. The same holds true for push-button calls.

At the top of the friction call heap, in my opinion, are the slate or glass calls, especially the newer ones that employ modern technology and design. I have a hard time trying to tell the difference between a live turkey and a good friction call if it's being run by a competent caller. I'm talking about a GOOD friction call. Here again, there are hundreds of slate and glass call manufacturers, and their calls all look good in the package but some of them sound like they were made by Mattel. Materials, manufacturing techniques and design are vital in the production of good slate and glass calls, so don't pay until you play. Most major call manufacturers make decent to good slate and glass calls, and there are a few great ones. Don't expect to get a good one for less than $25, and you can go as high as you can stand when you get into the custom calls made by guys like Bill Zearing or Tony Reynolds. Custom call makers might spend 20 or 30 hours on one call, and that can get expensive.

The mechanics of slate and glass calls are the personification of simplicity. A slate or glass surface, usually round, is bonded to a resonating chamber or "pot". A separate wooden peg or striker is drawn across the surface to create the sound in much the same fashion as writing with pen or pencil. The striker, the playing surface and the resonator are of equal importance in creating the sound. The volume and tone are altered by manipulating the pressure and position of the striker. That might sound complicated on paper, but it is easy. I do seminars all over the country, and I always get someone from the audience, usually a lady, up on the stage and teach that person how to make yelps on a slate call. In less than a minute they are making perfect hen yelps.

The two most important elements of slate calling are holding the striker at the proper angle and maintaining contact with the striker on the surface of the call. Don't pick it up!

Hold the pot up so it doesn't touch the palm of your left hand (if you're right handed) so as not to muffle the sound that usually comes from the bottom of the pot. Take the striker in your right hand as if you were holding a pencil. Place the heel of your hand on the edge of the pot at four o'clock if twelve o'clock is facing straight away. Set the striker down at eleven o'clock about an inch inside the edge of the pot. Point the handle of the striker slightly away from your body. The angle is 100 degrees, my son tells me. You are now poised to yelp.

With firm but gentle pressure on the striker, draw dime-sized counter-clock-wise circles (clock-wise if you're left handed or south of the Equator) on the surface of the call. If you are maintaining the proper angle, you are now making yelps. The top of the circle provides the "kee" or high note. As the striker descends, it should break over into the "youk" or second note of the yelp. Now you've got the idea; just keep trying to sound like a turkey.

Clucks, purrs, cutts, cackles and kee-kee runs can all be done to perfection on slate or glass calls with practice. It's there; you just have to get it out.

It's individual preference as to the difference between slate and glass, although I think slate makes better clucks and purrs and glass makes the best kee-kees. Some calls are double sided and give you a choice.

There are other calling surfaces available with a lot of unsubstantiated "techno-babble" touting their superiority, but I can make perfect hen yelps on slate or glass and turkeys respond better to other turkeys than anything else.

The striker plays a major role in friction calling, and the designs and materials available are too numerous to mention. The striker has to be balanced with enough weight on handle end to make the call surface vibrate. Hickory is the best all-around material I've found, although some of the carbon strikers are good for specialized calling. Carbon and plexiglass are both impervious to moisture, so I always have at least two kinds of strikers with me in case of rain, and because they also are easy to lose. I've got them scattered all over the country. Be sure you carry spares.

Friction calling has a down side — it takes both hands to operate most friction calls. That movement could easily be detected by the turkey, not to mention the motion made in having to put the call down and pick up your gun before you shoot. I'm often asked how

I deal with this problem. **I have a simple solution: when the turkey gets close enough to see me playing the call, I shoot him.** I'm not being facetious when I say that. You want to set up so that when you first see a turkey you can shoot him, and once the turkey starts closing ground he has made up his mind to investigate your calling. Put your call in your pocket and pick up your gun.

I use diaphragm, wingbones, and the other "air" calls when hunting and in competition. Turkey hunters use whatever it takes to get the job done. When I want to sound exactly like a turkey, I use a friction call. Knowing your calling is as good as or better than a real turkey does a lot for your confidence when nothing is answering. If you're just starting out, I suggest you start out with a friction call. They're easy to play, and they're accurate. If you can make good, clean hen yelps you will call some turkeys. So get yourself a call you can yelp on with confidence and get out there with them. I can teach you how to call; the turkeys will teach you how to hunt.

GARY SEFTON

Gary Sefton is a Tennessee-based expert game caller for turkeys and for deer. A competition caller as well as an active hunter, he has been a champion deer caller and holds several state and national titles in friction and open turkey calling contests. He has written articles on deer and turkey hunting and calling for several publications and appeared on radio and television outdoor programs. Sefton also serves on the board of directors of the Tennessee chapter of the National Wild Turkey Federation.

• *"One hour and ten minutes later .... He stepped out from behind a large tree, went into a full strut and drummed his way to the decoy. ... He stopped, raised his head a little, and I shot him at about 20 steps."* Photo by Karen Lollo.

> **D**on't mistake the pseudo-silent gobbler for the truly silent one. They are hunted differently.

by Bob Clark

Tactics for Silent Spring Gobblers

*I*F I've heard it once, I've heard it hundreds of times – "What's happening with these non-gobbling gobblers?"

The 'what' is increased hunting pressure, the maturing of wild gobblers, and in some areas, pre-season calling. In response to all that, gobblers will tend to gobble very little, and they will reduce their gobbling in general from these pressures. This is not an isolated phenomenon but a universal problem that will, in time, cause normally rational turkey hunters to think they have lost their minds or forgotten everything they ever learned about turkey hunting.

Don't doubt your ability and turkey hunting skills; silent gobblers are just another great aspect of turkey hunting. As ancient wisdom states, "You are never too old to learn". Meaning that if you don't change your ways of turkey hunting, you will not be able to handle these silent gobblers.

What is a silent gobbler? That's a legitimate question, because **silent gobblers come in many forms, In addition – and this is important – there's another situation frequently misinterpreted as a silent gobbler.** Let's look first at this pseudo-silent gobbler. Then we'll look at the truly silent gobbler and how to handle him?

The pseudo-silent gobbler will gobble several times on the roost, but then he shuts up, and that's when hunters mislabel the lack of further response.

This particular gobbler normally has several hens very close and can hear them calling to him. The hens normally drop down from their roost and walk directly to his tree, waiting for him to fly down to them. You, on the other hand, have called and thought he answered. He probably did gobble out to you, but then seemed to shut up.

What has really taken place is the immediate hens around him have been bred and the gobbler, thinking that all the hens have come to him, has taken them and left the area.

This gobbler can be called and killed if you will change your position a little. Move high or low or left or right about 75 yards, and then present a couple of fast yelps or a series of short cutts and clucks. The reasoning here is simple. After a period of time, most gobblers are revived and ready to look for more hens to breed. They will hear you and come to you when you call. I have been in this situation many times and, normally, the gobbler will take his time. Sometimes, such a gobbler will even gobble more than usual later in the morning. Don't be alarmed if, on the other hand, your gobbler of the morning may or may not gobble several times.

Normally, the hens will come to the gobbler off their roost and be bred, hang around for a few minutes and get on with their second primary duty, that of building a nest. So do not be surprised if you have any number of scenarios in this situation.

Earlier in the hunting season you also can encounter a pseudo-silent gobbler. The gobbler will have hens, and the hens have not left the gobblers for their duty of bringing a nest of eggs into young poults. When hens complete laying 14 eggs they normally will sit on their nest, leaving it only in a drought for water, and guard it until the eggs are hatched. State turkey hunting biologists gauge the estimated date of the opening for this period. Sometimes they hit it; sometimes (seems like most of the time) they do not.

Let me tell you about a turkey hunt I was on in New York State the final week of May, 1995. Note the week and month. Turkey hens would have been off their nests by then in southern states. Turkeys in New York State, Pennsylvania and Virginia all should have been on their nests. So why did the big New York State gobbler I killed that day have 14 hens with him? In addition, there also were three jakes in the group, making a flock of 18 birds. Under normal conditions, this should not have happened, right? Honestly, who really knows?

The key here is what you do in this and other types of situations? This is what wild turkey hunting is all about, and I have had success in 37 states by changing my way of thinking, calling and hunting. If you hunt long enough, you will run into more situations than you could imagine hunting wild turkeys. Every time you think you are a pretty good turkey hunter, some smart old gobbler will outsmart you badly.

The New York season had been in full swing for more than four weeks when I arrived, and all conditions and situations appeared to be normal. I was taken to the base of a mountain about 15 miles from the Baseball Hall of Fame city, Cooperstown. That is why this gobbler is dubbed the Hall of Fame Gobbler. At dawn, I heard no mature gobblers but did hear a young jake attempting to gobble. It was known that a large old gobbler had been seen in this area, but to date no one had heard it or was able to call it in.

A few minutes later, after setting up, a mature hen hit the ground and gave out five loud yelps. I could hear other birds flying in, but that was the extent of the calling. The situation was now similar to a fall turkey hunting scenario. I moved around my large tree and faced the flock, which was about 100 yards away. I sat silently and made no more calls. Every 10 minutes for almost an hour this old hen yelped five times and then became silent.

The flock fed and milled around the area for more than an hour and then out of nowhere, about 200 yards out to the left of the group, a deep gobble was heard. Under normal conditions, you would jump right on this gobbler with cuts and excited calls. I did this and again I had total silence for 30 minutes, with the exception of five yelps from the old hen every 10 minutes. No gobbles were heard.

Then he joined the group and made one gobble. I called again but there was silence. From this point on, about every 10 minutes the hen let out five yelps, but no other sounds were made by any of the turkeys in the group – not the jakes, not the hens, not the gobbler. I made no other calls and sat quietly. The hen yelps came by fives every 10 minutes for another half, hour and I answered her with five identical yelps each time she called.

Finally, all went silent. I could hear the flock walking away from me. I thought I had lost the day. As I watched and listened, the hen led the group in a large circle left and above me and then came on a slant, right at me. I was sitting facing them with my shotgun on my knee and tucked the gun into my shoulder in an aiming position.

As the birds came within several yards, I could see the jakes bringing up the rear. Except for one bird. Behind them I could see a magnificent gobbler. At 18 yards, he stopped, stretched his neck and I dropped him with one shot. I ran to him to make sure that he was not getting up, but the clean head shot had done the job. It was only when I picked him up to admire and show my respect to him that I noticed his extremely large spurs for a northern bird. He weighed 19-1/2 pounds, sported a 10-1/2 inch beard and had spurs of 1-11/16 inch and 1-9/16 inch, making him the third largest set of spurs recorded on a New York State gobbler.

It all depends on how you look at it. **Silent gobblers come in many forms, and no matter in which state you live, you can take solace in the fact that you are not alone with this problem.** The fact is, during the 1997 spring gobbler season, several states actually increased the length of their spring gobbler seasons because of this massive problem.

I hunt an area in my home state of Pennsylvania that in essence has been a silent gobbler area for well over five years due to hunting pressure, pre-season calling and the maturing of many smart gobblers.

How do you prepare to counter the silent gobbler problem?

First, if you can scout your area during the months of March and April, you can **locate a number of gobblers**, depending on weather conditions that can delay their normal breeding cycle. **Finding several gobblers simply gives you more opportunities.**

Second, as you **scout it is important to be in the general area that you plan to hunt prior to dawn, that you carry a topographical map to chart the exact location of the gobblers you hear.** This is important and will be of more importance in years to come. I have maps in a folder and use them in spring and fall as starting points for the upcoming season.

Look for turkey droppings which look like corn curls. These will be male droppings. Hen dropping look like cow patties or a tubular dropping curling over itself. This will be more information to add to your notes or topographical map – where you saw the male droppings. Gobblers have black tipped feathers and hens have brown tipped feathers. Finally, mature gobblers have a three-inch center toe; mature hens normally have two-inch toes. This is important information that you should add to your journal. Note where you found all turkey sign. **Good scouting will have you well prepared to handle silent gobblers.**

When your opening day arrives, or any other day during the season, with good scouting information, you will need to believe not only in yourself, but in the fact that, yes, there are mature gobblers in the area you hunt, and even if they do not gobble you can kill one.

How do you hunt a silent gobbler?

During a recent spring gobbler season, I had located more than eight mature gobblers in pre-season scouting. For 11 straight mornings, I arrived before dawn, generally set up in the area of the mountain that they were previously located, and made a loud fly down cackle at dawn. Then I shut up. For 11 days, no gobbling sound was made from dawn to noon, the hour at which I had to be out of the woods. On the twelfth day a gobbler made one gobble and went silent. I made no more calls and sat quietly, looking in the direction that I heard that one gobble. It took an hour and a half for that gobbler to quietly approach me. My guest shot it. To my surprise, it was a young gobbler. What made him so tough? I honestly don't know, except for the area and the previously described pressures.

This past spring, I walked into an area and not one, but five, gobblers gobbled at dawn in five locations. Two were on my side of the little valley and three were on the other side of the ridge across a small stream that had been dammed up by beavers. This was mid-season. I chose to move down and across the small valley and placed myself and two friends above the area where we heard the three gobblers. My plan was to place ourselves in a position where we possibly could call in two mature gobblers together. It took only about 20 minutes for us to be in position. We made no calls, listened and expected to hear any one of these gobblers. From dawn until 8 o'clock not one turkey sound was heard, although we did see a couple of hens. I felt comfortable in our position.

At eight o'clock, one of the gobblers on the other side let out one lone gobble. From past experience, I would have quickly moved down the ridge to the right or left of that gobbler and set him up for the kill. The fact that I had been in this position in the past dictated to me that I should respond with a single loud series of yelps and sit and wait. **The key to this and other similar situations — no matter the terrain — is to, above all, do very little calling, stay put and maintain lots of patience.**

One hour and 10 minutes later, a gobbler peeked out from under a hemlock tree in a small drain about 75 yards to my left and on my level on the ridge, looked straight at my single hen decoy and went into a full strut. He drummed and spun around but never made a gobble or any other sound. I watched him move directly to the hen. With my shotgun on my lap, I waited for an opportunity to bring the shotgun to my shoulder. Finally, after what seemed like several minutes, he disappeared behind a tree and up came my shotgun.

I settled in comfortably, knowing that if he came over the rise to the hen decoy, I could take him. This was the moment of truth that we all hunt the wild gobbler for. In time — this always is shorter than it seems — he stepped out from behind a large tree, went into a full strut and drummed his way to the decoy. (Sometimes it sounds more like an interrupted hum with hollow bursts of air and spitting.) He stopped, raised his head a little and I shot him at about 20 steps.

My two companions, both under 25 years of age, made it clear that they "would have been out of here an hour ago". Since I am about twice their age, I guess I have more patience, and **patience is what it takes if you are to be successful on silent gobblers.**

You do not have to be a great turkey caller or great turkey hunter to be a successful silent gobbler hunter. What you need to learn is when not to call, when to call, and that not calling can be more important than calling; where to sit (experience and woodsmanship) and above all, patience. In any turkey hunting situation, less calling and lots of patience will always win over more gobblers than too much calling and too little patience. In effect, most of the time you do what they do – make maybe one turkey sound to let them know you're there, then play it cool and silent.

Above all, turkey hunting can be a dangerous sport, and you must always place your safety above everything else. If you hear movement, do not be afraid to look to see what it is, even if you lose that gobbler. Know what it is. This one move could save your life. If you hear bluejays squawking, understand that something is moving in their area, and that "something" could be another turkey hunter trying to sneak up on your gobbler. Do not try to sneak up on a turkey, as 95 percent of the time those turkey sounds will be from hen turkeys. Gobblers gobble and make few other vocal sounds unless they are in a strut and you can hear them drumming.

Turkey hunting is a fascinating and most enjoyable sport. It is not a competition between you and other hunters. It is a hunt between you and one of the smartest and wisest of all of God's creatures. It should be conducted with all the respect due this magnificent bird.

> **S**ometimes you just have to be creative. If it works, it's not odd.

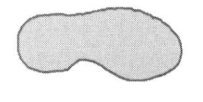

by Greg Abbas

Outsmarting Gobblers With Your Hunting Instincts

Nothing is more enjoyable to me than an old "classic" turkey hunt, the type of hunt you picture in your mind lying in bed the night before your hunt......

You are set up 80 yards from the roost at first light, just as the gobbler starts to wake the woods with his thundering gobbles. You are so excited that your leg trembles as you give your first tree yelps on your slate call. Twenty minutes go by before the mighty gobbler hits the ground and answers your call. You're giving excited cutts and yelps, and the gobbler answers with gobbles and double gobbles as he slowly approaches. When he reaches forty yards, you fear he will see the steam of your breath or hear your heartbeat. He closes on your decoy, dancing his dance and strutting his stuff. As he reaches twenty yards, you give a single cluck to bring him out of strut and expose his neck for the shot. You begin to squeeze the trigger...

RRRRRING!....the alarm goes off and you're wide awake. This dream doesn't always come true.

So what do you do when you've given your best calls and the gobbler ignores everything you do and runs off with his hens? Go home for some much needed sleep? No way! You need to reverse the situation, put it back in your favor, by using your natural hunting instincts as you would if you had to survive in the wilderness.

Being a turkey hunting guide has helped me come up with some of my own successful hunting tactics by using my instincts and observing wild turkey behavior. **Some of these tactics include ambush, drives, stalking, imitating the sounds of a flock of turkeys, and using the cautious nature of the wild turkey to my benefit.**

When all else has failed and I have nothing to lose, I drive turkeys. Have you ever heard of a turkey drive? Do you not drive other game? Why not turkeys?

This idea came while on a hunt with a client. We were hunting a smart trophy class gobbler which had lived its whole life on state land. If that doesn't educate a bird in a hurry, nothing does. As I called, the gobbler would answer with double gobbles but would not come in. This went on for about an hour. I then tried other tactics that have worked in the past, such as purring, and scratching the ground to make the gobbler think the hen was too busy feeding to come in. When that didn't work, I changed calling location, thinking maybe there was an obstacle in the gobbler's way. As I started calling with another type of call to sound like a different turkey, he double and triple gobbled, but still would not come any closer. This time I got up and walked in the opposite direction and pulled out a diaphragm call and a push-button call. I used them simultaneously to sound like two hens leaving the gobbler's territory. This usually gets them. What gobbler could resist the thought of strutting around with a "chick" under each wing? As I called, he let loose a mighty gobble, but then I also heard no less than two real hens firing up next to him. No wonder he wouldn't move. Now I really had to dig down and think hard. What could I do that the previous hundred hunters didn't do? Driving! Driving? Why not?

To have an effective turkey drive, it is important to try to use a natural barrier, such as a river, swamp or narrow woods, to pin the birds in on one side. So... Knowing that the turkeys probably would not cross the river they were following, I decided to try a one man turkey drive using the river as a barrier. I positioned my hunter thirty yards from the river and out of sight from the turkeys. I then put on a fluorescent orange hat for safety reasons and walked a big loop around the birds. Once in position, I showed myself to the birds, which were about 70 yards away. They quickly turned and hurried back the way they came, which I now find to be common on drives. I stayed 80 yards off the river and 80 to 100 yards behind the birds. If I had been on the river, they could have slipped between me and my hunter. If I would have run toward them, they would have taken to flight. I just walked slowly, and they moved in the direction I wanted them to move.

As they approached to within 80 yards of the hunter, I stopped and waited for the shot I hoped would come. It came, along with a lot of whooping and hollering. From that point on, this has been a deadly tactic.

Ambushing game has been around since the beginning of time,

yet you hardly hear of this highly successful method in turkey hunting. To use it to its fullest potential, it helps to have the bird's daily routine patterned. Turkeys are birds of habit, if undisturbed. They will pretty much follow the same routine day after day. To do this, I like to find a backwoods road that the turkeys are traveling. Once I find their tracks in the sand, I'll come back in the evening and brush them out. I'll return at 10 a.m. the next morning. If there are fresh tracks, I'll wipe them out again and come back at 8 a.m. the following morning. If there are no tracks at that time, I can assume the birds are coming through between sun-up and 8 a.m. I set up my ambush accordingly.

You also can ambush/stalk turkeys in more open areas such as farm fields, or open woods, by using terrain to your advantage. Ditches, river cuts and hills can hide your movements, allowing you to position yourself in front of the oncoming birds. Using the lay of the land and getting out in front of the birds are always keys to success on any turkey hunt.

One particular hunt comes to mind. A client and I had worked a gobbler who was with two hens for about an hour. The gobbler wasn't about to leave his hens for a turkey sound he heard in the woods. Therefore, I called out to the hens. I gave aggressive cutts trying to get one of the hens to challenge me. In the past, I've gotten them to come in, with the gobbler in tow, by using this method. Not this time. They just kept feeding slowly to the west. I did notice that they were moving toward a small creek that ran through the field. I figured if we got down on our hands and knees and crawled into a position in front of them, we would have a better than average chance of getting that gobbler. As we crawled into position, getting our gloves and pants soaked, I carefully peeked over the crest. The birds were only fifty yards away, coming straight at us. As they reached twenty yards, the shot rang out, the gobbler dropped, and high fives were in order.

Ridge runners, as I call them, are no exception. Ridge runners are birds that roost on ridge tops. They are fairly predictable in that when they fly down from the roost, they will run the ridge top for a while before going on with their daily routine.

The key here is to determine which way they go when they fly off the roost. Once this is determined, I like to set up eighty yards from the roost in the direction they want to travel. This can sometimes result in a short hunt. Again, we are using the hillside as a natural barrier. Turkeys do not like to go downhill. We are setting up in the direction they want to travel. If they circle you, they can do

Outsmarting Gobblers

it only in one direction, which is not a problem if you are positioned to swing your gun correctly.

Most of the time with the above mentioned tactics, I can harvest a ridge runner, but sometimes they humble me with a curveball. Such was the case on one of my own hunts. My father came along as my cameraman, trying to get the bowhunt on tape. The morning started off like most others, with the birds gobbling at the crack of dawn, sending chills down my spine. No matter how many hunts I go on, that sound never gets old.

I tree yelped to let the gobbler know that I was there. He responded with many gobbles. I figured we would have action as soon as the gobbler hit the ground. Well, this gobbler had six hens with him, and the hens didn't care to share their man with any more hens. They took off in the opposite direction.

The next morning found us set up on the other side of the roost. I decided not to do any calling and just let them come by. What do you think they did? Right! They went the other way. No wonder I'm losing my hair.

I had only one more day to hunt. I could have put my father on the other side of the roost and at the very least have had him drive the birds my way. I still wanted the hunt filmed, however. What we really needed was a third person, which we didn't have. My brother was supposed to be there, but he made a scheduling error and could not be there. I said, "Freddy is a dummy." My father said, "That's it. We'll use a dummy". We made a scarecrow, named it Freddy, and put it out that night on the far side of the roost.

As the birds woke up and gobbled, I gave a few tree yelps and fell silent. When it became fly down time, the birds went in the opposite direction again, only this time Freddy was there to greet them. I could just hear that gobbler as he saw Freddy...."What the hell...?"

The gobbler didn't want any part of Freddy, and he followed his tracks back to me. I drew my bow as he went behind a tree and released when he came out. The arrow flew 20 yards, found its mark, and the bird ran 20 yards.

Had it not been for some unusual tactics, this bird would still be out there.

There are few things more satisfying than seeing your own plans work, unconventional or not. I still prefer the "classic" turkey hunt when it presents itself, but for the times it doesn't, it's rewarding to be creative and use your hunting instincts and hunting skills to outsmart one of the most elusive creatures on this earth...the wild turkey.

TURKEY DRIVE ON RIVER

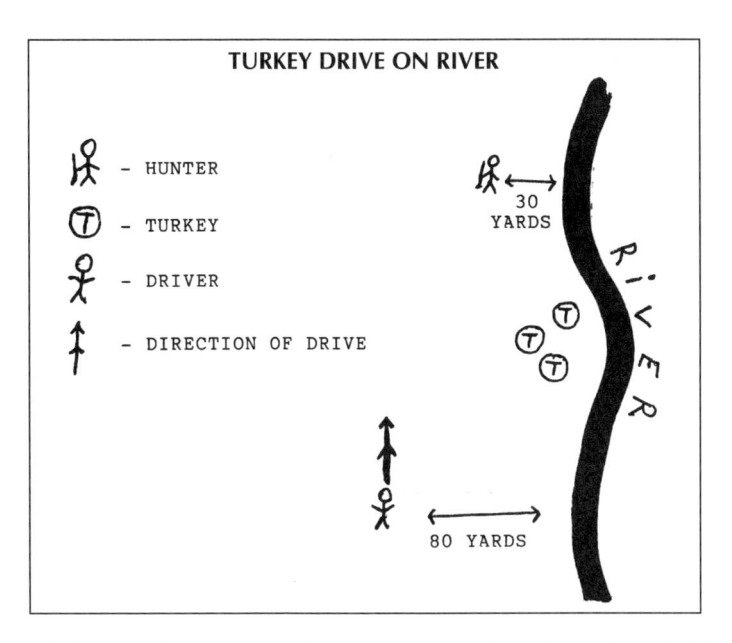

- 👤 – HUNTER
- Ⓣ – TURKEY
- 👤 – DRIVER
- ↑ – DIRECTION OF DRIVE

↔ 30 YARDS

RIVER

↔ 80 YARDS

TURKEY DRIVE IN NARROW WOODS

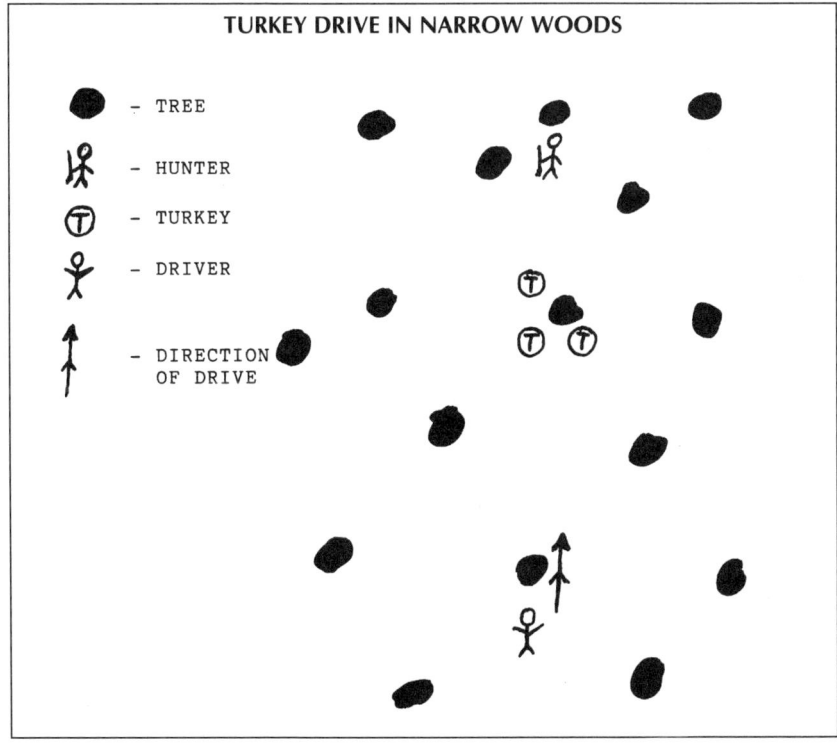

- ● – TREE
- 👤 – HUNTER
- Ⓣ – TURKEY
- 👤 – DRIVER
- ↑ – DIRECTION OF DRIVE

Outsmarting Gobblers 173

BUDDY SYSTEM

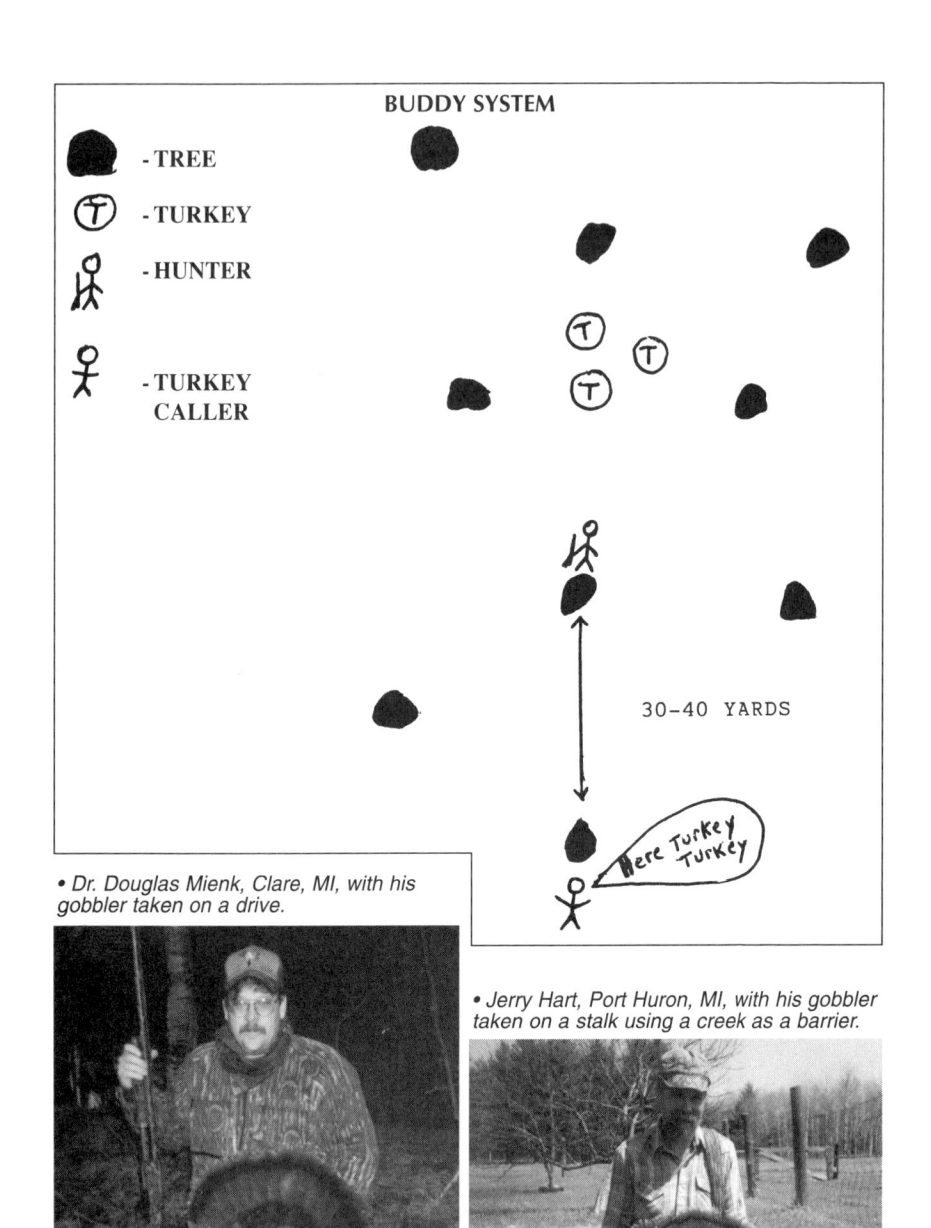

- 🌳 — TREE
- Ⓣ — TURKEY
- 🧍 — HUNTER
- 🧍 — TURKEY CALLER

30–40 YARDS

"Here Turkey Turkey"

• Dr. Douglas Mienk, Clare, MI, with his gobbler taken on a drive.

• Jerry Hart, Port Huron, MI, with his gobbler taken on a stalk using a creek as a barrier.

> **M**idwestern hunters may be living right in the middle of some of the best turkey hunting to be found.

by Steve Puppe

Hunting Midwestern Gobblers

Some of the greatest opportunities to be found for turkey hunting are in the Midwest, in states such as Wisconsin, Minnesota, Illinois and Iowa. I've hunted turkey across the country for the past 15 years, and that's my conclusion. The only problem is that you need to draw a tag to hunt. Missouri, Nebraska and South Dakota also offer great opportunities, and they offer over-the-counter licenses, except for the prairie units of South Dakota, which are draw. If you plan to travel to any of these states, preplanning and doing your homework will increase your odds for success. Even if you are a resident, doing some simple homework also will increase your percentages for drawing a tag.

Nebraska probably would be my first choice for the number of birds and the ease of harvesting a bird. Nebraska has a variety of wild turkey sub-species, with Merriams and Eastern and some hybrids. North Central near the Niobrara River offers some of the finest Merriams to be found. The better part of Nebraska is prairie, so when you find trees you probably will find turkeys. Most of the land is privately owned, and the landowners seem to be receptive to turkey hunters. If you can obtain permission on a ranch with cattle, look out, because you could be in for some real excitement. The first time I hunted in Nebraska, I was fortunate to find this situation. The first morning of my hunt, I probably heard 200 to 250 gobblers gobbling. It was incredible.

Northwestern Illinois along the Mississippi River would probably be my second choice. Illinois is a state in which you need to draw a tag. This state offers a challenging Eastern gobbler. These turkeys, like most Easterns, can be tough to call and are wary.

East Central Iowa and up the Mississippi toward the Minnesota border has some of Iowa's finest gobblers. This happens to be my home state now and has been most memorable. The better part of my experiences in the Hawkeye State have taken place in the northeastern corner where the numbers of birds seem to increase each year. The first time I had an opportunity to spend a day in the woods of northern Iowa, my buddy told me the night before that where we were going in the morning there would be turkeys everywhere in the valley. I thought "yeah, right."

As the sun brightened the eastern skyline, gobblers began to sound off one after another after another. I couldn't believe my ears. At that time, this was the most gobblers I had ever heard in any given location.

Now it is a tough choice whether we should head north or south. As far as obtaining a license is concerned, we probably should head south to the Show-Me state of Missouri. Licenses may be purchased over the counter and the entire state carries a good population of turkeys. Missouri also has most state-owned land tracts which hold good turkey populations. The flip side is that it also has a good number of turkey hunters. I have spent plenty of time in Missouri, north and south, and I would probably choose the northeast corner over the rest. Not only because of the number of birds, but because of their size. I harvested my personal best, a $26^1/_2$ pound bird, here.

I have seen several birds checked in that top the scales at or near the 30-pound mark. Not only in Missouri have I seen this, but also in Iowa, Illinois and Wisconsin. Thirty pounds is enormous.

Your best bet in Missouri is to find private land, mainly because of the pressure that the birds receive on public land. Wisconsin, in my opinion, has done the best job yet in its turkey restoration. For a northern state, it also has some of the most suitable habitats. Like everything "Cheeseheads" do, they give it 150%, no matter whether that's as football fans or as hunters. Every year it seems that Wisconsin gives out more tags in their lottery than the year before. In most areas of Wisconsin the birds have taken hold so well that obtaining permission from landowners is easy. My favorite area to hunt is the southwestern part of the state. Not only does this area hold good populations of birds, but it has some beautiful scenery. Along with the scenery comes other challenges. The bluffs near the Mississippi can test your endurance, so I would recommend that you be in good physical condition.

I grew up in Minnesota near Red Wing, and this is where it all began for this lifelong turkey hunter. My first gobbler was a Minnesota bird. It was the early 1980s, which may not seem that long ago time-wise, but experience-wise it is a different story, for in the years since I have spent as much time as possible, traveling to as many states as possible each year, after this wily bird.

I got the fever long before I had a tag. Between the time of the fever's onset and the arrival of a tag, time almost stands still, especially for an eager kid. That great day finally arrived ... I finally received my first turkey tag. Tags were a lot scarcer then than now; I look back and know how fortunate I was. This was the very first time I could even apply for a license because of my age, but I had the luck this time and this tag became an important part of my life. This dream of hunting turkeys become reality, it also became a love which has let me turn a hobby into a career.

I spent every available minute scouting; I learned everything I possibly could about the land I was going to hunt. I read every magazine article published about turkey hunting and even decided that I really should get serious about my turkey calling. I had purchased the first of many turkey calls several years before receiving this tag, but had never practiced as much as I was about to. Scouting is most important; if you can't find them, you can't call them.

My tag was for the first season that year, beginning in the middle of April. Three days before the season we had a late snow storm which left not just a blanket but a whole lot of snow. Ten inches in fact, but at that time of year the snow seems to melt rapidly.

Opening day arrived. Without a wink of sleep the night before, simply from excitement, I drove to the farm I had become so familiar with over the past month. As I headed across a field toward the woods where most of the turkeys spent most of their time, I eagerly listened to hear a gobble. Nothing! Finally I heard a gobble, but it was across the river from the farm I was on. It would take me at least 45 minutes to an hour to drive to that farm, on which I also had permission to hunt. The first day ended with no turkey encounters. The second and third days were the same; the turkeys always were on the other side of the river from where I chose to start my morning.

The fourth morning things began to change. I finally had turkeys on the land I had chosen to hunt. This early season the birds were still in flocks, and they just didn't want to respond to my call. At that time, I probably didn't even sound much like a turkey anyway. Patience and persistence paid off. I stayed with the turkeys all morning. As they went through their morning ritual, I tried to keep as close as possible. About 9:30, things started to happen. Turkeys had surrounded me but I still could not get that shot. Two large toms were fighting within 15 yards of my gun barrel, but they seemed always to be too close together. I could not squeeze the trigger for fear of downing two birds.

They finally disappeared, but just as suddenly one reappeared behind me. I eased around, raised my 12 gauge, and the boom silenced all the other sounds of spring as I harvested my first gobbler. He tipped the scales at 21 pounds and had a ten-inch beard. This bird had tags on a leg and a wing. Checking with the DNR, I found out that the gobbler was three years old and was one of the original transplanted birds in the area.

Since the early 1980's, things have really changed in southeastern Minnesota. Turkeys have adapted well, just like most everywhere. The turkey range is expanding, but the southeastern portion of the state from just north of Red Wing to the Iowa border boasts the best population and would be your best bet for success.

The Black Hills of South Dakota became my next target. At that time a nonresident license was twelve dollars; it has since gone up quite a bit. The Black Hills offer some of the most beautiful scenery and excitement of all the Midwestern states. The Merriam birds here are vocal and generally respond well to the call. A good portion of land is open to public hunting, and you may choose to travel the Hills differently from what most turkey hunting trips allow. Some outfitters in this area offer horseback hunts which can be fun, or you may even choose to travel the trails on a mountain bike.

Over the past four to five years, however, the turkey population has been declining because of severe winters. As noted earlier, the prairie units, with tags available on a drawing basis, hold good numbers of bird.

I prefer to hunt some of the later seasons in the northern states. I find that I would rather hunt birds that other hunters have harassed than try to pull them away from hens. That's something to keep in mind when you plan your hunt, but vacation time availability may decide for you. Always check with the state before you apply to see where your best odds are to draw a tag. Each state can tell you the permits available and the number of applicants for each zone and time period from the previous seasons.

Before you travel to another state, I would recommend that you send for topographical maps of the areas you plan to scout or hunt. If you have the opportunity to travel to your hunting ground before opening day, learn as much as possible about the land....where the fences are, logging roads, and any obstacles to turkey movement. Scouting is the most important part of any hunting; other articles in this book have good scouting details, so there's no sense repeating them here. Good luck and keep them gobbling.

The author calling on an Iowa hunt.

STEVE PUPPE

Steve Puppe, who grew up along the Mississippi River in southern Minnesota, has racked up 32 turkey calling contest wins, including seven straight Minnesota state calling championships 1990-1996. He has hunted turkeys since 1983; tagged his first deer when he was 12, and spent his free time during high school trapping and hunting. He is the director of the H. S. Strut Pro Staff.

- Jakes (immature males) are social and vocal. They like to travel in groups. Their calls are higher pitched. They are highly huntable. Photo by Bob Lollo.

- Campsites don't get much better than this, and the camaraderie of camp life is an important part of any hunt. Photo by Glenn Helgeland.

SECTION V:

OF
BEAR
&
ELK

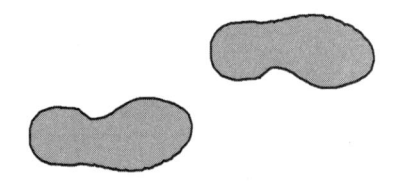

• Upper left. Where it is allowed, and if you have one, an ATV can be your best friend in transporting an elk. Here the author hauls an entire bull elk, including cape and antlers, back to camp.

• Above and left. A young, successful hunter with his first elk ... and 400 pounds of meat to take care of. The first of five trips with a loaded pack frame. Elk hunting is more work after the kill is made, but having the proper equipment and being prepared physically and mentally makes it much easier.

> **E**lk hunting is WORK. The sooner you realize that and prepare for it, the better your chances of success.

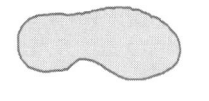

by Jay Verzuh

Elk Hunting Tips for Flatlanders

I killed my first elk when I was 14. I was excited and proud, but not overly so. It was a way of life for my family. My father killed an elk every year and had done so since he had returned from the service in 1944. He made a living guiding big game hunters and trapping, and he started my outdoor training early. So, when I was old enough to buy a license and killed that elk, it was no surprise. It was expected.

Many hunts have passed since that snowy day, and I have taken many elk, each a greater pleasure/reward than the previous. Recently I have taken to wondering why. Is it because as I grow older I have come to realize we only have a finite number of hunts, and as each comes to a close another chapter ends?

Elk are truly a magnificent animal to hunt. The country they live in, their regal manner, the haunting ability seemingly to appear and disappear like ghosts, and last and most spine-tingling, their vocalization. Bugling, squealing, grunting and sometimes roaring like an African lion, the rutting bull elk is exciting to hunt. It is an experience that every American sportsman dreams of — a dream hunt that can be exactly what you have dreamed of for years, or your worst nightmare.

EXPECTATIONS

I truly believe that the recent explosion in the hunting and outdoor video market is one of the hunter's best tools to get a feeling for the country and the animals he is going to hunt. Today, a hunter living in the Midwest who has never been west can actually watch and listen to bull elk bugling and squealing and chasing cows. He can hear the sounds a cow elk makes as she calls to her calf. All of this is valuable knowledge that can be put to use when hunting elk.

At the same time, these videos often are detrimental, as they develop a very "Hollywood" image of the hunt. I know. I have been involved in video production for both sales and television. We recently did an elk hunt for ESPN, a wonderful show with excellent elk footage, scenery and bugling, climaxing with the celebrity hunter killing a bull elk with an arrow. We had tips on hunting, calling and shooting the bow. Nevertheless, the real 'guts' of the show was calling in the bull and killing it. That is what sells and what a television audience wants to watch. Same reason they like to see car crashes and shoot-em-ups, I suppose; doesn't matter whether you're a hunter or not, only the action varies. The message the television audience received was "Go hunt elk with Jay Verzuh. He will call in bull after bull, and on about the third day you get a shot. It is perfect, and you ride off into the sunset."

It was a great hunt, but so was the one the year before when we saw lots of elk but never got one killed. Twenty rolls of video; no show. The 30-minute television show really was a combination of film from two hunts a year apart. What ended up on the editing room floor was footage of five different bulls being worked without getting a shot. Wind changes, bulls never presenting an open shot, and bulls too smart to come that last 30 yards – that's the real world, real excitement, REAL ELK HUNTING.

Plan to go west on a hunting trip, be prepared to kill an elk, go with the full intention of killing an elk, be disappointed if you do not kill an elk, but enjoy the trip for what it is – a HUNTING trip.

PLANNING YOUR HUNT

A successful hunting trip always begins with planning. Start researching at least a year in advance. First, contact state agencies for all licensing data and all hunting and camping regulations. It is important this be completed early enough to give you a chance to research all areas and get any necessary applications for special licenses. Some state agencies also will have statistics from previous years' harvests and game counts available, but you must request them. Often a fee is required.

There are four types of elk hunting trips available in most western states. You can choose from:
1) Outfitted hunt
2) Drop camp
3) Trespass fee hunt
4) Do-it-yourself hunt

The outfitted hunt offers the highest success rate of all the hunts and also the advantage of less time required. All your time is spent hunting. The outfitter takes care of all the work of the camp and caring for the meat, cape and antlers. The disadvantage is the cost. A successful outfitter has to pay all his expenses plus make a profit; it's a business, not a hobby.

Drop camps are offered for a lesser fee and provide a campsite in place with all the necessary equipment. These will vary from cabins to tents. You provide your own food, do your own cooking and camp chores, and pack and care for your own meat. These can be on private or on government ground.

Trespass fee hunts are on private property and all you are paying for is the right to hunt on this property. You provide all camp equipment and hunt on your own, again packing and caring for your meat, etc.

The do-it-yourself hunt is just that. You do it all yourself. This is the most difficult and by far the most work, but at the same time can be the most rewarding. A caution here – and often a caution also for the drop and trespass hunt – you are going to be hunting a 600 to 900 pound animal. You must be prepared to get this animal out of the mountains when you kill it. This is where the real work begins. Horses, back packs and ATVs – or a frying pan and salt – you must have some way to transport the meat to camp. Over the years, I have been confronted by several successful hunters and asked to get their meat out for them. They had killed an animal in a place where they had no idea, or equipment, to get it out. I'm sure some of it rotted in the woods, a waste and a violation of the law.

The do-it-yourself hunt often is most attractive because it is lowest cost. If you go this route, be prepared to invest several year's worth of elk hunting time to learn the ropes. Videos help, but nothing beats experience. On public land, there may be dozens of other hunters after the same elk you're hunting. There's not a bull elk on every mountainside.

PREPARE YOURSELF

Elk hunting is work. I have hunted from Alaska to Alabama, and elk hunting is as physically demanding as any type of hunting I have experienced. Plan for this. Nothing can totally prepare you for the physical exertion at the elevation that you will be hunting, but you can ease the pain. Get in the best physical shape possible. Run, walk, swim, work out at the gym – anything physical to work your muscles, lungs, ligaments, tendons, etc. I tell my clients to put 25 pounds in their day pack, put on their hunting boots, and go climb the stairs at the local sports stadium. Climb them many times.

The previously mentioned videos are also a good method of preparation in that one can learn a great deal about the animal behavior and some of the hunting techniques.

Your hunting tool of choice, be it a bow or rifle, should be one that you are very familiar with and comfortable with. You must know your capabilities and what your hunting tool is capable of. Practice often prior to your hunt, and do so with hunting clothes. Shoot from unusual positions and at odd angles. Far too many people come on their dream hunt and miss a shot that they should not. Some with a bow and some with a rifle. Too many rifle hunters have no idea where their rifle will hit at 325 yards, but will not hesitate to shoot at an elk at that distance. Elk hunters should practice at distances that they would shoot at an elk. Purchase one of the new laser range finders to use when practicing and when hunting. They are an invaluable aid for both bowhunters and rifle hunters.

Elk hunting is work. You MUST realize that. That will help you become mentally fit as well as physically fit. If your body can't handle it, your spirit wears down too. Neither come back very fast.

EQUIPMENT

Over the years of hunting elk, I have found the following to be indispensable:

- Quality optics, including top-of-the-line roof prism binoculars. Spend the money. It is a lifetime investment. Poor optics give you headaches. As for rifle scopes, my Dad said it all: "You can't shoot any better than you can see."
- Quality footwear. Again, you get what you pay for. It is hard to cover ground and hunt elk successfully when your feet hurt.
- Day pack with laser range finder and survival gear, including space blanket, flashlight, compass, fire starter, knife and steel, multi-purpose tool, canteen, first aid kit, 50 feet of nylon rope, spare calls and a small saw.
- Game bags big enough for a quarter of an elk and made of good quality cotton.
- Alaskan freighter pack frame.

Many items can be added to this list, depending upon whether you are bowhunting in the early season, hunting in cold weather, or hunting in wet weather and/or snow, but these are the ones I am never without.

KEYS TO SUCCESS

Each of the previous sections deserves to have a book or books written on the subject (and all have), rather than a few paragraphs, but remember this is just an elk hunting primer, just the beginning. It is intended to open your eyes, get you pointed in the right direction. Where you go from here is up to you. If I have just impressed upon you the importance of realistic expectations, planning and preparation, you can and will uncover all of the little details each area contains.

I say it again: Elk hunting is WORK.

The key? Remember, above all else, what you have learned from all your previous hunting experiences. An elk is a wild animal, and it will act accordingly. Use your whitetail knowledge, watch for natural funnels, heavy cover where they might bed, watch the wind, etc. With one big difference – whitetail can be anywhere, so you hunt accordingly, but with elk you first must find them, then you can hunt them. Many more acres...really rugged terrain...higher altitudes and thinner air...much more searching – important factors above and beyond hunting basics.

Do your homework, use previous knowledge and experience, and don't forget your camera.

• The author with one of his most recent elk, a magnificent 6x6 bull weighing more than 900 pounds, the fourth largest ever taken in Colorado with bow and arrow.

JAY VERZUH

Jay Verzuh is the owner/operator of Colorado Elite, an outfitting business, and an outdoor writer. He is a bowhunting advisor and columnist for *North American Hunter* magazine and is one of eight bowhunters honored as "Bowhunting All Stars" by Hoyt. Jay has hunted from Alaska to Alabama and has harvested numerous record book animals.

- Measuring the width of the front pad and adding one inch can give you a close estimate of what the bear will square. Square measurement is length of hide (nose tip to tail tip) plus width (tip of right front paw to tip of left front paw), divided by two. Any black bear squaring more than seven feet ought to have a skull measurement of around 18 inches or larger.

- A boar (male) often will mark some trees around the bait site, either by clawing them or biting them, as shown above and right. This marks his territory.

> . . . speaking of a bear and a sweet roll . . .

by Vicki Cianciarulo

Black Bears - Baiting & All

*T*he black bear is a fascinating animal ... shy and elusive, bold and powerful. I respect and admire the black bear. Because black bear hunting with bow and arrow is a close encounter hunt, it can be an exciting adventure .... punctuated by long periods of nothing but droning insects that want to sting or bite you into insanity. Not many women are bear hunters, but I'm one of them. I enjoy every minute of bear hunting – actually, every minute of every part of a bear hunt.

I didn't hunt before I met and married Ralph, but I sure do now. There's no question that the outdoors is in my blood. It's a lifestyle I took to like a duck to water ... or a bear to a sweet roll.

I'd like to think I have become a student of bear hunting with bow and arrow. Now it's my turn to be a teacher and pass along as much as I can of the fun and excitement — and hard work — of black bear hunting to those of you thinking you might like to try it.

So, speaking of a bear and a sweet roll....

Before I put a bait in the woods, I study topographical maps and locate solid-ground alleys running through major waterways or swamps. These runways are sure travel routes for not only bear but all types of game. Placing a bait on such higher, dry ground also dispenses the bait scent over a much broader area, down into the swampy, wetter areas bears love. The bait site needs to be in a position that will allow you to set up a tree stand 10 to 15 yards away for bowhunting, longer for firearms hunting.

We must also realize that these bears walking through their domain know that all of a sudden a bakery shop or butcher shop doesn't just drop out of the sky and into their back yard. They know something is up. However, they are much like us, but bigger and stronger. When we find a good restaurant, an easy snack shop, whatever is simple and convenient, do we not go there often? And if we're bigger and tougher than the other bears hitting the bait, don't we think it is our bait? Yes, we do. Therefore, **proper planning and set-up is critical to assure a convenient, active bait site.**

Bait. What is the best? This is a subject that many will argue ... meat, sweets, grains, popcorn ... the list goes on. No matter what you use, add some dry or liquid nutrients to the bait to help out the critters which frequent your bait sites. I personally favor sweets mixed with oats, corn and honey. I have found that sweets are a special treat to bears, and once they know sweets are there, they WILL be back.

For every bear you see at the bait, there probably are two to five bears you don't see, but you'll still be feeding them. Bait accordingly. If the bait is cleaned up, it might be a good idea to use more bait. You don't want to disappoint any bear; it may decide to stay away. Also, when more than one bear is hitting the bait, they get competitive and sometimes show up earlier. So keep them fed. Feed them 'til they burp.

The bait site should not be so thick that the only time you see the bear is when it is at the bait. It is better to relax a bit by watching the bear circle its prey – the bait. (Or maybe you. Just kidding. Even though most likely the bear knows you're there, it is accustomed to being woods boss, so you may make it cautious, but you probably won't scare it. Circling silently is a standard defense mechanism.)

On the other hand, I've seen bears come running right in, making all types of noise, but most of the time bears will come in without a sound. **Almost all of the time they will circle the bait, checking for unfamiliar odors.** We counter this defense by using a liquid smoke scent every time we bait to help mask our human presence. (Liquid smoke scent also attracts bears, so don't get it on yourself or your boots or hunting clothes unless you want company. In fact, don't get anything on your boots, clothes or hands which might attract bears. They are a curious animal and may decide to check out the lovely odor.)

The bait needs to be positioned so bears are forced to approach it at an angle which will give you a broadside or quartering-away shot. Wait for the bear to move its near front leg forward, then put one in the boiler room.

If the bear is nervous, don't rush things. A subordinate bear may grab a piece of bait and rush out into the brush to eat it, then return for more. The longer the bear eats, usually the more comfortable it will be and the more likely you will be to get a good shot.

If no shot presents itself, wait until next time. When you spook a bear, it may not return. When it isn't spooked, it may well return tomorrow, or later the same day.

What is an 'active' bait? Many outfitters will tell you that you are guaranteed an active bait. This means that the bait has been hit. To prove this to yourself, look for bear trails coming in and out of the bait site. The trail you walk in on should be worn down, telling you that the guide has done his part by baiting it often. The ground around the bait should be worn and dug up, telling you the degree of activity. Look for bear scat; grain and oats go through a bear quickly, so you should find this in their scat.

I have always used timing devices to help me tell when the bears are coming in. Not all bears hit the bait just before dark, so timers are a must for me. I have taken many bears in the morning or earlier afternoon because they set off the timers at those times on a regular basis. **If you ask me what is one of the most important tools for bear baiting and hunting, I will tell you the timers.**

A favorite time for many bears to hit the bait is just after the bait is re-stocked. When this happens, I walk into the bait with a hunter. As I re-bait, the hunter quietly climbs into the tree. As he gets ready, I finish the re-baiting. Then I walk out, sometimes fairly noisily, noisily throw the bait pail into the back of the truck. When I get into the truck, I slam the door and make whatever other noises I can, and then I drive away.

Many times the bears are waiting within hearing distance; all this noise is like the ringing of a dinner bell, and they come running.

Taking a bath or shower with scent free soap and spraying down with some type of scent-eliminating sprays will help. Spray your clothes, not your skin. Remember that we never can eliminate our odor completely, but for best hunting results we need to do everything we can. Using a scent-absorbing garment has helped in many situations.

I carry a small bottle of smoke scent or vanilla and spray it periodically while sitting in the stand.

Tree stand comfort is another highly important part of bear hunting. Being able to sit comfortably for a long time is just as critical now as during deer hunting. You will note that tree stands and their seats are getting larger, and the seat cushions are getting thicker. We're looking for more comfort. When we're comfortable, we can sit quieter and sit longer, which means we'll have more patience, enjoy the wait more, and be far less likely to spook incoming game. An uncomfortable tree stand makes our body numb and us fidgety. Neither is good.

- Ralph Cianciarulo with a good bear. Tracking line is an asset — orange is good in daylight hours, but white is best for night following.

- Early in the season, bears will hit but not eat all the bait.

- Timers are another asset, so you'll know whether you have a morning, mid-day or late afternoon bear hitting the bait.

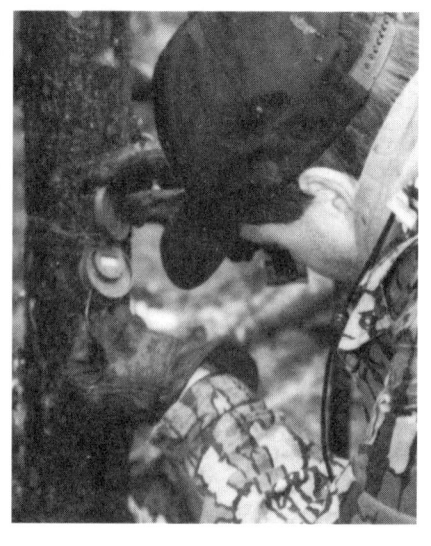

192   Steps Along the Hunter's Path

Many times you will be hunting within the pines, and you may have to do some cutting or trimming. Remember to remove any loose bark that you may brush up against, because pine bark can be noisy. The pines will leave a sticky sap, and if you lean up against any cut portion or just against a leaky area of the trunk, you will find it difficult to pull away for a shot without making a scratchy loud noise. To prevent this, I bring an old camo tee-shirt or small piece of camo fabric to the stand and cover the pine pitch area of the tree trunk.

Bugs ... bugs ... bugs. In the spring, in many bear hunting regions, you need to understand that they come with the territory and are part of the bear hunting scene. You can use repellent-impregnated suits; I've used the Bug Tamer brand with excellent results. You can put insect repellent on your skin – rub it on, don't just spray it on, and you can tape your sleeve cuffs to your gloves, your headnet to your turtleneck, and your pants cuffs to your boots. You also can wear two suits of clothes, making it more difficult for mosquitoes and black flies to get through to you. Fortunately, some parts of North America don't have much of a biting/stinging insect problem during spring bear hunting time.

I have found it hard to shoot with a headnet. So for a long time now, I have sprayed a small amount of 100% DEET at my stands every time I bait. This gets the bears acclimated to this odor, and since it is there when I'm not, it isn't an alarming odor to them. At the same time, this lets me and my hunters pull up our headnets right before the shot and not be dive-bombed by those pesky mosquitoes, black flies and no-see-ums.

As far as your equipment is concerned, it can be the same firearms or archery set-up you use for whitetails, or you might need to go a little heavier. Rifles in the .270 and larger calibers are good. Bow draw weights should be at least 55 pounds and 60 is better. The bears I have taken have been with less than 57 pounds. The bow I use now is set for 57 pounds at 27 inches of draw, shooting carbon arrows with three-blade 100-grain broadheads.

I have used a tracking string for most of my bears. Mounting this even with the arrow or above it will assure proper arrow flight. Especially in the spring, I use this, for the bears have a thick winter hide coming out of the den, which often will hold the blood and prevent a good blood trail.. I use a fiber-optic pin sight. This allows me to see my pins in low light conditions with no problem. The size of the bead is important. In today's market, there are too many sights with fiber-optic pins which are too big; they actually obscure the point at which you're aiming.

Bear hunting is a close encounter hunt. Make sure your equipment is noise free. When you draw your bow and the arrow makes a noise going past the rest, or the limb bases or something squeaks, those noises probably will be louder to the bear than to you. Those noises can and will spook a bear.

Judging bears is difficult, extremely difficult. There has been much written about this and many experts telling you how to judge them. The very best way is to watch and look at as many bears as possible. Young bears will come into a bait site with a cocky, bouncing gate. They will remind you of teenage kids walking through the mall. Many of their actions will not be as deliberate as those of a big bear. When a lesser bear comes in to the bait, many times it will take a piece of bait and run off, then return and do the same thing. This is telling you there is a more dominant bear in the area. Remember, this does not mean it is a bigger bear all the time, only a more dominant one.

I know you have heard this before: "If the ears look big, it is a small bear" … or "If there is not much light underneath the belly, shoot it." These are decent rules of thumb, but if you have not seen bears in the wild how can you judge? I recommend watching videos and going to the zoo or parks that have black bears. Watch them and learn to see these features before attempting to judge by any format. I have taken a few bears that would make Pope & Young which had big ears and some big flat-bellied bears that had a lot of light underneath them.

One of the best ways to judge a bear is to have a 55-gallon drum at your bait site. When the bear comes in and its back is even with or above the barrel, don't hesitate. That's a keeper. If you are using a five-gallon bucket and the bear's head fits into it with no problem, this is a young or small bear. Another thing you can do is to make a mark on the tree about hip height – your hip, not the bear's. Using an ax, I make a mark in a nearby tree and if the bear comes in and its back line is above the mark, I shoot it.

Bear activity at the bait can tell you many things. The size of the scat can tell you if it is a big bear, because that's one thing that is relative. Big bears make big piles of large-diameter scat. Scratch marks and bite marks on a nearby tree will signify a boar's presence. Look around to see if there are any small claw marks climbing up the trees or any abundance of small piles of scat, telling you of a sow with cubs.

So you're on stand, nice and relaxed, and suddenly you notice it is quiet. Too quiet. There's not a sound anywhere. Not even the birds are chirping. Uh oh, you tell yourself. Something's going on. I believe I'll commemorate this moment by having a heart attack. Then there's a silent, furry blob in the brush, and the next instant ... the next INSTANT ... there it is, approaching the bait. How tight can your mainspring wind? You'll find out. Enjoy the show; if the bear doesn't present a shot, you'll probably be treated to several minutes of close-up viewing of a black bear being a black bear. You'll hear it snuffing and snorting. You'll see it scooping out bait or reaching in and yanking out a chunk with its teeth.

And maybe you'll also be able to draw your bow and aim carefully....

Black bear hunting can be as rewarding as you make it. Don't just go to shoot a bear; go to learn and see bear.

VICKI CIANCIARULO

Vicki Cianciarulo is an experienced bowhunter and videographer. She has taken several black bear, three of which exceed Pope & Young Club record book minimum score, plus wild turkey, wild boar, javelina, whitetail deer (her 1997 buck greened 156-1/8), plus seven species of African game. She has taken an active role in getting more women and youth into the sport of archery and bowhunting. Vicki is on the field staffs of Hoyt USA, Beman USA, New Archery Products, Bowhunters Discount Warehouse, Fine-Line Inc., Loc-On Treestands, Trebark, Scent Shield and Spence's Targets.

• *Estimating bear sizes accurately is difficult. As a result, black bears are extremely susceptible to ground shrinkage – they are much smaller after they're shot than before they're shot. But just to give you an idea of how enormous they can be, this U.S. dollar bill helps put things in perspective. The bear field dressed at just over 350 pounds; it's skull measured 20-9/16. Glenn Helgeland photo.*

SECTION VI:

THE ROAD AHEAD

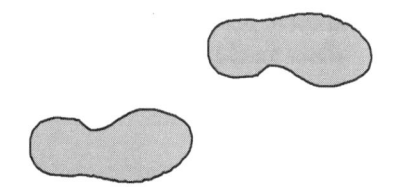

• Above, giraffe and zebra at the waterhole. Right, the blue wildebeest in perfect shot angle, and with all eyes directed elsewhere. Almost tailor-made.

198　　　　　　　　　　　　　　　　　　　　Steps Along the Hunter's Path

> The rush of being where you never know what species can come in is a thrill in itself.

by Ralph Cianciarulo

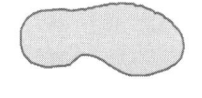

Affordable Adventure/ Affordable Safari

I looked at my watch. The time was 11:35 a.m. I had arrived in the blind at 7:30 a.m. and since then here is what had come to the water hole:
- 43 impala (four big rams)
- 19 gemsbok (a bunch of big ones)
- 31 red hartebeest (two big bulls)
- 4 nyala cows
- 2 blue wildebeest
- 6 eland (one giant bull)
- 9 kudu cows and calves
- 11 waterbuck (one big bull)
- A bunch of sand ground grouse and some Franklins

This is Africa. South Africa! This is the fastest growing hunting adventure going, and the best deal, too.

Do not compare this hunt with what you may be used to here in the States. All the hunting in South Africa is done on private ranches, called concessions. Most of the time you will stay in private chalets, with indoor plumbing. You will dine in the main lodge, and, yes, I said dine. Many times you have a full menu of some of the game you or a fellow hunter harvested.

While hunting Africa you experience many different things. The first day of our first safari, as the sun came up we heard birds calling that we had heard only on the Discovery Channel. We saw animals that we had seen only in zoos. You will sit in your blind and by noon you may have seen ten species of big game. The wildlife viewing is just great. The rush of being where you never know what species can come in is a thrill in itself.

One day I sat in my blind with my wife Vicki. We chose to sit the whole day. Our hosts, Jimmy and Linda Taljaard from Madiakgama Safaris, packed us a complete lunch, gave us a radio and dropped us off. By 1:30 p.m. we had seen a dozen big game species and more than 200-plus animals, 95 percent of them within 35 yards, with the average being 15-20 yards.

A few years ago, we were hunting from tree stands and Vicki and I were filming. A steenbok came in. We had been told we could not shoot steenbok in this area, so we just filmed him as he fed directly below us. Back at the lodge that evening, we showed the Professional Hunter (PH) the footage. He told us it was an exceptional common duiker and asked me why I didn't shoot. Since that day I have taken the time to learn about each animal and we always carry a pocket field guide for South African wildlife with us.

The first time I saw elephants in the wild I wanted to get as close to them as possible. No, make that "as close as practical". The sheer mass of these animals takes your breath away, especially when there's no safety barrier between them and you. It was amazing to put both my feet inside one footprint of these incredible animals.

It is a rush to get out of your blind and cut a fresh track of a lion or hyena that paced in back of your blind without making a sound..

There are times when you may wish you weren't there. One time my hunting partner, Brian Dayett, had just shot a beautiful gemsbok. His arrow had passed through the animal and disappeared into the bush. As we waited for the arrow to do its job, we watched a black mamba, one of the world's deadliest snakes, come out of the brush that Brian's arrow went into. The snake was 13 or 14 feet long. We watched it slither across the ground to get a drink at the water hole, and Brian and I, at that moment, wished we were not in Africa.

Many people (men and women) believe that Africa is not a place for women hunters. That is so far from the truth! The first animal Vicki ever harvested was a blesbok, stalking to within 30 yards and then putting a perfect shot on it. The misconception comes from thinking women cannot draw a heavy enough bow to harvest African game. Our feeling is that it is all shot placement, not poundage. Of course, you don't want to be under-bowed, but no amount of heavier draw weight can make up for poor shot placement. Vicki's blesbok was shot with a 42-pound bow and a 24-inch carbon arrow. The ram went down in 40 yards. Yes, for large-boned animals, a bowhunter needs more poundage, more like 65 pounds or higher.

Most of the hunting is from sun-up to sundown. I have taken a lot of clients out for evening hunting for duiker and steenbok. Most of the leopard hunting is at night. It is legal to hunt at night, but very few do it.

Blind hunting near water holes or trails is the best bet for archers. Your best opportunities come during the hottest parts of the day. Even though we all would love to stalk our quarry, most of the plains game species are very difficult to do so. These animals are constantly preyed upon by the big cats, and they run in herds. It makes for trying stalking.

However, stalking or stillhunting can be done with great results. My second Cape buffalo, I spotted him bedded in the shade along a dry river bed in Tanzania. Keeping the wind in my favor, I stalked in the long grass for over two hours and got to within 15 yards. There, bedded too close for comfort, lay this 2,000-pound buffalo chewing its cud. I drew my bow, held the crosshair right in back of his shoulder and released. The arrow sank all the way to the fletching. I was shooting a 70-pound bow, carbon arrow weighted with salt to get the necessary mass and 150-grain two-blade broadhead. As he stood up, brush flew everywhere. His left front leg broke what was left of my arrow as he ran off. He ran only 50 yards and went down. This was one of the largest adrenaline rushes I ever have had.

A few years ago, Jimmy Taljaard and I were hunting sable. This antelope is one of the most beautiful animals you will ever see. The colors of this animal are breathtaking. His horns go up and sweep back. The size of this animal can be compared to an elk. As usual, it is a strong herd animal. It took us numerous crawling and stalking attempts to get close to the bull; every time we began to get close, the wind would shift or some of the cows would catch us. After two days, things finally came into play. The sable bull stood for me. I got the distance and released. My arrow hit the mark. The bull spun and disappeared into the African bush. We waited for a short time and Jimmy and I got on the trail. Something that is a little different from hunting at home is you do not give the animal a long time after the shot. Especially if you are in an area with predators. It does not take these incredible predators long to find your trophy. As we got on the trail, the sign was good. After about 250 yards or so, we spotted my magnificent sable bull down.

Depending upon the area or concession (ranch) you are hunting, and if that concession has them, you may see some of the Big 6 (elephant, lion, rhino, Cape buffalo, leopard, hippo). Most of the time if you are hunting in Big 6 territory, you will be accompanied by your PH. They will not let you be in the field without protection.

• Above, Vicki Cianciarulo with her kudu bull. Above right, tree blind at a waterhole. Blinds generally are large enough for more than two people. Ground blind below. All blinds have solid roofs to keep out light and keep them cooler during the day. Lower right, an average impala ram coming to water. Impalas are among the wariest species at a waterhole; they can jump the string.

Steps Along the Hunter's Path

Last year I was sitting in a tree blind with Jacque Taljaard, and right at dark we heard grunting coming from the bush. Suddenly two giant white rhinos came in to water. It was like sitting right above a couple of dinosaurs. They came in cautiously, nothing like you would think these massive animals would do. After about five minutes of them drinking, we heard the jeep driving up, and all of a sudden we could feel the ground shake as those two incredible animals ran off into the seclusion of the brush.

One of Vicki's favorite hunts in South Africa is her red hartebeest.

"Ralph and I were sitting in a ground blind, situated about 15 yards from the water hole. We both had brought our bows that day, along with the video camera. Depending upon which species of game came in, we would determine who was to shoot and who was to film. Ralph did not care to shoot a red hartebeest. He said they are ugly. But I wanted one. As luck had it, a herd of hartebeest came to the water hole, including a really nice bull.

"Ralph whispered that he was on him with the camera and to take my time and pick a spot.

"The bull circled the water hole a couple of times, then presented me with a broadside shot at 15 yards. I placed my crosshair right behind the hartebeest's shoulder and released. The arrow hit right where I wanted it to and passed through the animal. The bull walked, not ran, about 20 yards and went down. I was so excited! This was the first time I had an arrow pass through an animal. Ralph caught the whole scene on tape, including the dance I did in the blind after the bull went down."

Costs & Such

Dollar for dollar you can't beat bowhunting over there. In most cases, if you do your homework, your South African trip will cost the same as a trophy hunt here in the Lower 48, and probably less than many Alaskan and Canadian hunts. When you go on a standard package, you can count on the cost being around $4,000 - $4,500, which would allow you the opportunity for four to five animals. That's normally a kudu, gemsbok, blesbok, impala and warthog. During your safari, if you do not take one of the animals you requested or whatever was in your package, the value of that animal is deducted from the cost of the package. Thus, even though you go on a package hunt for $4,500, for instance, if you don't shoot everything in that package, it will not cost you $4,500.

On the plains game animals, you are not charged for shooting a

Affordable Adventure Safari

better trophy-class animal. However, when you start going after the Big 6, you can surely pay more for the better animal. Elephant, for instance, is judged by the weight of the tusks; the heavier the tusks, the higher the fee.

South African Airlines (SAA) has a direct route from New York's JFK airport or from Miami straight to Johannesburg, South Africa. Rates vary, but $900 to $1,400 is the norm. The flight is about 14 hours. You leave in the evening and arrive early the following afternoon. Plenty of time to sleep. Take it from someone who's not fond of flying, it's not that bad. Other airlines fly to Johannesburg, but none of them fly direct.

When it comes to tipping your PH, most everyone I have dealt with gives around $100 or so, as long as the PH did what he or she said would be done. Normally, you ask the PH how much you should give the trackers and skinners. The norm is $25-$50. Also, here is where tee-shirts, clothes, flashlights and knives come in handy, using them instead of cash as tips.

All the concessions are gameproof, meaning that they are high fenced. All of South Africa is this way, and more countries are going this way….thousands and thousands of acres fenced in. They have realized that to manage their herds, they needed to have more control and at the same time try to patrol for poaching. A good example is Madiakgama Safaris. Their concession is over 15,000 acres, and they continually enlarge it.

Some concessions are small; they are the ones to stay away from. For example, I was invited to hunt a concession that was set up for bowhunting. We realized as we drove around that the area was very small. I asked to see where all the blinds were, and there were only two. They were within shouting distance of each other. It didn't take a rocket scientist to figure out we'd been had. For there is no actual hunting experience here.

Another concession operator invited us to visit while we were filming our Super Safari bowhunting video. They told us they were bowhunters and that they had built blinds by all the water holes. They even FAXed us photos of the blinds. Boy, were they nice. We felt it was worth our time to stop; it's a good thing we did. The blinds were 70-80 yards from the water.

In today's market, you can find a gamut of choices on who to hunt with. Prices vary. Services, experience, and quantity and quality of the game play a big role in your decision making. Make sure you talk to others who have hunted with the PH you plan to go with. Talk to many of his clients and then make up your mind.

Questions you should ask the references:
- Does the PH hunt with a bow himself?
- Where and how large is the concession you hunted?
- Did you see all the animals you were told you would?
- Were the blinds and set-ups set for your style of hunting?
- Did you receive all your trophies? Were they in good condition?
- Did the PH do everything he said he would?
- How were you treated, overall?
- Would you go back to that PH? (This is the biggest question.)

When is the best time to go to South Africa? Their seasons are exactly opposite our ours. Our fall is their spring; our summer is their winter. I recommend going in May-June-July-August. The foliage is down, water is scarce and activity is high. Most of all, the snakes are down or very inactive. Another benefit is that during this time of year, not many hunting seasons are open in the States.

The rainy season normally is October through January. You do not want to be there then, for if you are hunting over water holes you don't get much action. The animals can get water from all over without leaving cover or approaching a water hole.

In South Africa, depending upon the location of your hunt, the only precaution you may need is anti-malaria pills. You can buy them in the States, but if you talk to your Professional Hunter, he can purchase the pills for you there and save you 75 percent. The pills are the same. Most of the areas in South Africa, you won't need to worry about these pills. Another great thing – you don't need any shots or extra medication. Always check with your Professional Hunter before going over, in case you are going to hunt in an area where you may need something extra. South African medical doctors are available, and they're as good as anywhere.

What to bring?

Our first time, we packed two bags of camo gear, not knowing what to expect. We had more camo clothing than most retail shops. At most concessions, they offer, at no extra charge, daily laundry service. This eliminates the need for over-packing, or it should.

Affordable Adventure Safari

Here is a checklist that has taken us five safaris to come up with.

- ☐ Passport
- ☐ 2 camo shirts (button)
- ☐ 2 pair camo pants
- ☐ 1 med. weight camo jacket
- ☐ 1 camo cap
- ☐ 1 warm cap
- ☐ camp shoes
- ☐ light weight boots
- ☐ sunglasses
- ☐ lip balm
- ☐ tweezers
- ☐ sun block
- ☐ 220/110 power adapter
- ☐ Neck pillows (for plane ride)
- ☐ 5 pairs of socks
- ☐ underwear
- ☐ 2 pair shorts
- ☐ sweat pants
- ☐ 3 camo tee-shirts
- ☐ 1 pair camo gloves
- ☐ headnet or camo make-up
- ☐ duffel bag for clothes
- ☐ video camera w/ lots of tape
- ☐ 35mm camera w/ lots of film
- ☐ extras batteries for everything

A tip about packing underwear — pack enough for the whole trip. Most concessions wash the clothes by hand. The clothes are hung out to dry and then ironed (not with a steam iron, either). Sometimes they do not get all the soap out, and sometimes they starch things, including underwear. Wearing starched underwear is an experience.

Regulations concerning bow and gun differ for each country and the species of game you intend to hunt. The best thing to do is to contact Safari Club International. They have been the strongest organization to get results for international hunters. They can be reached at 4800 W. Gates Pass Rd., Tucson AZ 85745. Phone is 520-620-1220; FAX is 520-622-1205. They can keep you up-to-date on all restrictions and requirements.

Firearms hunters that I know bring their own hunting arms. They have not heard of anyone renting firearms from a PH, although I know some hunters super-concerned about airline regulations and such have considered that option. Many of the rifle hunts do cost more, due to the fact that the PH takes the hunters out and travels by vehicle most or all of the day until game is spotted. They don't really sit near water holes or stand hunt. Matter of fact, in all the cases I'm familiar with, no firearm hunter hunted near a water hole.

It is important to note that if you're planning to go there, do your homework. Once there, it is equally important that you listen to your PH's advice. Most wounded and lost game comes from poor shot placement due to not listening to the PH's advice. This is especially true on the huge, incredibly tough Cape buffalo. Your PH knows a lot more about those animals than you do.

I believe it is cheaper to have your taxidermy work done here. We tried all the ways you can thing of. Just have them treat the hides and send them to you. On average, it will cost $100 - $150 per animal. That may seem like a lot, but think about what it costs to bring home a caribou or moose rack on the plane.

Your PH handles all the hides once you have shot the animals. The PH takes them to the taxidermist who prepares the hides for dipping and crating. The PH also takes care of the paperwork to have the animals shipped back to the States. As long as you work with a good PH, you don't have to worry about the hides returning. We have learned that once you find a good PH, stick with him. That's just common sense.

RALPH CIANCIARULO

Ralph Cianciarulo promotes archery and bowhunting for a living as a video producer, seminar speaker, television personality and international bowhunter. He also is a guide/outfitter and has served as guide and shooting instructor to such athletes and celebrities as Bo Jackson, Walter Payton and Kurt Russell. Ralph was the first bowhunter to harvest a Eurasian brown bear, which he took in 1991 in Russia. He has made several hunting safaris to Africa. He is a member of the Hoyt USA "Hunting All-Star Team" and is on the field staffs of Hoyt USA, Beman USA, New Archery Products, Bowhunters Discount Warehouse, Fine-Line Inc., Loc-On Treestands, Trebark, Scent Shield and Spence's Targets.

Affordable Adventure Safari

KIDS- THE FUTURE

Kids are part of the natural world. Let's be sure they know, understand, appreciate and enjoy it.

Steps Along the Hunter's Path

Coming Soon???...
To a Ballot Box
near YOU????

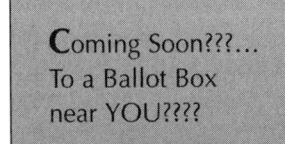

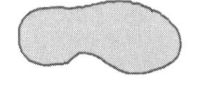

by Richard Smith

How Michigan ALMOST Lost Its Bear Hunting
....Blueprint for Beating the Anti's

*T*he measure was labeled Proposal D, and the anti's were at it again. It would have eliminated the use of bait and dogs for bear hunting and shortened bear season. In effect, it basically would have eliminated bear management, because bear hunting without dogs or bait in Michigan bear country would have made it impossible for hunters to harvest enough bruins on an annual basis to impact the population. Michigan hunters have been harvesting 1,200 to 1,400 bears a year recently. Without dogs and bait, that would have dropped by to only 280-360 bear, or fewer.

Similar proposals have passed in a number of other states, but Proposal D did not pass in Michigan. **How did the good guys and common sense – and the black bear in Michigan – win?** Lots of work by concerned, alarmed and unified sportsmen ... lots of money ... being proactive ... thousands of hours of volunteer effort by non-agency personnel ... giving voters both sides of the issue, so they could make an informed decision.

Here's how it all came about, and why you ought to read and remember this. **It or something like it could happen in your state tomorrow. Will you be ready? Will the sportsmen of your state be ready?**

During 1996, Michigan joined the list of states in which traditional wildlife management decision making was challenged at the polls. A measure – Proposal D – was put on the November ballot that, if passed, would have put wildlife management in the hands of voters and taken it away from the professionals in the Department of Natural Resources who are most qualified to make such decisions. Also on that ballot (to counter Proposal D) was Proposal G, which vested the authority for making wildlife management decisions in the hands of the Natural Resources Commission. This commission is the policy setting body for the state DNR, with members appointed by the Governor.

Proposal G gave the authority to the natural Resources Commission to make wildlife management decisions, with advice from DNR professionals. Specific wording requires that principals of sound wildlife management be used in making decisions. This measure also clearly provided for the opportunity for public input on wildlife issues before being acted on by the commission. Public input has been possible on wildlife management issues in Michigan for a long time, but many members of the public weren't aware of that opportunity.

It would have been possible for both proposals to be approved, but that did not happen. It appeared as though most voters clearly understood what they were voting for. Sixty-two percent of the people who went to the polls voted against Proposal D and 38 percent voted for it, for a 24 percent margin of victory. Proposal G was approved by a 38 percent margin, with 69 percent voting for it and 31 percent against it. Proposal D was defeated in every county in the state and Proposal G was approved in every county.

If both measures had passed, the proposal with the widest margin of votes would have taken precedence.

I'm pleased to have played a role in the defeat of Proposal D and passage of Proposal G. The fact that there are thousands of others like me in Michigan who are concerned about the proper management of wildlife such as bear, and were willing to get involved, is why it happened. **A tremendous team effort on the part of sportsmen and women across the state was responsible for educating voters about the best choices to make on their ballots.**

The fact that Michigan has a strong contingent of outdoor organizations was important. The understanding among residents of the state that Proposal D was not just about bear hunting was also important. **The passage of Proposal D would have set a dangerous precedent that could have eventually impacted any and all forms of hunting, trapping, fishing and other methods of management.** This realization mobilized a lot of people who otherwise might not have gotten involved.

Wildlife research by state or federal agencies and universities can also be negatively impacted by ballot initiatives, as Massachusetts found out during 1996. A proposal on that state's ballot that outlawed the use of hounds and snares for hunting and trapping also eliminated their use for research purposes. Bear dogs used to play an important role in bear research in that state, but that's no longer possible.

Michigan residents who are concerned about wildlife management also learned valuable lessons from what happened in Colorado and Oregon. Many hunters in those states did not believe that bear hunting proposals would make it on the ballot, much less be approved by voters. The threat wasn't taken seriously, if at all, until too late in those states.

That did not happen in Michigan. Our state's referendum was anticipated by at least two years by those who were paying attention. On a personal level, I had been planning to write a book about Michigan black bear, and the pending referendum gave me the incentive to do it, with the idea of using the referendum and its fallout as an educational tool. I have closely followed bear research and management in the state for many years as a hunter, writer and photographer, spending considerable time with state researchers.

My wife and I published *Understanding Michigan Black Bear* in 1995. We put as much information as possible about bears in the book. Thanks to the support of a dedicated group of bear hunters – the Upper Peninsula Bear Houndsmen – copies of the book were sent to all state legislators. I would like to think the information on its pages helped in the adoption of Proposal G.

Before the book was published, a coalition of hunting organizations formed the Citizens for Professional Wildlife Management (CPWM), which was the main group that campaigned against Proposal D and for Proposal G. One of the most important members of CPWM was the Michigan United Conservation Clubs (MUCC). The MUCC provided staff members and their office for fund raising and educational efforts. Michigan Chapters of Safari Club International also played a prominent role, as did many active hunting organizations in the state and one of Michigan's most prominent hunters - Ted Nugent.

Fund raising was the backbone for the successful campaign. Like any political campaign, and that's what this was, the amount of money in the war chest often separates winners from losers.

The Upper Peninsula Sportsmens Alliance, one of the member groups of CPWM, came up with the best fund-raising idea that helped lead to victory. The Alliance conducted a raffle that raised more than $1 million. The grand prize – 40 acres of recreational land with a log cabin kit to put on it – is what set this raffle apart from others.

The money raised from the raffle, auctions, banquets and from pledges made it possible to buy critical television time and ad space in newspapers to get the message to voters before the election. Long before Proposal D was officially on the ballot, bear hunting organizations were collecting pledges. A total of $1.8 million was collected, and most of it was used in the fight to protect professional wildlife management.

Most of the funding support for Proposal D came from two private individuals. The Michigan Humane Society and The Fund For Animals also provided some money for Proposal D. Few other private individuals contributed. About $800,000 was spent to pass Proposal D, and the effort ran out of money at least a month before the vote. It will never be known, of course, how the vote percentages may have differed had Proposal D's backers had enough money to continue their efforts up to voting time.

Reserving television time early is critical during an election year. If CPWM had waited until signatures were certified, it might have been too late to purchase the necessary TV time.

Besides ad time and space, Proposals D and G generated heavy news coverage. Members of CPWM met with the editorial boards of many major newspapers in the state and got the support of all but one of them. To the credit of the Detroit News, one of Michigan's largest newspapers, their editorial writer took the time to go on bear hunts with bait and dogs, to find out for herself what they were like.

A Seattle, Washington, crew from CNN (Cable News Network) did the same thing. I took the editorial writer and CNN crew on bait hunts and the Michigan Bear Hunters Association hosted them on hound hunts.

Michigan has its share of outdoor writers and outdoor television shows, most of which devoted space and time to the ballot proposals. On a personal note, I wrote more newspaper and magazine articles about black bear during 1996 than ever before, in an effort to get the truth out about bear hunting and management. Much of that work was spent countering false information distributed by the proponents of Proposal D.

Most of the campaign by the proponents of Proposal D was designed to deceive the public. We didn't let them get away with it.

•They maintained that eliminating bear hunting with bait and dogs would protect cubs. Cubs have been protected in Michigan since 1948. Sows in the company of cubs also are protected.

•They claimed that both hunting methods are unsporting, unethical and inhumane. Both hunting methods that were being challenged increase the opportunity for humane kills rather than decrease it. These hunting methods also offer hunters the best means of clearly identifying protected versus unprotected bears. I've always understood that two of the most important responsibilities of an ethical hunter are to identify the target and make a clean kill. I've also been told that non-hunters support hunting which meets these criteria.

Regarding success rates, approximately 25 percent of bait and dog hunters in Michigan shoot a bear. Any method that results in only one of four hunters filling a tag does not qualify as unsporting.

•Proponents of Proposal D also claimed that bait and dog hunting was hurting the state's bear population, another falsehood. The bear population has been increasing annually under a permit system started in 1990. Our permit system is similar to those in Minnesota and Wisconsin, limiting hunter numbers in specific management units, offering the best protection for bear numbers. Passage of Proposal D would have eliminated Michigan's very successful bear management system.

•Those who supported Proposal D also told voters they weren't against bear hunting, just the use of bait and dogs. Then the Make A Wish Foundation sent a youngster from Minnesota, who had a brain tumor, on an Alaskan brown bear hunt. That hunt, which involved neither bait nor dogs, was strongly opposed by The Fund For Animals, one of the groups seeking passage of Proposal D in Michigan.

The support of Governor John Engler and DNR Director K. L. Kool, who accepted the directorship about the time the referendum was heating up, also played a role in the defeat of Proposal D and passage of Proposal G. Director Cool appeared in commercials supporting Proposal G; he was able to do that because he is not classified as a civil servant, and no public funds were used to make the commercials.

Advice To Other States

If your state faces a referendum on wildlife management, it will be necessary to develop fund raising efforts by coalitions of sporting groups similar to CPWM as quickly as possible. The more time you have to raise money, the better. You'll need a big war chest.

I also suggest having measures like Michigan's Proposal G passed in your state before other hunting measures appear on the ballot. Michigan's Proposal G was passed by the state legislature.

Proposal D got on the ballot through the collection of voter signatures. People who circulated petitions to get Proposal D on the ballot were paid up to $2 per signature. Additionally, **there's no requirement that petition language be accurate to get a measure on** the ballot. **Wording on the Michigan petitions claimed that a ban on bear hunting with bait and dogs would protect cubs, which is false, but it helped get the signatures needed.** The petition language could have been challenged only after the election.

Another item which may help in the effort to protect professional wildlife management is solid research on the hunting methods that are being questioned. To my knowledge, little research effort has been spent gathering solid data on bear hunting with bait and dogs. It's time for that to change.

The Michigan United Conservation Clubs can provide additional advice for anyone who may face a similar referendum in the future. Rick Jameson is the Executive Director; Dennis Knapp also was actively involved in CPWM. MUCC's telephone number is 517-371-1041. The address is PO Box 30235, Lansing, MI 48909.

I would also be willing to help out in any way I can.

• Go the extra mile... slog it out ... not just in reaching a prime hunting spot, but also for the wildlife's sake and the future of hunting and good game management.

> Now there's an official name and program for something we hunters have been doing a long time ... watching and enjoying all sorts of wildlife year round.

by **Chip Gross**
Ohio Division of Wildlife

Watchable Wildlife Is Great Family Fun

"Ya know, you can use binoculars to watch birds and other stuff like that."

That statement by a friend, made to me as a kid growing up in the early 1960s, was a revelation. It had never occurred to me that the pair of binoculars my parents kept in a black case on the top shelf of the hall closet could be used for anything other than watching sporting events. At least, that's all my family ever used them for.

But one early-spring day after school, I got bold and sneaked the binoculars out of the house and went and laid down on my back in a weedy field. The first thing that happened to fly by was a red-tailed hawk, and training the field glasses on the bird, I watched, entranced, as it circled higher into the sky. Eventually it became only a dark speck and then completely disappeared.

I think the buzz phrase used today for such an experience is "defining moment", a moment in time when the way you look at life somehow changes forever. For me, that moment happened more than 30 years ago. I didn't realize it at the time, but watching that hawk disappear into the clouds helped set the direction of my life and what I would eventually make my life's work.

Since then I have earned a four-year degree in wildlife management from Ohio State University and worked during the past 21 years for the Ohio Division of Wildlife. For the past three of those years, I have had the privilege of initiating and coordinating the Ohio Watchable Wildlife Program.

The National Watchable Wildlife Program was officially created in 1990 by virtue of a memorandum of understanding signed by the USDA Forest Service, U.S. Fish and Wildlife Service, Bureau of Land Management, Department of Defense, International Association of

Fish and Wildlife Agencies, Defenders of Wildlife, and several other groups and agencies. The program is a cooperative, nationwide effort to establish a network of carefully chosen and officially designated wildlife viewing sites across the United States, and to put America's interest in wildlife-associated recreation to work for wildlife conservation. The program operates on the premise that if Americans are provided with ample opportunities to see and learn about wildlife in its natural habitat, these same people will become more knowledgeable and effective advocates for wildlife conservation.

The goals of the National Watchable Wildlife Program, as well as Ohio's, are four-fold: 1) wildlife-associated recreation; 2) economic development for the local communities near Watchable Wildlife sites; 3) education, and 4) conservation. To meet these goals, states are selecting wildlife viewing sites based on such criteria as reliability of wildlife viewing opportunities, access, ecological significance, and the ability of the site to withstand public use. To identify these sites and the routes leading to them, states are posting official Watchable Wildlife binocular-logo signs (white binoculars on a dark brown background) along area highways. Each participating state also is producing a state wildlife viewing guide describing the designated sites, including directions to each.

Many states, such as Ohio, have opted to produce their guides as part of the standardized Watchable Wildlife Series of viewing guides published and distributed by Falcon Press of Helena, Montana. Other states have chosen to produce their guides independently.

Fostering partnerships among state and federal agencies, conservation groups and private business is critical to the success of the National Watchable Wildlife Program. In Ohio, for example, no less than 24 constituent groups make up the Watchable Wildlife steering committee assembled by the Ohio Division of Wildlife.

But why is a National Watchable Wildlife Program needed? Mark Damian Duda states in his book *Watching Wildlife* that, "According to National Surveys of Fishing, Hunting and Wildlife-Associated Recreation, conducted by the U.S. Fish and Wildlife Service, the number of Americans who took trips for the specific purpose of watching wildlife increased 63 percent during the past decade. Today almost 30 million Americans take wildlife viewing trips each year." In addition, it is estimated that 76 million Americans now either watch, feed or photograph wildlife. It is with these wildlife enthusiasts in mind that the National Watchable Wildlife Program was initiated.

• The new Ohio Wildlife Viewing Guide, the completion of the first step in Ohio's Watchable Wildlife Program, lists and describes 80 of the best wildlife viewing sites in the state. It is available at local Ohio bookstores or by sending a $10 check or money order to: Ohio Division of Wildlife, Ohio Wildlife Viewing Guide, 1840 Belcher Drive, Columbus OH 43224-1329.

CHIP GROSS

W. H. "Chip" Gross is the editor of WILD OHIO magazine, book author and outdoor writer. He's also an avid turkey hunter and all-around outdoorsman.

EDITOR'S NOTE:
Wildlife watching? Hmmm. We spend hours at that every time we go afield, during hunting season and during the off-season. Many of our favorite anecdotes and memories are based on the things we learned and enjoyed as we observed ... yes, *watched*, quite possibly from a hunting stand ... wild animals and birds going about their daily lives. We sincerely hope that all non-hunting wildlife watchers understand that. There's a lot more to wildlife watching than a pair of binoculars and an open window of an automobile parked on the side of the road. As hunters afield, we have had to learn that before you can have wildlife watching you must have wildlife *spotting* – not just the whole cloth of an entire object magically in full and easy view, but the bits and pieces, the horizontal lines and the things out of place – and the wildlife *identifying* which naturally follows. You have to find it before you can watch it, and if it wants to remain camouflaged and hidden, that presents a fascinating challenge. Thus, knowing where to look, when to look, how to look, and what to look for are important elements leading to the maximum enjoyment of wildlife watching. Hunters know that better than anyone. We hope that no matter who it is or where it is, with watching comes awareness of the continuously fluctuating intricacies of that phenomenon mislabeled as the "balance" of nature, where the wildlife fits in it, where the habitat fits in it ... and where we fit in it as observers *and as participants*.

Watchable Wildlife

- *Oh .... My .... Goodness! That is a lot of antler! There is a reason even our ancient ancestors hung the largest antlers above their door. Photo by Troy Huffman.*

SECTION VII:

TROPHY & PHOTO CONTESTS

DEER DATA

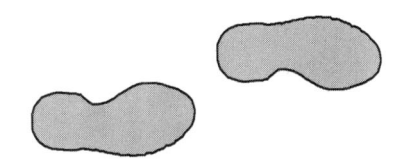

Thanks to the following organizations and agencies for providing the information which enabled us to produce the county-by-county summary data in this section—

ILLINOIS
Illinois Department of Natural Resources
Division of Constituency Services
Big Buck Recognition Program

MICHIGAN
Commemorative Bucks of Michigan

OHIO
Buckeye Big Buck Club

WISCONSIN
Wisconsin Buck & Bear Club

TENNESSEE
Tennessee Wildlife Resources Agency
Trophy Deer Registry

ILLINOIS
1996 Record Book Deer Kills (by county)

These are the trophy whitetail deer which were taken in 1996 and entered in Illinois Big Buck Recognition Program record books.

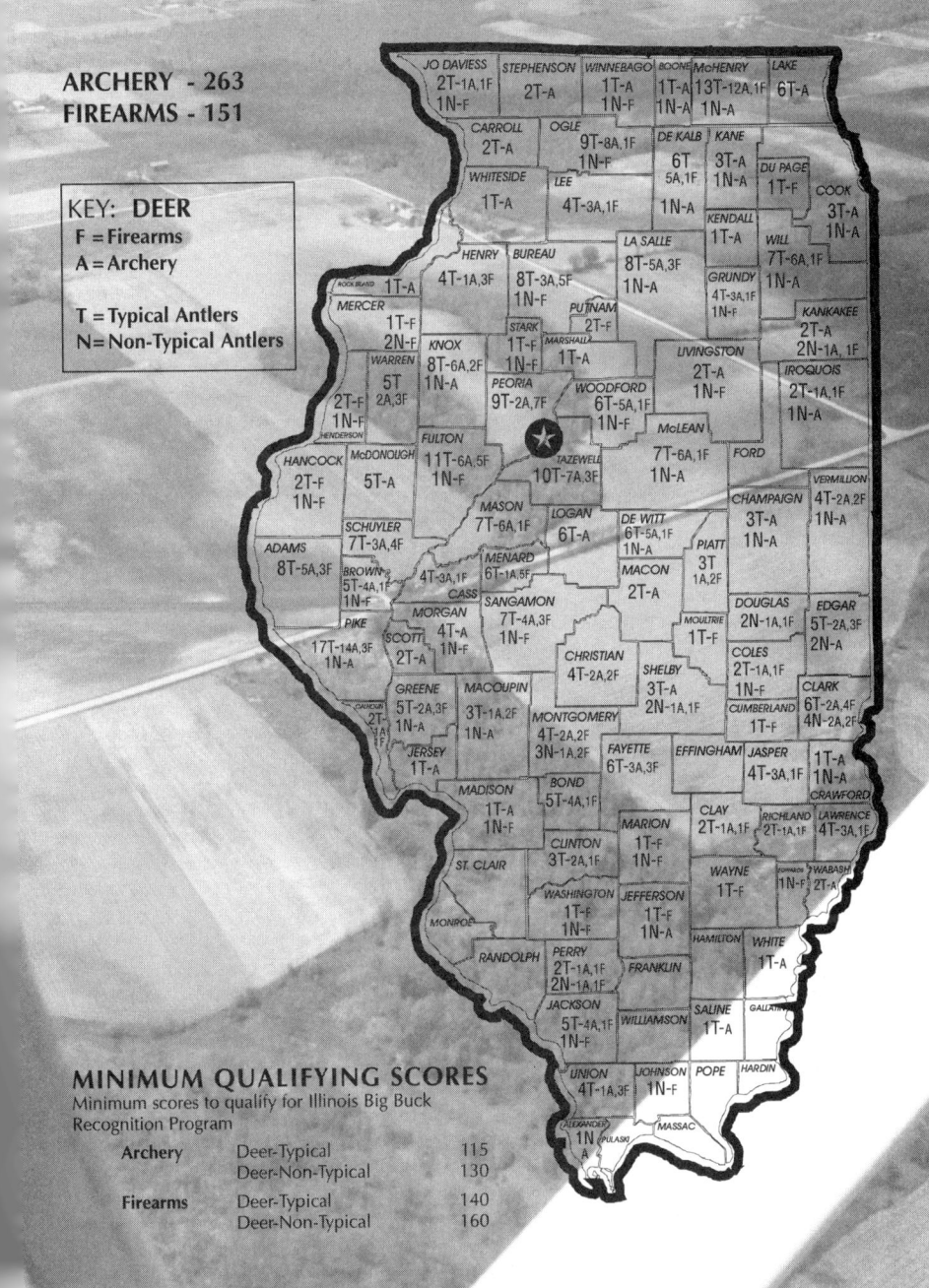

ARCHERY - 263
FIREARMS - 151

KEY: DEER
F = Firearms
A = Archery

T = Typical Antlers
N = Non-Typical Antlers

JO DAVIESS	2T-1A,1F / 1N-F
STEPHENSON	2T-A
WINNEBAGO	1T-A / 1N-F
BOONE	1T-A / 1N-A
McHENRY	13T-12A,1F / 1N-A
LAKE	6T-A
CARROLL	2T-A
OGLE	9T-8A,1F / 1N-F
DE KALB	6T / 5A,1F
KANE	3T-1A / 1N-A
DU PAGE	1T-F
COOK	3T-A / 1N-A
WHITESIDE	1T-A
LEE	4T-3A,1F
KENDALL	1T-A
WILL	7T-6A,1F
HENRY	4T-1A,3F
BUREAU	8T-3A,5F / 1N-F
LA SALLE	8T-5A,3F
GRUNDY	4T-3A,1F / 1N-F
KANKAKEE	2T-A / 2N-1A,1F
ROCK ISLAND	1T-A
MERCER	1T-F / 2N-F
PUTNAM	2T-F
STARK	1T-F
MARSHALL	1T-A
LIVINGSTON	2T-A / 1N-F
IROQUOIS	2T-1A,1F / 1N-A
KNOX	8T-6A,2F / 1N-A
WARREN	5T / 2A,3F
PEORIA	9T-2A,7F
WOODFORD	6T-5A,1F / 1N-F
HENDERSON	2T-F / 1N-F
McLEAN	7T-6A,1F
FORD	1N-A
HANCOCK	2T-F / 1N-F
McDONOUGH	5T-A
FULTON	11T-6A,5F / 1N-F
TAZEWELL	10T-7A,3F
VERMILION	4T-2A,2F / 1N-A
SCHUYLER	7T-3A,4F
MASON	7T-6A,1F
LOGAN	6T-A
DE WITT	6T-5A,1F / 1N-A
CHAMPAIGN	3T-A / 1N-A
ADAMS	8T-5A,3F
BROWN	5T-4A,1F / 1N-F
MENARD	6T-1A,5F
PIATT	3T / 1A,2F
CASS	4T-3A,1F
MACON	2T-A
DOUGLAS	2N-1A,1F
EDGAR	5T-2A,3F / 2N-A
PIKE	17T-14A,3F / 1N-A
SCOTT	2T-A
MORGAN	4T-1N-F
SANGAMON	7T-4A,3F / 1N-F
MOULTRIE	1T-F
COLES	2T-1A,1F / 1N-F
CLARK	6T-2A,4F / 4N-2A,2F
CALHOUN	2T-
GREENE	5T-2A,3F / 1N-A
MACOUPIN	3T-1A,2F / 1N-A
CHRISTIAN	4T-2A,2F
SHELBY	3T-A / 2N-1A,1F
CUMBERLAND	1T-F
JERSEY	1T-A
MONTGOMERY	4T-2A,2F / 3N-1A,2F
FAYETTE	6T-3A,3F
EFFINGHAM		JASPER	4T-3A,1F	CRAWFORD	1T-A / 1N-A
MADISON	1T-A / 1N-F
BOND	5T-4A,1F
CLAY	2T-1A,1F
RICHLAND	2T-1A,1F
LAWRENCE	4T-3A,1F
ST. CLAIR	CLINTON 3T-2A,1F
MARION	1T-F / 1N-F
WAYNE	1T-F
EDWARDS	1N-F
WABASH	2T-F
MONROE	WASHINGTON 1T-F / 1N-F
JEFFERSON	1T-F / 1N-A
HAMILTON		WHITE	1T-A
RANDOLPH	PERRY 2T-1A,1F / 2N-1A,1F
FRANKLIN	
JACKSON	5T-4A,1F / 1N-F
WILLIAMSON		SALINE	1T-A	GALLATIN	
UNION	4T-1A,3F
JOHNSON	1N-F
POPE		HARDIN	
ALEXANDER	1N-A
PULASKI		MASSAC	

MINIMUM QUALIFYING SCORES
Minimum scores to qualify for Illinois Big Buck Recognition Program

Archery	Deer-Typical	115
	Deer-Non-Typical	130
Firearms	Deer-Typical	140
	Deer-Non-Typical	160

WINNERS 1997
TROPHY CONTEST
DEER

ARCHERY - CURRENT YEAR (1996 season)
Score Name   County Taken
8 pt. Typical Antlers
154⁶/₈   Jeff Neuhalfen, Henry   Marshall
152¹/₈   Dave Voorhees, Peoria   Fulton
150²/₈   Kris Knox, Mahomet   Shelby
9 pt. Typical Antlers
148⁰/₈   Randy Ashman, Chatsworth   Livingston
142¹/₈   Andy Payne, Morton   Tazewell
139⁴/₈   Randy Pudik, Mapleton   Tazewell
10 pt. Typical Antlers
175⁵/₈   Dick Demay, East Moline   Knox
174⁰/₈   Mike Armstrong, Streator   La Salle
168⁵/₈   Michael Bily, Mahomet   Piatt
11 pt. Typical Antlers
161⁰/₈   Brian Kirkpatrick, Plainfield   Will
159⁶/₈   Bill Westlake, Riverton   Pike
12 pt. Typical Antlers
171²/₈   Jack Hoopes, Monmouth   Warren
170³/₈   Donald Hoey, Walworth, WI   McHenry
13+ pt. Typical Antlers
169⁴/₈   Robert Alfonso Jr., St. Charles   Grundy
165²/₈   Daran Harn, Sherman   Sangamon
Non-Typical Antlers
214⁴/₈   Kelly Riggs, Clinton   De Witt
195⁰/₈   Frank Bartels, Heyworth   McLean

FIREARMS - CURRENT YEAR (1996 season)
Score Name   County Taken
8 pt. Typical Antlers
148³/₈   Shane Heikes, Smithshire   Henderson
145²/₈   Dann Carroll, Bartonville   Peoria
144³/₈   Scott Shryock, Noble   Richland
9 pt. Typical Antlers
163³/₈   John Freidinger, Pekin   Schuyler
154²/₈   Bill Stewart, Canton   Fulton
10 pt. Typical Antlers
176³/₈   Jason McCulloch, Galesburg   Knox
169⁰/₈   Kory McAllister, Detroit   Pike
167⁰/₈   Gary Huson, Palmyra   Macoupin
11 pt. Typical Antlers
178⁶/₈   Carl Lee, LaHarpe   Hancock
161⁴/₈   Ronald Behrends, Tiskilwa   Bureau
157⁶/₈   Richard Huse, S. Pekin   Tazewell
12 pt. Typical Antlers
165⁰/₈   Alan J. Peterson, Colfax   McLean
13+ pt. Typical Antlers
177¹/₈   John Binz, Tiskilwa   Bureau
177⁴/₈   Steve Shields, Mt. Vernon   Jefferson
171⁷/₈   Kevin Winship, E. Peoria   Peoria
Non-Typical Antlers
203³/₈   Russell Whaite, Browning   Fulton
202¹/₈   Brent Blunier, Eureka   Woodford
197³/₈   Dwayne (Tex) Rogers, Madison   Perry

ARCHERY-HISTORICAL (1995 season / earlier)
Score Name   County Taken Year
8 pt. Typical Antlers
158⁷/₈   Todd Clayton, Galesburg   Knox   1995
156⁰/₈   Rick Carr, Meadowbrook   Saline   1993
155⁶/₈   Joe Schmitt, Paris   Edgar   1995
9 pt. Typical Antlers
168⁵/₈   Randy Zumwalt, Pittsfield   Pike   1995
160³/₈   Steve Tripp, Shelbyville   Shelby   1995
10 pt. Typical Antlers
164⁵/₈   Shawn Van Alsberg, Moline   Rock Island 1995
160²/₈   John Thomas, Grand Ridge   LaSalle   1987
155⁷/₈   Bret Epkins, Pekin   Fulton   1995
11 pt. Typical Antlers
173³/₈   James Meyer, Huntley   Kane   1995
164⁵/₈   Joe Schmitt, Paris   Edgar   1995
12 pt. Typical Antlers
175⁰/₈   Marc Anthony, Congerville   Schuyler 1995
13+ pt. Typical Antlers
158⁷/₈   Rusy Mitcheff Jr., Orland Park   Will   1990
Non-Typical Antlers
203⁰/₈   Kevin Moran, Lisle   DuPage   1995

FIREARMS-HISTORICAL (1995 season/earlier)
Score Name   County Taken Year
8 pt. Typical Antlers
153⁶/₈   Robert Schroen, Chatsworth   Livingston 1994
153⁴/₈   Alan Pullen, Smithshire   Henderson 1991
152²/₈   Larry Bielema, Washington   JoDaviess 1983
9 pt. Typical Antlers
152⁰/₈   Margaret Valley, Roseville   Warren   1995
150⁷/₈   Cliff Huddleston, Normal   Hancock   1977
147⁵/₈   Richard Collins, Chillicothe   Marshall 1995
10 pt. Typical Antlers
181⁵/₈   George Metcalf, Barry   Pike   1995
180⁵/₈   Ken Klauser, Quincy   Adams   1990
171⁴/₈   Tim Lantz, Springfield   Fayette   1995
11 pt. Typical Antlers
172¹/₈   Rich Farden, Pekin   Marshall 1991
167³/₈   Jay Brackunsick, Cassopolis   Adams   1989
163⁴/₈   Mark Henry, Oquawka   Hancock   1995
12 pt. Typical Antlers
189⁷/₈   Leo Romanotto, Springfield   Sangamon 1994
177¹/₈   Daniel Bouton, Stillman Valley   Ogle   1993
13+ pt. Typical Antlers
183²/₈   Bradley Wander, Knoxville   Knox   1995
175¹/₈   Robert Leckrone, Rushville   Adams   1995
168⁷/₈   Michael Bily, Mahomet   McLean   1994
Non-Typical Antlers
261²/₈   Ernest Hires, Metcalf   Edgar   1994
222¹/₈   Lewis Smith, Springfield   Macoupin 1993
213²/₈   Steve Shoopman, West Point   Hancock   1978

OTHER AWARDS
COLLECTED ANTLERS
Typical Antlers
155⁰/₈   Ronald Podik, Washington   Tazewell 1992
Non-Typical Antlers
243⁷/₈   Jeffrey A. Deuroy, Glenview   Cook   1995
193⁶/₈   Bollis A. Hamm, Astoria   Fulton   1996

222   Steps Along the Hunter's Path

ILLINOIS 1997 BEST of SHOW WINNERS TROPHY DEER CONTEST

ARCHERY TYPICAL ANTLERS
175 5/8 Dick Demay, E. Moline   Knox 1996
ARCHERY NON-TYPICAL ANTLERS
214 4/8 Kelly Riggs, Clinton   De Witt 1996
FIREARMS TYPICAL ANTLERS
189 7/8 Leo Romanotto, Springfield Sangamon 1994
FIREARMS NON-TYPICAL ANTLERS
261 0/8 Ernest Hires, Metcalf   Edgar 1994

• *Best of Show winners in the Budweiser Trophy Deer Contest at the 1997 Illinois Deer & Turkey Classic were, left to right, Leo Romanotto, Springfield, Firearms - Typical Antlers; Dick Demay, East Moline, Archery - Typical Antlers; Ernest Hires, Metcalf, Firearms - Non-Typical Antlers; Kelly Riggs, Clinton, Archery - Non-Typical Antlers.*

Illinois

Illinois 1997 Outdoor Photo Contest

Wildlife
1) Scott Bianchini, Beloit, WI
2) Gary Pettus, Decatur, IL
3) Scott Bianchini, Beloit, WI

Scenic
1) Cindy Lance, Victoria, IL
2) Richard Spagnolo, Chicago, IL
3) Bill Reuscher, Magnolia, IL

People
1) Todd Radek, Grayslake, IL
2) Terry Hoeft, Manito, IL

1st Scenic

Cindy Lance, Victoria, IL

224   Steps Along the Hunter's Path

1st Wildlife

Scott Bianchini,
Beloit, WI

1st People

Todd Radek,
Grayslake, IL

Illinois

MICHIGAN

County by county report of bucks taken in 1996 hunting seasons which have been entered in Commemorative Bucks of Michigan records.

MINIMUM QUALIFYING SCORES
Minimum scores to qualify for Commemorative Bucks of Michigan record book.

Archery		Firearms	
Black Bear	18	Black Bear	19
Deer-Typical	125	Deer-Typical	150
Deer-Non-Typical	155	Deer-Non-Typical	175
Elk-Typical	240	Elk-Typical	240
Elk-Non-Typical	265	Elk-Non-Typical	265
Turkey	8	Turkey	12

ARCHERY - 248
SHOTGUN/RIFLE - 272
MUZZLELOADER - 16
HANDGUN - 6

KEY:
DEER/BEAR/ELK
F = Firearms
M = Muzzleloader
A = Archery
H = Handgun
T = Typical Antlers
N = Non-Typical Antlers

TURKEY
S = Single Beard
M = Multiple Beard
F = Firearm
A = Archery

Upper Peninsula

KEWEENAW
HOUGHTON D-1T-F B-5F
ONTONAGON D-6T-1A,4F,1M B-1A,1F
GOGEBIC D-3T-1A,2F
BARAGA D-2T-F B-5A
MARQUETTE D-1T-A B-2F
IRON B-1F
ALGER D-3T-2F,1H B-1F
LUCE B-1A,1F
SCHOOLCRAFT D-1T-F
CHIPPEWA D-3T-2A,1M
MACKINAC D-1T-F
DICKINSON D-1T-A B-1A,1F
DELTA D-2T-F 2N-A B-1A
MENOMINEE D-1T-F 1N-A B-1A,2F

Lower Peninsula

EMMET D-3T-1A 1F,1M B-1A
CHEBOYGAN D-1T-F T-1S-F E-2T-F
PRESQUE ISLE B-1A,2F
CHARLEVOIX -1T-F T-1S-F
OTSEGO D-2T-1A,1F E-5T-F 1N-A
MONTMORENCY E-3T-F B-1F
ALPENA D-2T-F T-1S-F
ANTRIM D-3T-2A,1F T-3S-F
LEELANAU 2S-1A,1F
BENZIE D-1T-F T-1S-F
GR TRAVERSE D-1T-A T-1S-F
KALKASKA D-1T-A T-2S-F
CRAWFORD D-1T-F T-1S-F 1M-F
OSCODA D-1T-F T-1S-F B-1F
ALCONA D-5T-2A,1F T-1S-F
MANISTEE D-3T-2A, 1F
WEXFORD D-1T-A T-1S-F
MISSAUKEE D-1T-A
ROSCOMMON D-1T-A T-1S-F
OGEMAW T-1F
IOSCO T-1S-F
MASON D-1T-A
LAKE D-1T-F
OSCEOLA D-1T-A T-3S-1A,2F 1M-F
CLARE D-2T-1A, 1F
GLADWIN D-2T-A
ARENAC T-1S-F
HURON D-3T-2A,1F 1N-F T-1M-F
OCEANA T-1S-F
NEWAYGO D-3T-1A,2F T-3S-F
MECOSTA D-1T-F
ISABELLA D-5T-3A, 2F
MIDLAND D-5T-2A 2F,1A 1M-F
BAY D-6T-6A 1N-A
TUSCOLA D-7T-5A,2F T-2S-F
SANILAC D-8T-4A,4F T-1S-F
MUSKEGON D-3T- 1A,1F,1H
MONTCALM D-5T-4A,1M
GRATIOT D-4T-2A,2F T-4S-F
SAGINAW D-7T-5A,1F,1M T-15S-F
LAPEER
KENT D-11T- 6A,4F,1M
IONIA D-11T-A T-3S-F
CLINTON D-4T-A T-3S-1A,2F 1M-F
SHIAWASSEE D-12T-7A, 2F T-2S-F 2M-F
GENESEE D-8T-6A,2F
ST. CLAIR D-13T-7A,6F D-11T- 3A,7F,1M T-1S-F
OTTAWA D-7T-4A,3F
OAKLAND D-12T-10A,2F 1N-H T-3S-2A,1F
MACOMB D-7T- 5A,1F,1M
ALLEGAN D-10T-4A,6F T-5S-F 2M-F
BARRY D-15T- 12A,2F,1M
EATON D-7T-4A,1F T-3S-F
INGHAM D-9T-6A,3F T-3S-1A,2F
LIVINGSTON D-10T- 6A,2F,2M
WAYNE D-6T-3A,3F 1N-A
VAN BUREN D-11T- 3A,5F,2M,1H 3N-F T-3S-F
KALAMAZOO D-5T-3A,2F T-2S-F
CALHOUN D-16T-14A,2F 2N-F T-3S-F
JACKSON D-19T-9A,9F,1H 4N-1A,3F
WASHTENAW D-26T-9A,15F,2M 1N-1A
BERRIEN D-13T- 9A,4F T-4S-F
CASS D-7T-5A,2F 3N-F T-3S-F 3M-F
ST. JOSEPH D-3T-A
BRANCH D-16T-9A,7F 1N-A T-1S-F
HILLSDALE D-11T-5A,6F 2N-1A,1F T-4S-2A,2F 1M-F
LENAWEE D-14T-7A,7F
MONROE D-3T-1A,2F

WINNERS 1997
TROPHY CONTEST
DEER / BEAR / ELK

ARCHERY - TYPICAL ANTLERS - CURRENT YEAR (1996 season)

Score	Name	County Taken
8 pt. Typical Antlers		
$136^{0}/_{8}$	Thomas Osborne, Pewamo	Clinton
$133^{7}/_{8}$	Danny Hargett, Burr Oak,	St. Joseph
$132^{2}/_{8}$	Jack Armstrong, Three Rivers,	St. Joseph
9 pt. Typical Antlers		
$149^{4}/_{8}$	Keith Benton, Haslet	Shiawassee
$132^{3}/_{8}$	Don Shepard, Lowell	Ionia
10 pt. Typical Antlers		
$172^{7}/_{8}$	Charles Conaway, E. Greenwich, RI	Lapeer
$164^{7}/_{8}$	Mike Turk, Charleston	Lapeer
11 pt. Typical Antlers		
$137^{0}/_{8}$	Mark A. Wilson, Jackson	Jackson
12 pt. Typical Antlers		
$163^{4}/_{8}$	Troy Satterthwaite, Chelsea	Washtenaw
$162^{2}/_{8}$	John Ykimoff, Jackson	Jackson
13+ pt. Typical Antlers		
$158^{5}/_{8}$	Shawn Crocker, Jackson	Jackson

FIREARMS – TYPICAL ANTLERS — CURRENT YEAR (1996 season)

Score	Name	County Taken
8 pt. Typical Antlers		
$164^{0}/_{8}$	Keith Sircey, Belleville	Wayne
$162^{0}/_{8}$	John Tackitt, Sawyer	Berrien
9 pt. Typical Antlers		
$152^{6}/_{8}$	Daryl A. Zuk, Eaton Rapids	Jackson
10 pt. Typical Antlers		
$158^{2}/_{8}$	David Halsey, Adrian	Lenawee
$151^{0}/_{8}$	Dick Wever, Okemos	Ingham
11 pt. Typical Antlers		
$156^{3}/_{8}$	Mike Toncevich, Ann Arbor	Washtenaw
12 pt. Typical Antlers		
$154^{0}/_{8}$	Steven Reader, Jackson	Jackson
13+ pt. Typical Antlers		
$198^{0}/_{8}$	Troy Stephens, Jackson	Jackson
	(new state record firearm typical antlers)	

ARCHERY – TYPICAL ANTLERS HISTORICAL (1995 season and earlier)

Score	Name	County Taken	Year
8 pt. Typical Antlers			
$159^{1}/_{8}$	Greg Kuhn, Northville	Washtenaw	1990
$138^{0}/_{8}$	Nicky Charnoske, Alger	Arenac	1982
9 pt. Typical Antlers			
$138^{2}/_{8}$	Gerald Jacobson, Coldwater	Branch	1995
$135^{5}/_{8}$	Ronald Perkins, Adrian	Lenawee	1995
10 pt. Typical Antlers			
$156^{0}/_{8}$	Cora Fink, Quincy	Hillsdale	1995
$143^{5}/_{8}$	Pat Rankin, Eaton	Eaton	1994
$142^{6}/_{8}$	Nicky Charnoske, Alger	Arenac	1988
11 pt. Typical Antlers			
$154^{0}/_{8}$	Roger Hughes, Burlington	Calhoun	1995
12 pt. Typical Antlers – No Entries			
13+ pt. Typical Antlers – No Entries			

FIREARMS – TYPICAL ANTLERS - HISTORICAL (1995 season or earlier)

Score	Name	County Taken	Year
8 pt. Typical Antlers			
$149^{0}/_{8}$	Marcus Smith, Lansing	Eaton	1994
$126^{0}/_{8}$	William McCarty, Holland	Allegan	1988
9 pt. Typical Antlers			
$156^{7}/_{8}$	Timothy Smith, Dundee	Monroe	1995
$149^{1}/_{8}$	Wade Phillips, Lapeer	Lapeer	1995
10 pt. Typical Antlers			
$171^{1}/_{8}$	Floyd Lee, Woodhaven	Ingham	1995
$170^{1}/_{8}$	Jeffrey Stauffer, Shipshewana, IN	Branch	1995
11 pt. Typical Antlers			
$165^{2}/_{8}$	Jerry Marlatt, Lenawee	Lenawee	1995
$163^{2}/_{8}$	Micheal Judd, Muskegon	Muskegon	1984
$154^{5}/_{8}$	Alan Jourdan, Sturgis	St. Joseph	1991
12 pt. Typical Antlers			
$174^{1}/_{8}$	Delores Kassuba, Livingston	Livingston	1995
	(state record gun kill by a woman)		
13+ pt. Typical Antlers			
$154^{0}/_{8}$	Russell Bucknor, Livingston	Livingston	1944

BLACK POWDER –TYPICAL ANTLERS -ALL

Score	Name	County Taken	Year
8 pt. Typical Antlers			
$119^{0}/_{8}$	Christy Powaga, Leslie	Ingham	1996
9 pt. Typical Antlers			
$128^{0}/_{8}$	Richard Powell, St. Clair	St. Clair	1996
10 pt. Typical Antlers			
$169^{7}/_{8}$	Barry Boyes, Washtenaw	Washtenaw	1996
11 pt. Typical Antlers – No Entries			
12 pt. Typical Antlers			
$143^{2}/_{8}$	John Hodge (hunter) Roger Hughes, Marshall (exhibitor)	Barry	1984
13+ pt. Typical Antlers			
$169^{0}/_{8}$	Chad Minnock, Ortonville	Oakland	1995

NON-TYPICAL ANTLERS — FIREARMS / ARCHERY / BLACK POWDER – ALL YEARS

$211^{0}/_{8}$	Paul Kintner, Adrian (bow)	Lenawee (new state record)	1996
$203^{6}/_{8}$	Ronald Chabot, (bow)	Dexter (new #2 in state)	1996
$201^{1}/_{8}$	Steven Crocker, Jackson (firearm)	Jackson	1989

OTHER AWARDS

BEAR

Firearms			
$19^{10}/_{16}$	Kevin Krupp, Chesaning	Newberry	1996
Archery			
$20^{10}/_{16}$	Scott Merchant, Charlotte	Delta	1996

ELK

Typical Antlers			
$306^{3}/_{8}$	Katie Dilks, Kalamazoo	Otsego	1996
$301^{0}/_{8}$	Howard Chupp, Bellevue	Otsego	1996

COLLECTED ANTLERS

Typical Antlers			
$171^{6}/_{8}$	Terry Amos, Vicksburg	Saskatchewan, Can.	Unk.
$171^{0}/_{8}$	Kenneth Bryan, Springport	Vinton Co, OH	1996
$167^{3}/_{8}$	Jay Brakensick, Dowagiac	Adams Co., IL	1987
Non-Typical Antlers			
$213^{3}/_{8}$	Keith Lundberg, Diamondale	Unk.	Unk.

Best of Show Winners
Trophy Deer Contest

ARCHERY — TYPICAL ANTLERS
172⁷⁄₈   Charles Conaway, E.Greenwich,RI   Lapeer Co.   1996

FIREARMS — TYPICAL ANTLERS
198⁰⁄₈   Troy Stephens, Jackson   Jackson Co.   1996

BLACK POWDER — TYPICAL ANTLERS
169⁷⁄₈   Barry Boyes, Washtenaw   Washtenaw   1996

NON-TYPICAL ANTLERS
211⁰⁄₈   Paul Kintner, Adrian   Lenawee County   1996

• Best of Show winners of the trophy deer contest at the 1997 Michigan Deer & Turkey Spectacular were, left to right, Barry Boyes, Washtenaw, Black Powder - Typical Antlers; Troy Stephens, Jackson, Firearms - Typical Antlers; Paul Kintner, Adrian, Non-Typical Antlers; Charles Conaway, E. Greenwich, Rhode Island, Archery - Typical Antlers. Conaway's brother-in-law, Zane Walker, exhibited the antlers and stood in for Conaway in this photo.   Stephens' buck is the new Michigan state record typical antlers taken with firearm.

CBM BEST of '96 WINNERS

COMMEMORATIVE BUCKS OF MICHIGAN

1996-SEASON AWARDS

Archery Typical Antlers
172⅝ Charles Conaway, E.Greenwich,RI Lapeer 1996

Archery Non-Typical Antlers
211⅝ Paul Kintner, Adrian Lenawee 1996

Firearms Typical Antlers
198⅝ Troy Stephens, Jackson Jackson 1996

Firearms Non-Typical Antlers
179⅞ James Hamilton, Osseo Hillsdale 1996

- Winners of the Commemorative Bucks of Michigan "Best of 1996" awards at the 1997 Michigan Deer & Turkey Spectacular in Lansing were, left to right, David Blaker, exhibitor, James Hamilton, Osseo, hunter, Firearms - Non-Typical Antlers; Troy Stephens, Jackson, Firearms - Typical Antlers; Paul Kintner, Adrian, Archery Non-Typical Antlers; Charles Conaway, E. Greenwich, Rhode Island, Archery - Typical Antlers. Conaway's brother-in-law, Zane Walker, exhibited the antlers and stood in for Conaway in this photo. All deer were taken during the 1996 season. Stephens' buck is the new Michigan state record typical antlers taken with firearm.

Michigan

MICHIGAN 1997 OUTDOOR PHOTO CONTEST

Wildlife
1) Greg Teyson, Mackinaw City, MI
2) Don Cox, Grass Lake, MI
3) Doug Randall, Sumner, MI

Scenic
1) Ron St. Germain, Lansing, MI
2) Lurie Rentschler, Mattawan, MI
3) Judy Porritt, Flint, MI

People
No Winners

Greg Teyson,
Mackinaw City, MI

Steps Along the Hunter's Path

Ron St. Germain
Lansing, MI

1st Scenic

TURKEY BEARDS & SPURS
MULTIPLE BEARDS
1) Jim Dawson, DeWitt, MI   3 beards (23 $^3/_8$")
2) Jim Dawson, DeWitt, MI   2 beards (18 $^5/_8$")
3) Robert Burns, Hubbardston, MI   2 beards (18")

SINGLE BEARD
1) Dale Gardell, St. Joseph, MI   13 $^1/_2$"
2) Frank Lloyd, Alanson, MI   11 $^1/_4$"
3) Dan J. Miller, Bancroft, MI   11 $^5/_8$"

SPURS
1) Scott Phillips, Hillsdale, MI   1 $^{11}/_{16}$"
2) Todd Granger, Alanson, MI   1 $^1/_2$"
3) Brian Bucknarish, Harrison, MI 1 $^1/_2$"

(Five entries were tied at 1 1/2". Names were drawn to fill the 2nd and 3rd places. Since there was no entry fee, this seemed a fair way to do it.)

OHIO

County by county report of bucks taken in 1996 hunting seasons which have been entered in Buckeye Big Buck Club records.

MINIMUM QUALIFYING SCORES
- Typical: 140
- Non-Typical: 160

WILLIAMS	1T-S
FULTON	1T-S
LUCAS	1T-S
DEFIANCE	1T-S, 1N-S
WOOD	2T-1S,1M
SANDUSKY	1T-L
LAKE	1T-S
ASHTABULA	6T-4S,4S,1L,1C
GEAUGA	1T-S
CUYAHOGA	1N-S
PORTAGE	3T-1L,2C
TRUMBULL	1T-S
SENECA	1T-1S,2L
HURON	1T-S
MEDINA	2T-S, 1N-M
SUMMIT	3T-2L,1C
HANCOCK	1T-S
MAHONING	3T-1S,2C
ALLEN	1T-S
WYANDOT	2T-1L,1C
CRAWFORD	2T-S
RICHLAND	3T-2S,1L, 1N-S
ASHLAND	4T-2S,1L,1C, 3N-S
WAYNE	1T-S, 2N-1S,1C
STARK	2T-L
COLUMBIANA	1T-C
HARDIN	2T-1L,1C
MARION	2T-1S,1C
HOLMES	1T-S
CARROLL	4T-2S,1L
LOGAN	2T-1S,1L,2M
UNION	1T-L
DELAWARE	4T-2S,2C, 2N-1S,1C
KNOX	3T-2S,1M, 2N-1L,1M
COSHOCTON	7T-5S,1L,1C, 1N-S
TUSCARAWAS	3T-1S,1L,1C
JEFFERSON	5T-1S,1C,2M,1R
HARRISON	—
SHELBY	1N-M
MIAMI	6T-1S,4L, 1N-S
CHAMPAIGN	2T-1L,1C
CLARK	1N-S
MADISON	1T-S
FRANKLIN	4T-2L,2C
LICKING	17T-8S,3L,5C,1M, 5N-4S,1L
MUSKINGUM	9T-6S,2L,1C
GUERNSEY	8T-5S,2S,1C, 1N-S
BELMONT	1T-S
DARKE	1T-S, 1N-S
PREBLE	—
MONTGOMERY	—
GREENE	1T-S, 1N-S
FAYETTE	2T-1S,1L
PICKAWAY	4T-3S,1L
FAIRFIELD	6T-3S,2L,1C, 4N-2S,2M
PERRY	8T-5S,1L,1C,1M
MORGAN	4T-4S,1L, 2N-S
NOBLE	5T-4S,1L
MONROE	2T-S
BUTLER	2T-1S,1L
WARREN	1T-C, 1N-C
CLINTON	1T-L
ROSS	5T-2S,2L,1C
HOCKING	13T-9S,2L,1C,1R, 2N-1S,1L
ATHENS	8T-5S,2L,1C
WASHINGTON	5T-4S,1C
HAMILTON	3T-1S,1L,1C
CLERMONT	4T-1S,1L,1C,1M
BROWN	2T-1L,1C
ADAMS	2T-1S,1L
HIGHLAND	2T-1L,1U
PIKE	3T-S
SCIOTO	2T-S, 1N-S
JACKSON	5T-3S,2C, 1N-L
VINTON	7T-6S,1C
MEIGS	6T-3S,1L,1C,2M
GALLIA	5T-4S,1L
LAWRENCE	1T-L

TOTAL 283

KEY: DEER
- T = Typical Antlers
- N = Non-Typical Antlers
- S = Shotgun
- L = Longbow
- C = Crossbow
- M = Muzzleloader
- A = Archery
- H = Handgun
- R = Rifle

WINNERS 1997 TROPHY CONTEST DEER

Ohio DEER & TURKEY EXPO

ARCHERY - CURRENT YEAR (1996-97 season)
Score	Name/Hometown	County Taken
8 pt. Typical Antlers		
165 5/8	Sheldon Sparks, West Union	Adams
156 4/8	John Zaayer, Baltimore	Coshocton
9 pt. Typical Antlers		
163 1/8	Steven Allen Wallace, Batavia	Clermont
125 7/8	Doug Reed, Jr., Westerville	Hocking
10 pt. Typical Antlers		
170 0/8	Douglas Parker, Waverly	Pike
168 6/8	Jeff Tigner, Newark	Licking
166 6/8	Dan Mace, Bellville	Richland
11 pt. Typical Antlers		
163 0/8	Mike Florea, Wilmington	Clinton
161 5/8	Craig Bonham, Delaware	Franklin
12 pt. Typical Antlers		
174 2/8	Mike Newman, Troy	Miami
170 1/8	Steve Orchard, Danville	Ashland
13+ pts. Typical Antlers		
147 6/8	Kerry Proctor, Newark	Licking
Non-Typical Antlers		
179 2/8	Rod Stufflebeam, Lewis Center	Licking
178 5/8	Shane Roop, Rockbridge	Hocking

ARCHERY - HISTORICAL (1995 season or earlier)
Score	Name/Hometown	County Taken	Year
8 pt. Typical Antlers			
131 7/8	Troy Gillespie, Cleves	Hamilton	1994
127 0/8	Johnny Holbrook, Waterloo	Lawrence	1995
9 pt. Typical Antlers			
149 0/8	Kenny Hedges, Circleville	Pickaway	1992
140 7/8	Jerry Rhodes, Canal Winchester	Pickaway	1993
10 pt. Typical Antlers			
164 0/8	Cliff Henderson, Peebles	Pike	1992
162 0/8	Steve French, Buckeye Lake	Noble	1995
161 1/8	Steve Doggett, New Carlisle	Adams	
11 pt. Typical Antlers			
145 6/8	Ray Iames, Pataskala	Licking	1995
12 pt. Typical Antlers			
132 3/8	Larry Brown, Yellow Springs	Clark	1995
13+ pt. Typical Antlers			
170 7/8	Shannon Wolfe, Peebles	Pike	1995
Non-Typical Antlers			
180 1/8	Kelly Banny, Columbus	Franklin	1994

FIREARMS - CURRENT YEAR (1996-97 season)
Score	Name/Hometown	County Taken
8 pt. Typical Antlers		
160 2/8	Duwayne Howard, Waverly	Pike
153 4/8	Brad Wilhelm, Mt. Vernon	Knox
9 pt. Typical Antlers		
154 0/8	Jeff Herald, Chillicothe	Ross
138 0/8	James Meyer, Houston	Shelby
10 pt. Typical Antlers		
166 4/8	Matt Baker, Shiloh	Richland
160 0/8	Lonnie Murray, Waverly	Pike
156 7/8	Nate Johnson, Stryker	Williams
11 pt. Typical Antlers		
169 2/8	Robert Clark Jr., Marietta	Washington
168 5/8	Randy Shaeffer Sr., Lancaster	Fairfield
167 4/8	Troy Stone, Columbus	Hocking
12 pt. Typical Antlers		
174 4/8	Mike Anthony, Mt. Sterling	Madison
13+ pt. Typical Antlers		
157 7/8	Marvin Combs, Middletown	Butler
Non-Typical Antlers		
212 0/8	Frank Squires, Powell	Delaware
201 3/8	Richard Steen, Spring Valley	Greene
189 7/8	Greg D. Lemon, Holmesville	Wayne

FIREARMS - HISTORICAL (1995 season or earlier)
Score	Name/Hometown	County Taken	Year
8 pt. Typical Antlers			
161 1/8	Joe Gassaway, Lucas	Richland	1992
144 0/8	Jim Middlesetter II, Lagrange	Knox	1988
143 3/8	L. Forest Stapleton, Walhonding	Coshocton	1976
9 pt. Typical Antlers			
162 1/8	Jason Sauders, New Vienna	Highland	
156 1/8	Bonnie Skaggs, South Salem	Ross	1995
152 3/8	John Decker, Tallmadge	Noble	1995
10 pt. Typical Antlers			
166 0/8	Don Hurst, Mechanicsburg	Champaign	1977
163 7/8	Mack Steinbrook, Chillicothe	Ross	1995
162 3/8	Jeff Ison, Columbus	Washington	1986
11 pt. Typical Antlers			
170 2/8	Walter Gibson, Chandlersville	Muskingum	1995
150 7/8	Michael Bauerle, Pataskala	Licking	1994
12 pt. Typical Antlers			
158 6/8	David Lauer, Columbus	Hocking	1993
157 1/8	William Rice, Hamilton	Franklin	1995
13+ pt. Typical Antlers			
159 3/8	William Gee, Columbus	Ross	1991
153 1/8	Carl Reeves, Waynesville	Warren	1995
Non-Typical Antlers			
192 0/8	Robin Hazenfield, Moscow	Clermont	1995
169 7/8	Larry Shaw, Scio	Carroll	1995

BUCKEYE BIG BUCK CLUB

Ohio

BLACK POWDER (ALL YEARS)
Score Name/Hometown   County Taken   Year
8 pt. Typical Antlers
154²/₈ Dale Ameling, Bowling Green   Wood   1996
143⁷/₈ Ron Gleason, Junction City   Perry 1996
9 pt. Typical Antlers
148⁵/₈ Don Krieg, Wapakoneta   Logan 1996
10 pt. Typical Antlers
188⁶/₈ Dale Bevington, Troy   Miami   1996
157⁵/₈ Jerry Rhodes, Canal Winchester   Licking 1984
11 pt. Typical Antlers
163⁵/₈ Martin McAllister, Rarden   Pike   1995
12 pt. Typical Antlers
No Entries
13+ pt. Typical Antlers
137³/₈ John Hunt, Lancaster   Fairfield 1996
Non-Typical Antlers
186⁵/₈ George Korn, Carroll   Meigs   1996
177¹/₈ Michael P. Lanning, Lancaster   Fairfield

CROSSBOW (ALL YEARS)
Score Name/Hometown   County Taken   Year
8 pt. Typical Antlers
145³/₈ Michael Hickman, Pataskala   Franklin   1996
142⁵/₈ Don Dozer, Lancaster   Fairfield 1996
9 pt. Typical Antlers
152⁰/₈ Randy Hines, Ashley   Delaware   1996
151⁵/₈ Ray Justice, Columbus   Delaware   1995
10 pt. Typical Antlers
173¹/₈ Mark Thompson, McArthur   Vinton   1995
155⁴/₈ Terry Wells, Franklin   Warren   1996
11 pt. Typical Antlers
162¹/₈ Mark Hedge, Windham   Portage   1996
12 pt. Typical Antlers
183³/₈ Mark Newman, Cleves   Hamilton   1996
        (new state crossbow typical-antler record)
166¹/₈ David Chapman, West Union   Adams   1995
13+ pt. Typical Antlers
159⁶/₈ Michael Hobbs, Lucasville   1995
Non-Typical Antlers
145¹/₈ Robert Jackson, Springfield   Clark   1996

OTHER AWARDS

COLLECTED ANTLERS
Typical Antlers
174⁴/₈ Toy Hazenfield, Moscow   Wolfe   1993
163⁵/₈ Nick Stidham, Gallipolis   Gallia   1979
161⁰/₈ Bruce Bowman, Hillsboro   Highland
Non-Typical Antlers
226⁶/₈ Jerry Mock, Baltimore   Fairfield 1992

OHIO 1997 BEST of SHOW WINNERS TROPHY DEER CONTEST

TYPICAL ANTLERS

Firearm
174 4/8   Mike Anthony, Mt. Sterling   Madison 1996
Archery
174 2/8   Mike Newman, Troy   Miami 1996
Crossbow
183 3/8   Mark Newman, Cleves   Hamilton 1996
Black Powder.
188 6/8   Dale Bevington, Troy   Miami 1996

TYPICAL ANTLERS

*   *"Best of Show" winners in the Typical Antlers segment of the trophy deer contest at the 1997 Ohio Deer & Turkey Expo in Columbus were, left to right, Mark Newman, Cleves, Crossbow; Mike Newman, Troy, Archery; Dale Bevington, Troy, Black Powder. Not present was Mike Anthony, Mt. Sterling, Firearms.*

Ohio

NON-TYPICAL

"Best of Show" winners in the Non-Typical Antlers segment of the trophy deer contest at the 1997 Ohio Deer & Turkey Expo in Columbus were, left to right, Robert Jackson, Springfield, Crossbow; Frank Squires, Powell, Firearms; Kelly Bandy, Columbus, Archery. Not present was George Korn, Carroll, Black Powder.

NON-TYPICAL ANTLERS

Firearm
212⁰/₈ Frank Squires, Powell   Delaware   1996

Archery
180¹/₈ Kelly Bandy, Columbus   Franklin   1994

Crossbow
145¹/₈ Robert Jackson, Springfield   Clark   1996

Black Powder
186⁵/₈ George Korn, Carroll   Meigs   1996

OHIO 1997 OUTDOOR PHOTO CONTEST

Wildlife
1) Ray McMillen, Mansfield, OH
2) Molly Sue Rouse, Martins Ferry, OH
3) Marty Long, Millfield, OH

Scenic
1) Fred Bakies, Logan, OH
2) Marty Long, Millfield, OH

People
1) Kathi Wilson, Franklin, OH

Ray McMillen
Mansfield, OH

1st Wildlife

Ohio

1st People

Kathy Wilson
Franklin, OH

1st Scenic

Fred Bakies
Logan, OH

Steps Along the Hunter's Path

TENNESSEE
1996 Record Book Deer Kills (by county)

These are the trophy whitetail deer which were taken in 1996 and entered in Tennessee Deer Registry records as of deadline time for this book.

ARCHERY - 12
FIREARMS - 32

County entries on map:

- Reelfoot-WMA: 1T-A
- LBL WMA: 3T-F
- Fort Campbell: 2T-F, 1N-F
- Unknown: 1T-A
- Obion: 1T-F
- Dyer: 1T-F
- Fayette: 2T-F
- Shelby: 1T-F
- Chester / McNairy area: 1T-F
- Hardeman: 2T-F
- Hardin: 2T-1A,1F
- Benton: 1NT-F
- Decatur: 1T-F
- Perry: 1NT-F
- Humphreys: 1T-A
- Stewart: 1T-F
- Houston: 1A,1F
- Montgomery: 2T
- Robertson: 1T-A
- Davidson: 1T-F
- Cheatham: 1T-F
- Williamson: 3T-1A,2F
- Rutherford: 3T-1A,2F
- Bedford: 1T-F
- Lincoln: 2T-1A,1F
- Overton: 1T-A
- Fentress: 3T-1A,2F
- White: 1T-F
- Hamblen: 1T-F
- Marion: 1T-F

KEY: DEER
- F = Firearms
- A = Archery
- T = Typical Antlers
- N = Non-Typical Antlers
- WMA = Wildlife Management Area
- LBL = Land Between the Lakes

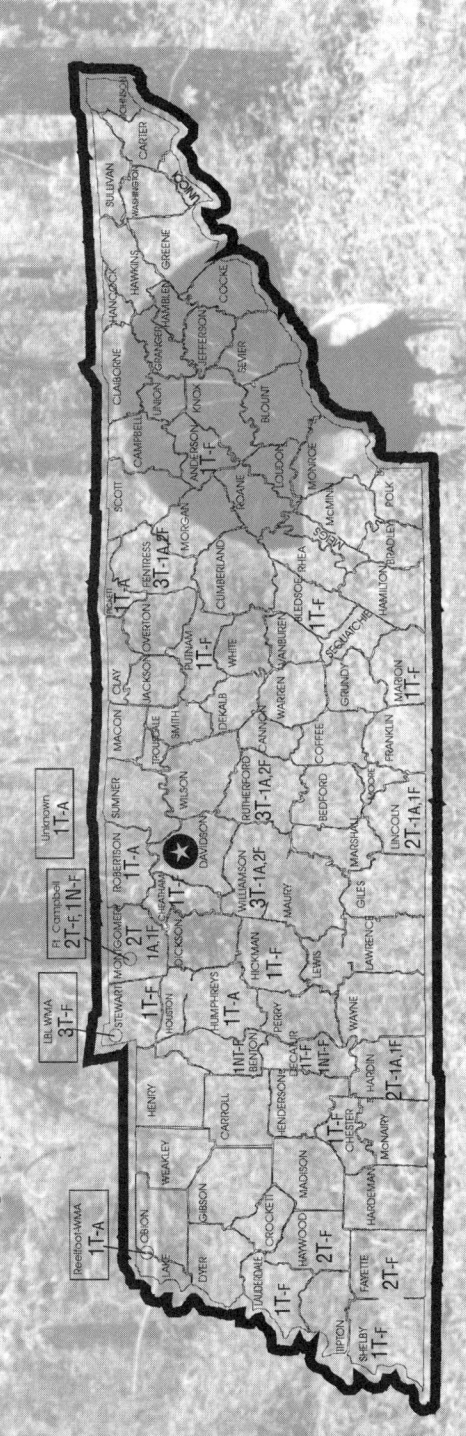

MINIMUM QUALIFYING SCORES
Minimum scores to qualify for Tennessee Deer Registry

Archery	Deer-Typical	115
	Deer-Non-Typical	140
Firearms	Deer-Typical	140
	Deer-Non-Typical	165

WINNERS 1997 TROPHY CONTEST DEER

FIREARMS - CURRENT YEAR Category
(1996 Season)
Score   Name, Hometown   County
8 pt. Typical Antlers
135⁴/₈   Billy Mathis, Dover   Stewart
132²/₈   Herschel L. Rich Sr., Milton   Rutherford
9 pt. Typical Antlers
125²/₈   Terry L. Cartwright, Shelbyville   Bedford
118⁵/₈   Randy Wright, Old Hickory   Stewart
10 pt. Typical Antlers
168¹/₈   Richard Edmons, Pikeville   Bledsoe
158⁵/₈   Robert Alexander, Brentwood   Decatur
146⁶/₈   Bryon Divis, Fayetteville   Lincoln
11 pt. Typical Antlers
176¹/₈   Alan Jackson, Henderson   Stewart
142⁶/₈   Ronald Carney, Joelton   Cheatham
12 pt. Typical Antlers
163²/₈   Steve Holden, Bell Buckle   Rutherford
13+ pt. Typical Antlers
168³/₈   Robert McPeake, Parsons   Benton
153⁴/₈   Johnny Thompson, Monterey   Fentress

FIREARMS - HISTORICAL Category
(1995 & Earlier)
Score   Name, Hometown   County   Year
8 pt. Typical Antlers
132¹/₈   Melvin Gamble, Iron City   Wayne   1993
128¹/₈   Gary Hardcastle, Lebanon   Davidson   1995
9 pt. Typical Antlers
144⁴/₈   Dwight Spicer, Clarksville   Montgomery 1967
10 pt. Typical Antlers
144⁵/₈   Jay Graves, Gallatin   Sumner   1994
134⁵/₈   Jeff Winningham, Clarksville   Montgomery 1995
11 pt. Typical Antlers
172⁵/₈   Michael Bowers, White Bluff   Stewart   1992
159⁵/₈   Kevin Grogan, Smyrna   Cumberland 1958
12 pt. Typical Antlers
166⁵/₈   Roy Pulley, Chapmanboro   Cheatham   1993
13+ pt. Typical Antlers
131¹/₈   Thomas Shadix, Pleasant View   Montgomery 1994

ARCHERY Category (All Years)
Score   Name, Hometown, State   County   Year
8 pt. Typical Antlers
143⁵/₈   Edgar Parker, Jamestown   Fentress   1996
134⁵/₈   Scott Stamps, Pleasant View   Cheatham   1996
9 pt. Typical Antlers
No Entries
10 pt. Typical Antlers
135²/₈   Steve Crabtree, Jamestown   Fentress   1992
133⁵/₈   Tim Byrd, Dover   Stewart   1996
11 pt. Typical Antlers
122⁴/₈   Scott Weber, Brentwood   Williamson 1996
12 pt. Typical Antlers
142⁵/₈   Franklin Bledsoe, Jamestown   Fentress   1995
13+ pt. Typical Antlers
125³/₈   Eddie Stinson, Pickett   Pickett   1996

BLACK POWDER Category (All Years)
Score   Name, Hometown, State   County   Year
8 pt. Typical Antlers
144⁴/₈   Lee Gault, Fayetteville   Lincoln   1995
129¹/₈   James Jones, Bon Aqua   Williamson 1996
9 pt. Typical Antlers
149²/₈   Mark Bottom, Lebanon   Wilson   1988
128⁰/₈   Gary Faulkner, Hendersonville   Davidson   1996
10 pt. Typical Antlers
161⁶/₈   Gerald Crabtree, Allardt   Fentress   1996
152⁶/₈   Chris Collingsworth, Ashland City Montgomery 1993
152⁴/₈   Lucas Norman, Springfield   Davidson   1995
11 pt. Typical Antlers
151³/₈   James Smith, Dickson   Williamson 1996
12 pt. Typical Antlers
160⁰/₈   Kipp Holt, Jamestown   Jackson   1989
13+ pt. Typical Antlers
146⁴/₈   Franklin James Bledsoe, Jamestown Fentress   1996

NON-TYPICAL ANTLERS Category
(All Hunting Tools, All Years)
Score   Name, Hometown   County   Year
177³/₈   Bruce Fox, Knoxville   Anderson   1996
175⁰/₈   Daniel Conatser, Ashland City   Cheatham   1991

OTHER AWARDS

OUT-OF-STATE
Typical Antlers — Firearms
174⁴/₈   Toy E. Hazenfield, Moscow, OH   Wolfe/KY   1993
166⁷/₈   Douglas Carrigan, Murfreesboro   Rutherford
157⁴/₈   John Barnwell Sr., Princeton, KY   Caldwell/KY 1992
Typical Antlers – Archery
164³/₈   John Barnwell Sr., Princeton, KY   Cumberland/KY 1990
159⁵/₈   John Barnwell, Princeton, KY   Caldwell/KY 1989
Non-Typical Antlers — Firearms
192⁶/₈   Robin Hazenfield, Moscow, OH   Clermont/OH 1995
Non-Typical Antlers – Archery
No Entries

COLLECTED
Typical Antlers
141⁴/₈   Debra Terry, Clarksville   Montgomery 1943
Non-Typical Antlers
175⁷/₈   Wayne Davis, Nashville   Davidson   Unk.

TENNESSEE 1997
BEST of SHOW WINNERS
TROPHY DEER CONTEST

TYPICAL ANTLERS — FIREARMS
176 1/8   Alan Jackson, Henderson, TN   Stewart 1996

TYPICAL ANTLERS — ARCHERY
143 5/8   Edgar Parker, Jamestown, TN   Fentress 1996

TYPICAL ANTLERS — BLACK POWDER
161 6/8   Gerald Crabtree, Allardt, TN   Fentress 1996

NON-TYPICAL ANTLERS
177 3/8   Bruce Fox, Knoxville, TN   Anderson 1996

• *Best of Show winners of the Trophy Deer Contest at the 1997 Tennessee Deer & Turkey Expo were, left to right, Alan Jackson, Henderson, Typical Antlers - Firearms; Edgar Parker, Jamestown, Typical Antlers - Archery; Gerald Crabtree, Allardt, Typical Antlers - Black Powder, Bruce Fox, Knoxville, Non-Typical Antlers.*

TENNESSEE 1997 OUTDOOR PHOTO CONTEST

Wildlife
1) Gary Russell, Dickson, TN
2) Kathy Butt, Portland, TN
3) Kam S. Sandstrom, Murfreesboro, TN

Scenic
1) Kam S. Sandstrom, Murfreesboro, TN
2) Mike Hampton, Dickson, TN

People
No Entries

1st Wildlife

Gary Russell
Dickson, TN

Kam Sandstrom
Murfreesboro, TN

1st Scenic

Tennessee

WISCONSIN

County by county report of bucks taken in 1996 hunting seasons which have been entered in Wisconsin Buck & Bear Club records.

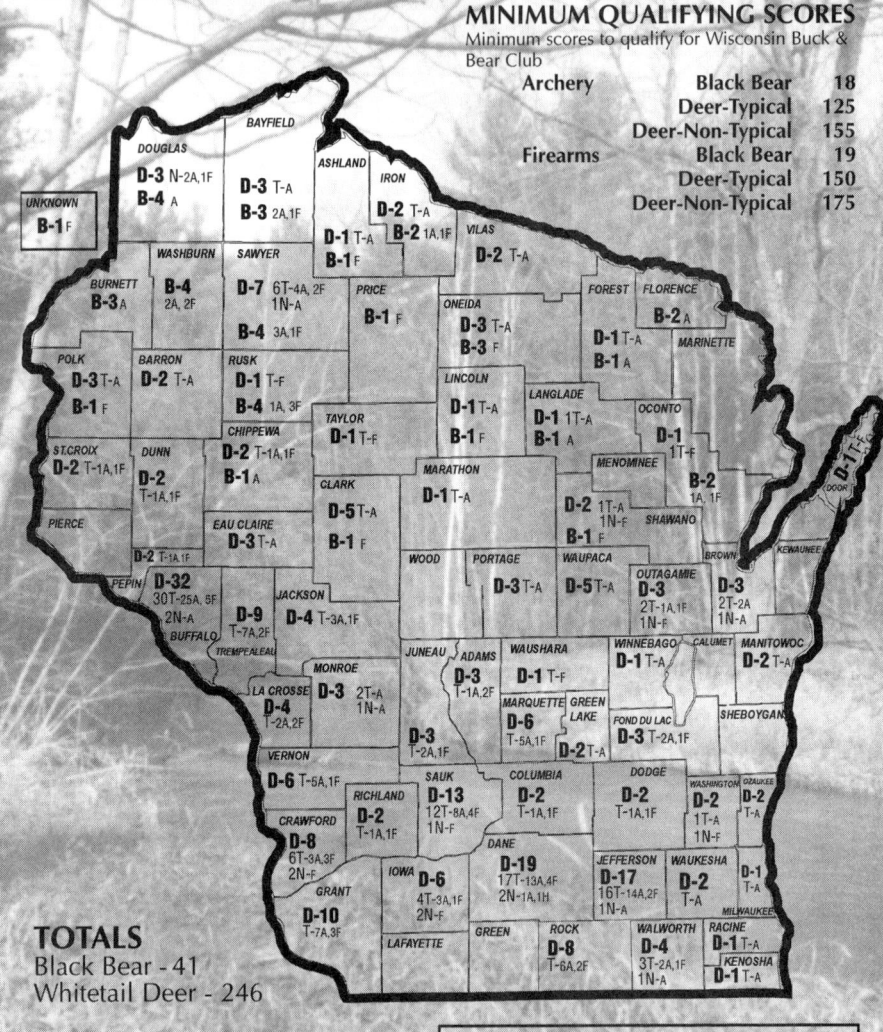

MINIMUM QUALIFYING SCORES
Minimum scores to qualify for Wisconsin Buck & Bear Club

Archery		
Black Bear		18
Deer-Typical		125
Deer-Non-Typical		155
Firearms		
Black Bear		19
Deer-Typical		150
Deer-Non-Typical		175

UNKNOWN B-1 F

DOUGLAS D-3 N-2A,1F B-4 A
BAYFIELD D-3 T-A B-3 2A,1F
ASHLAND D-1 T-A
IRON D-2 T-A B-2 1A,1F
VILAS D-2 T-A
WASHBURN B-4 2A,2F
SAWYER D-7 6T-4A,2F 1N-A B-4 3A,1F
PRICE B-1 F
ONEIDA D-3 T-A B-3 F
FOREST B-2 A
FLORENCE D-1 T-A B-1 A
MARINETTE
BURNETT B-3 A
POLK D-3 T-A B-1 F
BARRON D-2 T-A
RUSK D-1 T-F B-4 1A,3F
CHIPPEWA D-2 T-1A,1F B-1 A
TAYLOR D-1 T-F
LINCOLN D-1 T-A B-1 F
LANGLADE D-1 1T-A
OCONTO D-1 1T-F
MENOMINEE
SHAWANO B-2 1A,1F
ST.CROIX D-2 T-1A,1F
DUNN D-2 T-1A,1F
EAU CLAIRE D-3 T-A
CLARK D-5 T-A B-1 F
MARATHON D-1 T-A
WOOD D-3 T-A
PORTAGE D-5 T-A
WAUPACA
OUTAGAMIE D-3 2T-2A,1N-F
BROWN D-3 2T-2A,1N-A
DOOR D-1 T-F
KEWAUNEE
PIERCE D-2 T-1A,1F
PEPIN D-32 30T-25A,5F 2N-A
BUFFALO D-7 7A,2F
TREMPEALEAU D-9
JACKSON D-4 T-3A,1F
LA CROSSE D-4 T-2A,2F
MONROE D-3 2T-1A,1N-A
JUNEAU D-3 T-1A,2F
ADAMS D-1 T-F
WAUSHARA
MARQUETTE D-6 T-5A,1F
GREEN LAKE
WINNEBAGO D-1 T-A
CALUMET
FOND DU LAC D-3 T-2A,1F
MANITOWOC D-2 T-A
SHEBOYGAN
VERNON D-6 T-5A,1F
CRAWFORD D-8 6T-3A,3F 2N-F
RICHLAND D-2 T-1A,1F
SAUK D-13 12T-8A,4F 1N-F
COLUMBIA D-2 T-1A,1F
DODGE D-2 T-1A,1F
WASHINGTON D-2 1T-A 1N-F
OZAUKEE D-2 T-A
GRANT D-10 T-7A,3F
IOWA D-6 4T-3A,1F 2N-F
DANE D-19 17T-13A,4F 2N-1A,1H
JEFFERSON D-17 16T-14A,2F 1N-A
WAUKESHA D-2 T-A
MILWAUKEE D-1 T-A
LAFAYETTE
GREEN D-8 T-6A,2F
ROCK D-4 3T-2A,1F 1N-A
WALWORTH D-1 T-A
RACINE D-1 T-A
KENOSHA D-1 T-A

TOTALS
Black Bear - 41
Whitetail Deer - 246

KEY
DEER - D
BLACK BEAR - B

T=Typical Antlers
N=Non-Typical Antlers

F=Firearm (Inc. Blackpowder)
A=Archery
H=Handgun

WINNERS 1997
TROPHY CONTEST
DEER / BEAR

ARCHERY - HISTORICAL (1995 season or earlier)

Score	Name/Hometown	County Taken	Year
8 pt. Typical Antlers			
No Entries			
9 pt. Typical Antlers			
124⁴/₈	Gary Inman, Milwaukee	Marinette	1995
10 pt. Typical Antlers			
163⁰/₈	Bill Lawrence, Brodhead	Rock	1994
159³/₈	Jeffrey Eder, Milwaukee	Ozaukee	1994
11 pt. Typical Antlers			
180²/₈	Randy Latsch, Jefferson	Jefferson	1995
12 pt. Typical Antlers			
148³/₈	John Charles, Winona, MN	Buffalo	1994
125³/₈	Mark DeSmet, Blue Mound	Iowa	1995
13+ pt. Typical Antlers			
118³/₈	Shannon Swiggum, Janesville	Crawford	1995
Non-Typical Antlers			
190⁴/₈	Dean Goecks, Stoughton	Dane	1995
187⁰/₈	Travis Althoff, Fountain City	Buffalo	1995

ARCHERY - CURRENT YEAR (1996 season)

Score	Name/Hometown	County
8 pt. Typical Antlers		
151⁷/₈	Dennis Messmann, Jefferson	Jefferson
144⁴/₈	Dan DiMaggio, Madison	Dane
140⁵/₈	John Charles, Winona, MN	Buffalo
9 pt. Typical Antlers		
139⁶/₈	Scott Sprecher, Middleton	Sauk
136⅝	Dan Kaiser, Madison	Dane
10 pt. Typical Antlers		
181⁰/₈	Fred Koehn, Burlington	Jefferson
156¹/₈	Rory Rossman, McFarland	Dane
150⁶/₈	Dean Goecks, Stoughton	Dane
11 pt. Typical Antlers		
173³/₈	Eric Sorge, North Freedom	Sauk
154⁰/₈	Scott Moran, Fort Atkinson	Dane
12 pt. Typical Antlers		
139³/₈	Randall Nash, Prairie du Chien	Crawford
13+ pt. Typical Antlers		
181⁴/₈	Charles Fralick, Glen Haven	Grant
Non-Typical Antlers		
214²/₈	Paul Borowick, Eau Claire	Buffalo
206⁶/₈	Monte Nichols, Eleva	Buffalo

FIREARMS - HISTORICAL (1995 season or earlier)

Score	Name/Hometown	County	Year
8 pt. Typical Antlers			
154⁷/₈	Craig McGinnis, Gratiot	Lafayette	1988
139⁵/₈	Roger Krentz, Lancaster	Grant	1985
135⁶/₈	John Inman, Milwaukee	Marinette	1948
9 pt. Typical Antlers			
148⁷/₈	Pat Foley, Boscobel	Crawford	1993
145⁰/₈	Sue Ebbert, Fort Atkinson	Jefferson	1995
10 pt. Typical Antlers			
184⁶/₈	Jeffrey Wilson, Sauk City	Sauk	1995
161³/₈	Jerry Kendhammer, LaCrosse	LaCrosse	1995
157⁰/₈	Jonathon Walsh, Mukwonago	Richland	1994
11 pt. Typical Antlers			
188⁶/₈	Eli Randall, Chicago, IL	Crawford	1995
158⁴/₈	Randall Nash, Prairie du Chien	Crawford	1995
158³/₈	Matthew Bayley, Racine	Racine	1995
12 pt. Typical Antlers			
162³/₈	Russell Wildes, Watertown	Jefferson	1994
155¹/₈	Yvonne Loe, Brookfield	Richland	1995
13+ pt. Typical Antlers			
176³/₈	Guy Hansen, Arcadia	Buffalo	1995
168⁰/₈	Paul Leitza, Schofield	Marathon	1995
Non-Typical Antlers			
207³/₈	Todd DeForest, Stoughton	Dane	1989
202⁴/₈	Scott Lucey, Lancaster	Crawford	1992
195³/₈	Dennis Losey, Beloit	Rock	1995

FIREARMS - CURRENT YEAR (1996 season)

Score	Name/Hometown	County Taken
8 pt. Typical Antlers		
151¹/₈	Tim Liegel, Spring Green	Iowa
144¹/₈	Richard Rose, Hartford	Rusk
141⁴/₈	Mike McClurg, Viroqua	Vernon
141⁴/₈	George Callow, Whitewater	Pierce
9 pt. Typical Antlers		
145²/₈	Darrel Quamme, DeForest	Columbia
144¹/₈	Randy Hartt, Beaver Dam	Dodge
10 pt. Typical Antlers		
171³/₈	Dave Kitzman, Alma	Buffalo
171¹/₈	Miles Weaver, Oregon	Dane
165⁰/₈	Lawrence Yapp, Oxford	Marquette
11 pt. Typical Antlers		
171⁴/₈	Bradley Hering, Lake Mills	Jefferson
166⁶/₈	Allen Lehman, Grand marsh	Adams
163¹/₈	Ken Harris, Cobb	Crawford
12 pt. Typical Antlers		
170²/₈	Gaylord Downing, Janesville	Juneau
155²/₈	John Koch, Muwonago	Walworth
13+ pt. Typical Antlers		
178³/₈	John Hausz, Fort Atkinson	Jefferson
163³/₈	Matthew Healy, Merrimac	Sauk
160²/₈	Thomas Kempf, Delavan	Sawyer
Non-Typical Antlers		
207¹/₈	Neil Hagen, Superior	Douglas
190³/₈	Scott Pludeman, Green Bay	Shawano
188⁵/₈	Brian Swiggum, Soldiers Grove	Crawford

OTHER AWARDS
WISCONSIN BLACK BEAR
Firearms
20⁴/₁₆ Mike Bodden, Lodi   Langlade 1995
Archery
19¹⁰/₁₆ David Fetting, Stoddard   Sayyer 1996

OUT-OF-STATE ANTLERS (2)
Typical Antlers
170⁵/₈ Donald E. Hoey, Watertown   McHenry, IL 1996
166⁰/₈ Jaime Marsden, Galena, IL   JoDaviess, IL 1994
165⁴/₈ Jacob Marsden, Galena, IL   JoDaviess, IL 1996
Non-Typical Antlers
191²/₈ Tim Laurie, Elgin, IL   Kane, IL 1990

COLLECTED ANTLERS (3)
Typical Antlers
178¹/₈ Dave Mueller, Waukesha   Unk. 1960
Non-Typical Antlers
222⁰/₈ Brant Mueller, Waukesha   Unk. Unk.

(1) Due to an administrative error, the Firearms Non-Typical Best of Show award was first given to Neil Hagen's buck. When the error was discovered and corrected, the most equitable thing to do was to let Hagen's buck remain as a co-winner.
(2) Must be from Minnesota, Iowa, Illinois or Michigan - states contiguous to Wisconsin.
(3) Can be found, purchased, road kill, hunter unknown; entrant must own the antlers; can be from any state; can be a legally taken deer by the hunter/entrant from states non-contiguous to Wisconsin or from a Canadian province or Mexico.

ACE Sauk Prairie
TURKEY CALLING CONTEST

• Winners of the 1997 Turkey Calling Contest were, front row, left to right, Steve Davis, Onalaska, 1st Hunter Division; Joe Frost, Stevens Point, 2nd Hunter Division; Chad Quinlan, Madison, 3rd Hunter Division. Second row, l-r, Zeb Degenhardt, Boscobel, 1st Junion Division; Logan Degenhardt, Boscobel, 2nd Junior Division; Matt Engels, Mason City, IA, 3rd Junior Division. Back row, l-r, Rick White, Cedar Rapids, IA, 1st Open Division; Jim Fink, Nora Springs, IA, 2nd Open Division; Wade Feiner, Milwaukee, 3rd Open Division. The contest was sponsored by the National Wild Turkey Federation / Wisconsin Chapter and co-sponsored by ACE-Sauk Prairie

WISCONSIN 1997 BEST of SHOW WINNERS TROPHY DEER CONTEST

TYPICAL ANTLERS
Firearms
188 6/8 Eli Randall, Chicago, IL   Crawford 1995
Archery
181 4/8 Charles Fralick, Glen Haven   Grant 1996

NON-TYPICAL ANTLERS
Firearms(1)
207 3/8 Todd DeForest, Stoughton   Dane 1989
207 1/8 Neil Hagen, Superior   Douglas 1996
Archery
214 2/8 Paul Borowick, Eau Claire   Buffalo 1996

• "Best of Show" winners of the Budweiser Trophy Deer Contest at the 1997 Wisconsin Deer & Turkey Expo were, front row left to right, Todd DeForest, Stoughton, co-winner of Firearms - Non-Typical Antlers; Neil Hagen, Superior, co-winner of Firearms Non-Typical Antlers; Paul Borowick, Eau Claire, Archery - Non-Typical Antlers. Back row, left, Charles Fralick, Glen Haven, Archery - Typical Antlers; Eli Randall, right, Firearms - Typical Antlers. Hagen and DeForest were declared co-winners because an administrative error mistakenly designated Hagen's buck as the winner and the error wasn't caught until the awards were announced.

Wisconsin

WISCONSIN 1997 OUTDOOR PHOTO CONTEST

People
1) Jerry Davis, La Crosse, WI
2) Jason Joers, Madison, WI
3) Jerry Kendhammer, La Crosse, WI

Scenic
1) Erin Kerch, Wausau, WI
2) Bill Cross, Madison, WI

Wildlife
1) Scott Bianchini, Beloit, WI
2) Scott Bianchini, Beloit, WI
3) Jerry Davis, La Crosse, WI

Scott Bianchini, Beloit, WI

1st Wildlife

Steps Along the Hunter's Path

1st Scenic

Erin Kerch
Wausau, WI

1st People

Jerry Davis
LaCrosse, WI

Wisconsin

249

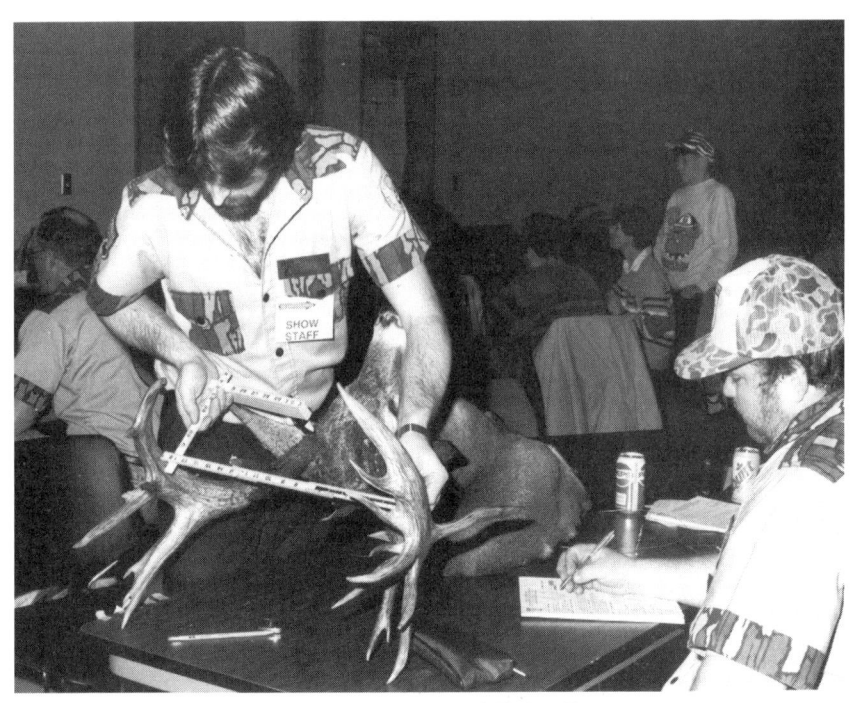

Measuring a non-typical whitetail rack at a Deer & Turkey Expo.

> How big is your trophy? Will it qualify for state and national lists?

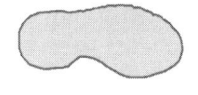

by Richard Smith

How to Enter Your Trophy In The Record Book

*H*ere's what you need to know about entering your trophy in the records, both state and national.

NATIONAL ORGANIZATIONS

There are three national record keeping organizations for big game, all of which use the same measuring system, plus one for turkeys. The minimum score to qualify for listing varies from one organization to the next, and the type of hunting tool used is a consideration for two of the record-keeping systems.

• The **Pope and Young Club**, PO Box 548, Chatfield MN 55923 (507-867-4144) maintains records of big game taken with bow and arrow.

• The **Longhunter Society**, PO Box 67, Friendship IN 47021 (812-667-5131) compiles records of trophies taken with muzzleloading firearms.

• The **Boone and Crockett Club**, Old Milwaukee Depot, 250 Station Dr., Missoula MT 59801 (406-542-1888) considers any big game animal (hunter taken, picked up, hunter unknown) for its records that meets its stringent standards.

The minimum qualifying scores for entry in Boone and Crockett records are the highest among the three national record-keeping organizations.

Deer bagged anywhere in North American can be entered in national records, providing necessary qualifications are met. In some cases, bucks could qualify for listing with two of the three record-keeping organizations. High-scoring whitetails taken with bow and arrow or with muzzleloader could qualify for their respective record books as well as those maintained by the Boone and Crockett Club.

Enter Your Trophy

• The **National Wild Turkey Federation**, PO Box 530, Edgefield SC 29824 (803-637-3106) also has a trophy scoring system for big gobblers. To enter a trophy bird in their records, you must be a member of the NWTF; you can join when you submit your bird's measurement details. The formula for determining the bird's total score: Weight (lbs. & oz.) plus 10 times spur length (r & l) plus two times beard length. Each beard must be measured from the center point of the protrusion from the skin to the end of the longest bristle. Spurs must be measured along the outside center, from the point at which the spur protrudes from the scaled leg skin to the tip of the spur. All measurements are recorded in sixteenths of an inch. Subspecies categories: Eastern, Florida, Rio Grande, Merriam's, Domestic Feral and Hybrid. Entry forms and other details are available from the NWTF; their address and phone number are given later with other national organizations.

STATE ORGANIZATIONS

There are organizations or programs in each of the five states in which Target Communications produces Deer & Turkey shows – Michigan, Ohio, Illinois, Wisconsin and Tennessee. This means whitetails in Tennessee, Illinois and Ohio; whitetails and black bear in Wisconsin; whitetails, black bear and elk in Michigan. Michigan also maintains state turkey records; the other states do not.

The minimum scores for entry into state records often, but not always, are lower than those of national organizations, increasing the odds of qualifying for a listing. A statewide network of scorers has been set up in each of these states for measuring big game trophies taken by hunters. In addition, some state organizations have begun keeping records on turkeys, using some combination of beard length, spur length and/or weight. The combination varies.

Some measurers who are certified to score trophies for state records are qualified to perform the same duties for one or more national record-keeping organizations, simplifying the process of entering qualifying trophies in more than one record book.

It must be noted here that entering your trophy whitetail, black bear or elk in the trophy contest at the appropriate state show, and having it measured there, qualifies it ONLY for that state's record book if it meets that state's minimum scores. Even if your trophy meets the minimum qualifying score for a national organization, entering it in that national organization's record book is another, totally separate step. In addition, the trophy must be measured and scored by a person officially qualified to measure and score for the appropriate national organization. National record-keeping organizations always charge a reasonable amount for entries to help cover the cost of the paperwork. B&C, P&Y and the Longhunter Society charge $25 for entries that meet their qualifications.

Here's the list of state organizations/programs/contacts:

MICHIGAN: Commemorative Bucks of Michigan (CBM) maintains big game records for Michigan. A list of measurers is available at Department of Natural Resources offices and from the CBM itself. For more information, within Michigan call 1-800-298-2825, and outside Michigan call 1-810-796-2925. CBM's mailing address is 3215 Old Farm Lane, Walled Lake, MI 48390.

Although CBM's record-keeping activities revolve around the hundreds of deer entered each year, the organization also scores black bear, elk and turkeys bagged in the state. Cleaned skulls are measured for bear. Beard and spur lengths are determined for gobblers.

CBM has differing minimums for deer entries, based upon whether bucks were taken with firearms (including black powder) or bow and arrow.

Trophy entry fee: $5.00

Annual recognition program: Entry deadline is March 31 for bucks tagged the preceding fall. However, trophies can be entered in the all-time records at any time.

ILLINOIS: Illinois' Big Buck Records are maintained by the Division of Constituency Services within the Department of Natural Resources (DNR). To get in touch with one of the volunteer measurers closest to you, contact your local DNR office or Noel Laurent, Director, Big Buck Recognition Program, Division of Constituency Services, DNR, 524 S. Second St., Room 500, Springfield IL 62701. Telephone: 217-782-4963.

Illinois has different minimum scores for archery kills and for firearms (including black powder) kills.

Trophy entry fee: None

WISCONSIN: The Wisconsin Buck & Bear Club (WB&BC) maintains big game (whitetail deer and black bear) records for Wisconsin. A list of measurers can be obtained at Wisconsin DNR offices or directly from the Buck & Bear Club at PO Box 20881, Greenfield WI 53220-0881. Telephone: 414-545-0984

The Buck & Bear Club has different minimum qualifying scores for deer and bear according to the hunting tool used to tag the animal. Cleaned skulls are measured for bear.

Records have divisions for firearms (including black powder) and archery kills.

Trophy entry fee: None

OHIO: The Buckeye Big Buck Club (BBBC) maintains big game records for Ohio. A list of measurers is available from Ohio Division of Wildlife offices throughout the state or from the BBBC, PO Box 2009, Heath OH 43056. Telephone is 614-928-1644.

The BBBC has one set of minimum scores for its record book for all whitetails bagged within its boundaries, no matter how the individual deer were taken. It has divisions for shotgun, longbow, crossbow, handgun and black powder trophies.

Trophy entry fee: $25, includes certificate and one-year magazine subscription.

Annual recognition program: Entry deadline is September 1 of the year after the deer is tagged. However, trophies can be entered in the all-time records at any time.

TENNESSEE: The Tennessee Deer Registry has three goals: 1) To provide the Tennessee Wildlife Resources Agency (TWRA) with a meaningful and understandable record of the number of quality whitetail deer taken annually in Tennessee; 2) to provide important data concerning Tennessee's expanding deer herd; 3) to recognize successful deer hunters who bag quality deer. The TWRA measures and keeps appropriate records of each entry. Deer Registry rules specify that all entries must have been taken in Tennessee by sport hunting.

For more information on the Tennessee Deer Registry Program or for the name of the official measurer/scorer nearest you, contact the appropriate TWRA Regional Office: Region I - 1-800-372-3928; Region II - 1-800-624-7406; Region III - 1-800-262-6704; Region IV - 1-800-332-0900. Or contact the Tennessee Deer Registry, TWRA, PO Box 20747, Nashville TN 37204. Telephone: 615-781-6612.

Trophy entry fee: None

MEASURING REQUIREMENTS

Antlers and skulls must air dry for a minimum of 60 days before they can be officially scored. As that time nears, if you believe your trophy may qualify for state and/or national records, contact a measurer and make an appointment.

Of course, the easiest way to get your trophy measured might be to bring it to your respective state Deer & Turkey show and enter it in the trophy contest. Entry fee is $12, but in return you get a three-day pass, which has a $24 value. The most economical way to see the show is to enter a trophy in the show's contest. Qualified measurers will be available at every show.

Antler classification:
Whitetail antlers are classified in two ways – typical and non-typical. Typical antlers have all or nearly all the tines growing vertically from left and right main beams, usually with the same number of tines on each beam. The more symmetrical, the better, in comparing left side and right side of the rack. The huge majority of bucks grow typical antlers. Non-typical antlers often have more points than typical antlers, with many of them growing in abnormal locations, such as from other tines and/or at odd angles from main beams. If your trophy deer has non-typical points, consult with the measurer to decide whether it should be scored as a typical or a non-typical. In a few instances, racks will score well both ways.

To qualify for official measuring/scoring:
Antlers must have a solid skull plate; the plate cannot be flexible or broken. Broken antler times which have been repaired are measured only to the break point. If your trophy has broken tine tips, it's best to get the rack officially measured and scored, then do whatever cosmetic repairs you want. Or not have them done at all. This is preferred. Antlers can be measured on mounted deer.

Bear skulls must be in one piece, with unbroken nose and back of skull and unbroken eye ridges. If you're a firearm hunter and concerned about getting your trophy officially scored, it is NOT a good idea to shoot it in the head.

MINIMUM ENTRY SCORES (for all-time records)

Organization	Whitetail Deer Typ	Non-Typ	Black Bear	Rocky Mountain Elk Typ	Non-Typ	Turkey
Boone & Crockett	170	195	21	375	385	
Pope & Young	125	155	18	260	335	
Longhunter Society	130	160	18	255	265	
National Wild Turkey Fed'n						No Min.
Illinois - Archery	115	140				
Illinois - Firearms	140	160				
Michigan - Archery	100	125	18	240	265	8
Michigan - Firearms	125	150	18	240	265	12
Michigan - Pick-ups	140	165	18	240	265	
Ohio - All	140	160				
Tennessee - Archery	115	140				
Tennessee - Firearms	140	165				
Wisconsin - Archery	125	150	18			
Wisconsin - Firearms	150	170	19			

Enter Your Trophy

• A rare photograph of the even rarer beast known as the whitetail deer Push Me-Pull You. Location of this animal is super secret. We're trying to get a full-color photograph of it, but it will be difficult. Photograph by Troy Huffman.

SECTION VIII:

FROSTING ON THE CAKE

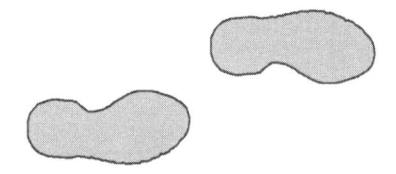

> For ultimate enjoyment of the game you take....and because wild game is better for you than domestic meats.

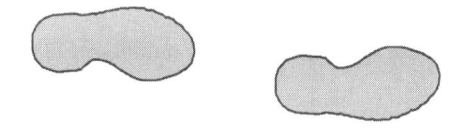

TURKEY & VENISON RECIPES

*T*ime afield and in the woods is great. Filling your tag is too. But there's more to it than that. Much more! Far beyond the mounted-for-display trophy deer and/or gobbler. People throughout history have used antlers for residential ornamentation. Deer hide becomes clothing, gloves, mittens, footwear, purses, coin purses, even briefcases and more. Deer hair, attached to a hook, catches fish. Antlers are carved and drilled for cribbage boards; they become door handles on rustic cabins, lamp and lantern bases, chandeliers and more. Gobbler fans make colorful wall displays. We've seen turkey feet made into interesting lamp bases and put to other display uses.

It is, however, as table fare that the deer and turkey – and all wild game – gain most glory. Simply stated, wild game tastes great (whether or not it's less filling is up to you) when properly processed, stored and prepared. Wild game is healthy food, with less of the bad-for-us fats and carbohydrates and other things, and much more of the trace elements vital to our well-being.

North American Indians understood and revered the "Circle of Life". For good reason....we're all in this together. Let's treat all game with the respect it deserves. In our home state of Wisconsin, Thanksgiving Day occurs during the firearms deer season. We kind of like that; it's fitting.

Enjoy!

Suggestion: Copy the recipes on the following pages. Cut and paste into your favorite wild game recipe file.

BARBECUED TURKEY

1 turkey, about 8 pounds
Liquid Smoke, if desired
2 coarsely chopped onions
1 recipe barbecue sauce
salt and pepper
celery leaves from 1 bunch celery
½ - ¾ c. salad oil

Remove turkey neck if still attached, but leave skin. Rub cavity of bird with salt and brush with about 1-1/2 tsp. Liquid Smoke. Stuff with celery leaves and onion. Truss bird. Add 1 tsp. Liquid Smoke to salad oil; brush on bird. Sprinkle well with salt and pepper. Place on rack in roasting pan and roast at 325°F about 3-1/2 hours or until tender. Brush with oil mixture several times during cooking. Add remaining mixture to hot barbecue sauce about 30 minutes before cooking is completed. Brush bird with sauce several times during last 30 minutes. (Sauce recipe below.)

Barbecue Sauce

1 c. catsup
2-3 dashes hot sauce
1 c. water
¼ c. vinegar
1 tbsp. Worcestershire sauce
1 tbsp. sugar
1 tsp. salt

Combine all ingredients. Heat to boiling and simmer 30 minutes.

J. Wayne Fears
Heflin, AL

HUNTER'S TURKEY

1 wild turkey
2 tbsp. olive oil
¼ c. water
1 clove garlic
1 tsp. black pepper

Skin turkey and filet out the breast halves and allow to cool. Rub breast halves with split garlic clove and sprinkle half of pepper on each half. Fry in hot oil 2 minutes on each side. Add water, cover and simmer 10 minutes. Serve with hot biscuits. Serves 4.

Norman B. Bates
Thompson's Station, TN

K.C. BEST VENISON JERKY

3-4 lbs. venison strips
1 (12 oz.) can beer
¾ c. Worcestershire sauce
¾ c. Tabasco sauce (optional)
2 tbsp. onion powder
¾ c. soy sauce
2 c. (1 pint) cheap whiskey
1 6-oz. bottle Wright's Hickory Smoke Flavor
¾ c. Durkee's red hot sauce (optional)
2 tbsp. black pepper
2 tbsp. garlic powder
fresh ground black pepper - save for after soaking

Mix together all ingredients in glass or plastic bowl. Add venison. Refrigerate contents in covered bowl. Remix twice daily for 4-6 days depending on desired strength of flavor. Drain mixture from meat. Place meat on racks and blacken both sides with fresh ground black pepper. Place on racks in smoker or oven at about 100°F until dried to preferred moisture content (about 8-10 hours). Place foil under racks to catch drips and save on clean up.

Kevin W. Cranick
Petoskey, MI

SAM'S VENISON SALAMI

For every 5 lbs. of venison add:
1 lb. suet
3 tsp. hickory smoke salt
3 tsp. Liquid Smoke
5 heaping tsp. Morton Tender Quick
3 tsp. coarse ground black pepper

Mix and refrigerate. Once a day for 3 days knead for 5 minutes. On fourth day, shape into 1-1/2 pound rolls. Place on rack in oven. Bake 4-1/2 hours at 160°F. Turn rolls, bake 4-1/2 hours more. Let cool, wrap in freezer paper and freeze.

Sam Rice
Toulon, IL

PATRICK'S VENISON CHILI

4 lbs. venison round steak
1 (10-3/4 oz.) can tomato soup
3-4 tbsp. chili powder
2 (15-1/2 oz.) cans chili beans
1 (46 oz.) can tomato juice
6 oz. noodles, uncooked

Cut venison into one-inch squares, brown in large pan. Add browned venison, tomato juice, chili powder, tomato soup, 2 cans of water (tomato soup can). Cook 3-3-1/2 hours. Add chili beans and cook 20 minutes. Cook noodles and add when you add beans. Serves 10-12.

Patrick J. Rice
Shiocton, WI

GREAT VENISON ROAST

1 3-6 lb. roast
1 tbsp. chili powder
½ tsp. celery salt
3-4 onions, sliced
¼ c. red wine
½ tsp. Worcestershire sauce

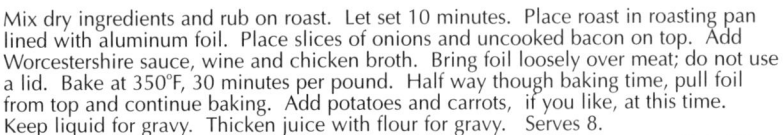

salt, pepper, garlic powder to taste
¼ tsp. dry mustard
dash of red pepper
5 slices bacon
2 c. chicken broth or bouillon

Mix dry ingredients and rub on roast. Let set 10 minutes. Place roast in roasting pan lined with aluminum foil. Place slices of onions and uncooked bacon on top. Add Worcestershire sauce, wine and chicken broth. Bring foil loosely over meat; do not use a lid. Bake at 350°F, 30 minutes per pound. Half way though baking time, pull foil from top and continue baking. Add potatoes and carrots, if you like, at this time. Keep liquid for gravy. Thicken juice with flour for gravy. Serves 8.

Bob Cloar
Munfordville, KY

LUCA'S GARLIC SAUCE

2 tbsp. butter or margarine
5 garlic cloves, crushed
1 tsp. onion salt

2 tbsp. flour
½ c. milk
1 tbsp. cream

Heat butter or margarine in pan. Add flour and garlic over medium heat. Add milk and stir until thick. Add onion salt and cream. Good over any red meat.

Steve Gillhouse, World Adventures
Sarona, WI

FRESH MILD-HOT VENISON ITALIAN SAUSAGE

2-1/2 lbs. venison
2-1/2 tbsp. salt
1-1/2 tsp. cracked fennel seed
1 tsp. hot peppers, crushed
½ tsp. coriander

2 1/2 lbs. pork butt
1 c. water
1-1/2 tsp. sugar
½ tsp. caraway seed

Grind venison and pork butt through 3/16-inch plate on a grinder and mix well with all ingredients. Stuff into hog casings or make into patties. Great for grilling, frying or on pizza.

Adrian Rush Erhard, Erhard's Sausage Supplies
Hopkins, MN

VENISON POT PIE

1-½ lbs. venison, cubed
2 tbsp. olive oil
1 tsp. Lawry's Seasoned Salt
1 10-oz. pkg. frozen peas
1 c. cooked potatoes, diced
½ c. onion, diced

1 c. Lawry's Seasoned Marinade
1 tsp. Lawry's Garlic pepper
2 1-oz. pkg. Lawry's Brown Gravy
1 10 oz. pkg. frozen carrots
1 c. sliced mushrooms
pie dough or prepared pie crust

In a resealable plastic bag or container, place venison and Lawry's Seasoned Marinade. Marinate in refrigerator 30 minutes to 2 hours. Heat oil in a large fry pan. Add venison and sprinkle with Lawry's Seasoned Pepper and Seasoned Salt; cook until onions are tender and venison is browned. Lower heat, cover and simmer about 30 minutes or until tender, adding additional liquid as needed. While meat is simmering, in a medium-size sauce pan, make Lawry's Gravy mix according to package directions. Add peas, carrots, potatoes, mushrooms and onions; mix well.

Line two 8-inch pie pans with pie dough, spoon in meat and vegetable mixture. Top with remaining dough and pinch edges to seal. Using a sharp knife, make vent holes in crust. Bake in 350°F oven 30-40 minutes or until top of crust is browned.

TIP: Substitute other fresh, frozen or canned vegetables. Great cooked around the campfire, just use a cast iron Dutch oven. Make individual pies and freeze them ahead.

VENISON PEPPER STEAK

1-1/2 lbs. venison steaks
1-1/2 c. catsup
dash garlic powder
dash salt & pepper
2 tbsp. Worcestershire sauce
1 green pepper

3 cans (10-3/4 oz) French onion soup
2 c. flour
dash lemon pepper
dash parsley
1 onion
3 c. rice, cooked

Add spices to flour. Tenderize venison steak with meat mallet. Coat meat with flour and brown in a little vegetable oil in a pan. Mix French onion soup, catsup, Worcestershire sauce and spices in separate pan. Add meat. Simmer 1 hour. Cut onion & green pepper in strips. Add, simmer 1/2 hour. Serve over hot rice. Serves 4-6.

Jon & Debbie Jones
Algonac MI

Our thanks to the great wild game cooks who's recipes are used here. They are from a wild game cookbook – "The Wild Pantry" – we will be publishing in mid-1998. That cookbook will have 250+ recipes, great wild game meals, anecdotes about hunting camp meals good and bad, and such additional things which make a cookbook much more than a recipe book, and thus fun to read.

Recipes

The "On Target" Series of Outdoor / Shooting / Hunting Books

UNDERSTANDING WINNING ARCHERY, by Al Henderson, coach of the 1976 U.S. Olympic Archery Team, international coach and shooting consultant. Mental control means easier archery gear set-up, more-productive practices, and winning archery – for target, field and hunting shooters. ISBN: 0-913305-00-6. Library of Congress Catalog Card Number (LCCN): 82-074190. TCC (Target Communications Corporation) Book #01-001; $9.95.

TAKING TROPHY WHITETAILS (2nd Edition), by Bob Fratzke with Glenn Helgeland. In-depth, detailed information on year-round scouting (and its huge payoff), scrape hunting, rut hunting, late season hunting, camo, use of scents plus entire new chapter on mock scraping and licking branches. Learn why this consistent trophy-taker says, "I spend 90% of my time in the woods scouting and 10% hunting." ISBN #: 0-913305-02-2. LCCN: 83-050905. TCC Book #01-003; $10.95.

TO HECK WITH GRAVY wild game cookbook, by Glenn and Judy Helgeland. Gourmet results from quick, easy recipes. Includes 209 recipes (roasts, steaks, marinades, soups/stews, ground meat, fish and birds), plus meat field dressing tips, handling and /processing tips, spice chart, low-sodium diet tips and more. ISBN: 0-913305-05-7. LCCN: 85-179767. TCC Book #01-005; $12.95.

TASTY JERKY RECIPES FOR EVERYONE, by Glenn and Judy Helgeland. Spicy, mild, sweet and no-sodium recipes for three different meat cut thicknesses and tenderness. Make in oven, smoker, dehydrator or microwave. Book #01-006; $2.00 plus stamped, addressed #10 return envelope.

TUNING YOUR COMPOUND BOW (2nd Edition), by Larry Wise, the recognized master at understanding and interpreting the mechanics of compound bows. Includes pre-use bow preparation, draw stroke, power stroke, shooting from the valley, fine tuning, test shooting, plus tuning the Fast Flite cable system, building and tuning aluminum and carbon arrows. ISBN: 0-913305-07-3. LCCN: 85-051883. TCC Book #01-008; $10.95.

TUNING YOUR BROADHEADS & Entire Bow/Arrow Hunting System (2nd Edition), by Larry Wise. Problem-solving information on fitting the bow to your body and shooting form for optimum results; broadhead effects on arrow flight; noise reduction; aiming and shooting strategies; proper practice; plus tuning the Fast Flite cable system, building and tuning aluminum and carbon arrows. ISBN: 0-913305-08-1. LCCN: 89-50077. TCC Book #01-009; $10.95.

TUNING & SHOOTING YOUR 3-D BOW, by Larry Wise. Explains the 3-D archery game and who shoots it; arrow speed – the 3-D advantage; 3-D archery and bowhunting. Detailed information on choosing the right equipment, the force-draw curve of a cam, choosing and tuning 3-D arrows, shooting your 3-D bow. Practice strategies for 3-D and for bowhunting, and shooting 3-D competition. ISBN: 0-913305-10-3. LCCN: 92-83910. TCC Book #01-010; $10.95.

BECOME THE ARROW (the Art of Modern Barebow Shooting), by Byron Ferguson with Glenn Helgeland. Details the "become the arrow" philosophy; walks you step-by-step through that shooting system; explains how to visualize arrow flight path and sight picture; shooting form practice and mental exercises (and discipline); how to develop the necessary focus and concentration; tuning for barebow shooting; bowhunting details on moon phases and other advanced items; most-commonly asked questions, building a longbow. ISBN: 0-913305-09-X. LCCN: 92-83909. TCC Book #01-011; $12.95.

MUZZLELOADING FOR WHITETAILS & Other Big Game, by Toby Bridges, the nation's foremost black powder hunter/writer. Black powder technology and rifles have changed dramatically the past ten years with the introduction of the percussion in-line style. More and better black powder hunting seasons now are the big draw. Here's the most up-to-date technical data on black powder rifles (new and traditional) and accessories, plus detailed, no-nonsense black powder hunting tips. ISBN: 0-913305-12-X. LCCN: 94-49359. TCC Book #01-012; $12.95.

STEPS ALONG THE HUNTER'S PATH (Volume 1). A new kind of book. Based on seminars given by some of today's finest deer and turkey hunters at the five 1998 Deer & Turkey Expos produced by Target Communications in Michigan, Illinois, Ohio, Wisconsin and Tennessee. This book greatly expands that material into a wealth of hunting information, offering the combined wisdom of literally a "who's who" of expert hunters in the country. Also includes complete trophy contest winners' lists from all five of the 1997 Deer & Turkey Expos; county by county trophy information – what was taken and what it was taken with; more than two dozen venison recipes; listing of the Outdoor Photo Contest winners (with photos) from all five 1997 Expos; how/where to get your trophy scored and entered in record books, and more. ISBN: 0-913305-14-6. LCCN: 97-52714. TCC BOOK #01-014; $19.95.

SHIPPING & HANDLING — $2.75 All prices (books and s/h) are in U.S. funds. Wisconsin residents add 5.6% tax.

SEE YOUR DEALER
or order directly from the publisher.
(MC/VISA accepted)

Write or call for a FREE catalog:
TARGET COMMUNICATIONS CORPORATION
7626 W. Donges Bay Rd., Mequon WI 53097
414-242-3990 • 1-800-324-3337